THE EUROPEAN UNION SERIES

General Editors: Neill Nugent, William E. Paterson, Vincent Wright

The European Union series is designed to provide an authoritative library on the European Union, ranging from general introductory texts to definitive assessments of key institutions and actors, policies and policy processes, and the role of member states.

Books in the series are written by leading scholars in their fields and reflect the most up-to-date research and debate. Particular attention is paid to accessibility and clear presentation for a wide audience of students, practitioners and interested general readers.

The series consists of four major strands:

- general textbooks
- the major institutions and actors
- the main areas of policy
- the member states and the Union

Published titles

Wyn Grant
The Common Agricultural Policy

Justin Greenwood
Representing Interests in the European Union

Fiona Hayes-Renshaw and Helen Wallace
The Council of Ministers

Simon Hix and Christopher Lord
Political Parties in the European Union

Brigid Laffan
The Finances of the European Union

Janne Haaland Matláry
Energy Policy in the European Union

Forthcoming

Simon Bulmer and Drew Scott
European Union: Economics, Policy and Politics

David Millar, Neill Nugent and William E. Paterson (eds)
The European Union Source Book

John Peterson and Elizabeth Bomberg
Decision-making in the European Union

Ben Rosamond
Theories of European Integration

Richard Sinnott
Understanding European Integration

●   ●   ●   ●

Simon Bulmer and Wolfgang Wessels
The European Council (Second Edition)

Renaud Dehousse
The Court of Justice: A Brief Introduction

David Earnshaw and David Judge
The European Parliament

Neill Nugent
The European Commission

Anne Stevens
The Administration of the European Union

●   ●   ●   ●

David Allen and Geoffrey Edwards
The External Economic Relations of the European Union

Michelle Cini and Lee McGowan
Competition Policy in the European Union

Martin Holland
The European Union and the Third World

Anand Menon
Defence Policy and the European Union

James Mitchell and Paul McAleavey
Regionalism and Regional Policy in the European Union

John Redmond, René Schwok and Lee Miles
Enlarging the European Union

Margaret Sharp and John Peterson
Technology Policy in the European Union

Hazel Smith
The Foreign Policy of the European Union

Mark Thatcher
The Politics of European High Technology

Rüdiger Wurzel
Environmental Policy in the European Union

●   ●   ●   ●

Simon Bulmer and William E. Paterson
Germany and the European Union

Phil Daniels and Ella Ritchie
Britain and the European Union

Alain Guyomarch, Howard Machin and Ella Ritchie
France in the European Union

Other titles planned include

European Union: A Brief Introduction
The History of the European Union
The European Union Reader
The Political Economy of the European Union

●   ●   ●   ●

Social Policy
Monetary Union
Political Union
The USA and the European Union

●   ●   ●   ●

The European Union and its Member States
Reshaping the States of the Union
Italy and the European Union
Spain and the European Union

Representing Interests in the European Union

Justin Greenwood

St. Martin's Press
New York

t published in the United States of America in 1997

This book is printed on paper suitable for recycling and
made from fully managed and sustained forest sources.

Printed in Hong Kong

ISBN 0–312–17288–5

Library of Congress Cataloging-in-Publication Data
Greenwood, Justin.
Representing interests in the European Union / Justin Greenwood.
p.   cm.
Includes bibliographical references (p.   ) and index.
ISBN 0–312–17288–5 (cloth)
1. Lobbying—European Union countries.   2. Pressure groups–
–European Union countries.   I. Title.
JN36.G74   1997
328.4'078—dc20
                                                    96–36917
                                                       CIP

To my mother, and father

Contents

List of Tables and Figures[*]

Figures

---

* All tables drawn from original data collection have percentages rounded up
or down to nearest per cent.

List of Abbreviations

ACEA	Association of European Automobile Constructors
AEBR	Association of European Border Regions
AECM	European Independent Business Confederation
AER	Assembly of European Regions
AIRLINE	Aerospace Industry Regional and Local Authority Network
AMCHAM-EU	EU Committee of the American Chamber of Commerce
AMUE	Association for the Monetary Union of Europe
ANEC	European Association for the Co-ordination of Consumer Representation in Standardisation
APPE	Association of Petroleum Producers and Exporters
BCC	Biotechnology Co-ordinating Committee
BEUC	Bureau Européen des Unions de Consommateurs
CAOBISCO	Association of the Chocolate, Biscuit and Confectionery Industries of the EEC
CAP	Common Agricultural Policy
CCBE	Council of European Bar and Law Societies of the European Communities
CC	Consumers' Committee
CCC	Consumers' Contact Committee
CCC	Consumers' Consultative Committee
CCC	Coalfield Communities Campaign
CCMC	Committee of Common Market Automobile Constructors
CCRLA	Consultative Council of Regional and Local Authorities

CEA	European Insurance Committee
CEAT	Coordination Européenne des Amis de la Terre
CEBSR	Combined European Bureau for Social Development
CEC	Confédération Européenne des Cadres
CEDAG	Comité Européen des Associations d'intérêt Général.
CEDI	Confédération Européenne des Independents
CEEP	European Centre of Public Enterprises
CEFIC	European Chemical Industry Council
CEG	Consumers in Europe Group
CEMR	Council of European Municipalities and Regions
CEN	Committee for European Normalisation
CENELEC	European Committee for Electrotechnical Standardisation
CENPO	Centre for Non Profit Organisations
CEOs	Chief Executive Officers
CERCLE	European Local Authorities Research and Study Centre
CESI	European Confederation of Independent Unions
CFDT	Confédération Française Démocratique du Travail
CGT	Confédération Général du Travail
CIAA	Confederation of Food and Drink Industries of the EEC
CLCA	Liaison Committee of the Automobile Industry of the Countries of the European Communities
COAST	Co-ordinated Action for Seaside Towns
COFACE	Confederation of Family Organisations in the EC
COGECA	General Committee of Agricultural Co-operation in the EEC
COLIPA	European Cosmetics, Toiletry and Perfume Association
CONCAWE	The Oil Companies European Organisation for Environmental and Health Protection

COPA	Committee of Agricultural Organisations in the EC
CoR	Committee of the Regions
COREPER	Committee of Permanent Representatives
CPMR	Conference of Peripheral Maritime Regions
CPS	Consumer Protection Service
CREW	Centre for Research on European Women
CRP	Committee on Rules of Procedure and the Verification of Credentials and Immunities
EACEM	European Association of Consumer Electronics Manufacturers
EAGGF	European Agriculture Guidance and Guarantee Fund
EARLIE	European Aerospace Regional and Local Authority Information Exchange
EBA	European Business Agenda
EBCG	European Biotechnology Co-ordinating Group
EBIS	European Biotechnology Information Service
ECAS	European Citizens Action Service
ECJ	European Court of Justice
ECOSA	European Consumer Safety Association
ECTAA	Group of National Travel Agents' and Tour Operators' Associations within the EEC
ECTEL	Association of the European Telecommunications and Professional Electronics Industry
ECU	European Currency Unit
EEA	European Environmental Agency
EEA	European Economic Area
EEB	European Environmental Bureau
EEC	European Economic Community
EEF	European Environmental Federation
EEG	European Enterprise Group
EFAH	European Forum for the Arts and Heritage
EFL	European Federation of Lobbyists
EFPIA	European Federation of Pharmaceutical Industry Associations
EIB	European Investment Bank

EIC	European Middle-Sized Cities Network
EICs	European Information Centres
EMSU	European Medium and Small Business Union
EMU	Economic and Monetary Union
ENOW	European Network of Women
EP	European Parliament
EPAL	European Parlimaentary Affairs Lobbyists
EPHA	European Public Health Alliance
ERAF	European Roundtable of Associations and Federations
ERDF	European Regional Development Fund
ERRA	European Recovery and Recycling Association
ERT	European Round Table of Industrialists
ESAN	European Social Action Network
ESC	Economic and Social Committee
ESF	European Social Fund
ESNBA	European Secretariat of National Biotechnology Associations
ETOA	European Tour Operators' Association
ETSI	European Telecommunications Standards Institute
ETUC	European Trade Union Confederation
EU	European Union
EURADA	European Association of (Regional) Development Agencies
EURO-FIET	European Regional Organisation of the International Federation of Commercial, Clerical, Professional & Technical Employees
EUROBIT	European Association of Manufacturers of Business Machines and Information Technology
EUROCADRES	Council of European Professional and Managerial Staff
EUROCARE	European Concern on Alcohol
EUROCHAMBRES	Association of European Chambers of Commerce and Industry
EUROCOMMERCE	European Federation of Retailing and Distribution

EUROCOOP	European Community of Consumer Co-operatives
EUROFER	European Confederation of Iron and Steel Industries
EUROPECHE	Association of National Organisations of Fishing Enterprises in the EEC
EUROPEN	European Organisation for Packaging and the Environment
EUROPMI	European Committee for Small and Medium-Sized Independent Companies
EUROPOL	European Police Office
EUROSYNET	European Network for Cross National Co-operation on Public Procurement and the promotion of Small and Medium Sized Enterprises
EWL	European Women's Lobby
FEANI	Federation Européenne d'Associations Nationales d'Ingénieurs
FEANTSA	European Federation of National Organisations Working with the Homeless
FEE	Federation of European Accountants
FEM	Federation of European Motorcyclists
FGSD	First General Systems Directive
FIET	International Federation of Commercial, Clerical, Professional & Technical Employees
FoE	Friends of the Earth
GATT	General Agreement on Tariffs and Trade
HAI	Health Action International
HDTV	High Definition Television
HOTREC	Confederation of the National Hotel and Restaurant Associations in the European Community
ICON	Interregional Cultural Network
ICSW	International Council on Social Welfare
IEIC	Institut Européen Interégional de la Consommateur
IFPMA	International Federation of Pharmaceutical Manufacturers' Associations
IFS	International Federation of Settlements and Neighbourhood Centres European Network

IGC	Inter Governmental Conference
INTERREG	Cross-border and Inter-regional Cooperation
ISCO	International Standard Classification Organisation
ISO	International Standards Organisation
IT	Information Technology
IULA	International Union of Local Authorities
LEDA	Local Economic Development Action
MEP	Member of the European Parliament
MILAN	Motor Industry Local Authority Network
NCVO	National Council for Voluntary Organisations
NET	Network of European Private Entrepreneurs in the Tourism Sector
OECD	Organisation for Economic Cooperation and Development
ORGALIME	Liaison Organisation for the European Mechanical, Electrical and Electronic Engineering and Metalwork Industries
PCF	Packaging Chain Forum
PEFRIFRA	Special Programme Supporting Communities in Border Regions and Sensitive Areas
PhRMA	Pharmaceutical Research and Manufacturers of America
QMV	qualified majority voting
RECHAR	Reconversion of Coal Basins
RECITE	Regions and Cities of Europe
REEN	European Third Sector Training Network
RENAVAL	Conversion of Shipbuilding Areas
RETI	Regions of Industrial Technology
SAGB	Senior Advisory Group Biotechnology
SEA	Single European Act
SEPLIS	European Secretariat of the Liberal, Independent and Social Professions
SGSD	Second General Systems Directive
SME	small and medium sized enterprise
SPEC	Support Programme for Employment Creation

T&E	European Federation for Transport and the Environment
TENs	Trans European Networks
TERN	Trans European Rural Network
TEU	Treaty on European Union
UEAPME	European Association of Craft, Small and Medium-Sized Enterprises
UNICE	Union of Industrial and Employers' Confederations of Europe
VAT	value added tax
VOICE	Voluntary Organisations in a Citizens' Europe
WCL	World Confederation of Labour
WFTU	World Federation of Trade Unions
WHO	World Health Organisation
WWF	World Wide Fund for Nature
YES	Young Entrepreneurs for Europe

List of Directorates-General

Acknowledgements

I want to record debts of gratitude to universities and a number of research foundations in providing money, time, resources and opportunities to conduct and develop the research on which this book is based. I owe a great deal to my present employer, the School of Public Administration and Law at the Robert Gordon University, Aberdeen, and to the University of Teesside, the European Commission, the British Academy, the Carnegie Foundation, and to the European Consortium for Political Research.

I am also conscious of the considerable intellectual support and stimulation provided by valued colleagues throughout Europe and the USA with whom I have collaborated in research projects and in publishing since 1990. I am also grateful to my publisher, Steven Kennedy, to Neill Nugent as series editor, and to the many specialists who have provided helpful comments on draft chapters. Equally, many organisations and individuals have been extremely generous in providing me with their time and information. I want to thank them all, and to record my regret that they are too numerous to mention.

Finally, particular thanks are due to Rachel Stewart, Lara Stancich, Linda Strangward and Ruth Webster, who have provided impressive research assistance and helped generate important information for me during the past three years in the production of this manuscript.

JUSTIN GREENWOOD

1

Introduction

The representation of public and private interests plays a key part in the functioning of the European Union (EU). As long ago as 1958, Ernst Haas suggested that the activities of interest groups could partly explain the development and functioning of the (then) European Economic Community (EEC). First, they could form an important means of contact between the rather remote central institutions of the EEC, then chronically lacking in democratic structures, and the populations of the member states. In so doing, interest groups could play a key role in legitimising the decisions of the EEC, and in relieving the 'democratic deficit' so characteristic of the early days of the Community. Second, in trying to take advantage of the opportunities presented by a European single market envisaged in the Treaty of Rome, business interest groups, Haas suggested, would encourage the progressive transfer of competencies from the national to the European level. Indeed, the 'relaunching of Europe', culminating in the Single European Act (SEA) of 1986, arose in part from the demands of a group of business leaders from Europe's largest companies, worried about losing out in global competition to Japan, America and the newly industrialising countries of south-east Asia. For the businesses they represented, a European single market was, at the bottom line, a strategy for survival. It therefore came to be widely recognised by Europe's political leaders as an essential step to take.

Today, the performance of key business sectors in Europe would be undermined without the willing and collective involvement of firms with public authorities in the governance of their affairs, because the quality of public policy decisions depends upon the specialist input and co-operation of the powerful interests they affect. The European Commission is so small that there might be just one official with responsibility for the affairs of an entire business domain – such as the multi-billion European currency unit (ECU) motor insurance business. It has therefore become dependent upon input from specialist outside interests, sometimes to the extent that European business interest groups write Commission reports. Indeed, a recent report from the Commission recorded in its opening paragraph that

> The Commission has always been an institution open to outside input. The Commission believes this process to be fundamental to the development of its policies. This dialogue has proved valuable to both the Commission and to interested outside parties. Commission officials acknowledge the need for such outside input and welcome it (Commission of the European Communities, 1992a, p. 3).

For non-business interests, however, the impact of interest representation activities at the European level, has on the whole, been less dramatic, although there are a growing and significant number of exceptions, and a number of contexts in which these interests can operate on a level playing field with business interests (Chapter 8). Taken as a whole, neither the outputs (purposive and non-purposive action and inaction), nor the outcomes (end-results), of European public policies can be understood without reference to, and analysis of, the behaviour and perspectives of those with interests in them. Similarly, the development of the EU cannot be fully understood without considering the role which key interests have played in encouraging the growth of European-level competencies.

The variety of interests in Europe

The variety of interests with a stake in European public affairs is vast. It includes firms, professions, employers and labour groups, consumer, cause, social/community, citizen and environmental interests, at European, national and subnational levels of organisation, and territorial interests themselves, such as regional and local government. On a visit to Brussels and Strasbourg it is possible to come across every imaginable type of interest, from multinational firms to aquarium trustees and handwriting analysts, motorcyclists to municipalities, trade unionists to topical campaign groups, craftsmen to citizens and consumers, and bird-lovers to beer-drinkers.

Collective interests at the European-level range from formal associations through to networks as informal as a regular lunch club, although interests are also represented through non-collective formats (such as firms acting alone). However, to the outsider the most

identifiable form of European interest representation is that associated with groups, and expressed by a variety of non-group actors,
such as 'hired-hands' lobbyists. Formal associations represent either
'peak' (such as employers or union confederations, organised across
sectors, with claims to represent constituency-wide interests), cross-
sectoral (again, organised across sectors but with direct affiliation
from units such as firms, rather than confederations, and which may
specialise in organising a particular type of interest, such as large
firms) or sectoral (such as car manufacturers). The Commission has
estimated that there are some 3000 interest groups in Brussels seeking
to exert influence on European public affairs, including more than
500 European and international federations, and that some 10 000
individuals are involved in interest representation, working on behalf
of either collective or non-collective interests (Commission of the
European Communities, 1992a). Provided such an estimate is accurate, as Grant (1995) observes, there is thus a ratio of approximately
one person in the interest representation arena for every Commission
official, if translators and secretarial staff are excluded from the latter.

The range of groups is considered in the section which follows,
ahead of special analysis of them which is provided in Chapter 3. Full
examination of particular types of interests is provided in Chapter 5
(business interests), Chapter 6 (the professions), Chapter 7 (labour
interests), Chapter 8 (consumer, environmental and social/citizen
concerns) and Chapter 9 (territorial interests).

Groups

In order to encourage interests to organise on a Europe-wide basis the
Commission, in its early days, operated a policy of dialogue only with
European-level (Euro) groups. In practice this proved unworkable,
because the presence of Euro groups was patchy and, where they
existed, some were unrepresentative, weak in building meaningful
platforms among their members or little more than symbolic pre-
sences. In response, the Commission found that where it needed
sensible dialogue with interests it might have to trawl around the
national capitals to find it (Caporaso, 1974). Although these problems
have not altogether disappeared today, the enhanced competence of
the EU, and the efforts of the Commission in the early 1980s to work
closely with industry and other interests, have resulted in the development of a number of highly effective Euro groups at the sectoral and

cross-sectoral levels of business, and in some non-producer domains, to the extent that they have a significant impact upon public policy outputs, and in some cases outcomes (Chapters 3, 5 and 8).

Today, the Commission still retains its policy of favouring inter-action with Euro groups where possible. Places on its advisory committees are handed out to Euro groups first. Drafts of directives and other policy initiatives are often given to European business sector associations to comment on. Although single-firm representa-tions to the Commission are heard, the firm concerned is usually told that the Commission would wish to explore the issue further by talking to the interest group concerned in order to ensure that it gets a more representative opinion. Where significant interactions occur between the Commission and single interests, it tends to be where collective interests are largely unaffected, or because the Euro group is weak, or where a single firm is so large or strategically important to the EU that it can bring more resources to the Commission than can a Euro group. However, on the whole, if the Euro group is strong and representative, the Commission's preferred strategy is to seek princi-pal forms of dialogue there. A well-organised Euro group can make itself indispensable to the Commission by bringing representative opinion and other resources from one source. The Commission far prefers this scenario to having to talk to a plethora of interests within the same field.

The large, cross-sectoral groups are among the best known of all interest groups working in Brussels. These include: UNICE (Union of Industrial and Employers' Confederations of Europe), comprising national federations; ERT (the European Round Table of Industri-alists) and AMCHAM-EU (the EU Committee of the American Chamber of Commerce), both representing primarily large firms, and probably the most influential of all Euro groups; EUROCHAM-BRES (the Association of European Chambers of Commerce and Industry), representing Chambers of Commerce; and, among those representing small firm interests, UEAPME (European Association of Craft, Small and Medium-sized Enterprises) and EUROPMI (Eur-opean Committee for Small and Medium-sized Enterprises) (Chap-ter 5). Public-sector employers are represented by CEEP (European Centre of Public Enterprises), while ETUC (European Trade Union Confederation) represents worker interests (Chapter 7), and SEPLIS (European Secretariat of the Liberal, Independent and Social Profes-sions), CEC (Confédération Européene des Cadres) and EURO-CADRES (Council of European Professional and Managerial Staff) those of the professions (Chapter 6). Cross-sectoral public interests are represented by a host of organisations, including the EEB (European Environmental Bureau), ECAS (European Citizens Action Service), and a number of well-established organisations representing consumer interests, including BEUC (Bureau Européen des Unions de Consommateurs), COFACE (Confederation of Family Organisations in the European Community), and EUROCOOP (European Community of Consumer Cooperatives) (Chapter 8). Subnational interests are represented through the CEMR (Council of European Municipalities and Regions) and the Assembly of European Regions (AER) (Chapter 9). These are described in some detail within the discrete chapters which follow, together with the other associations present within each of these interest arenas.

For any student seeking to locate the influence of private interests upon public policies, the first starting point is often to examine the sectoral organisation of business interests, and the representation of these interests in public policies, through groups, fora and individual firms, by European, national and territorial levels of interaction. Many of these actors have become indispensable to public policy-making and implementation in Europe because of the types of resources they bring to these arenas, becoming institutionally involved with European public policy-making and implementation. Brussels is very much an insider's town, where operating effectively depends upon a dense network of interpersonal and interorganisational links. It is very difficult for outsiders to arrive, win the day through persuasion, and go home again.

Lobbyists

Well known in concept are the commerical lobbyists, who interact with the European institutions on behalf of their clients. In the three years following the entry into force of the SEA in 1987 these are estimated to have tripled in number (see Gorges, 1993), although there has been some pruning back since (Stern, 1994). Their number includes those working for an estimated 160 law and 140 accountancy firms engaged on European public affairs (Grant, 1995), and specialist public-affairs consultancies, varying in size from one-man bands to firms of well over twenty employees. Although there is a core of highly respected public affairs firms led by impressive, well-established individuals with invaluable contacts and inside knowledge of the working of the Union, taken as a whole it is a transient community with a high turnover of personnel. Sometimes lobbyists are recent graduates whose later career paths are likely to involve the European interface, or working for the institutions themselves, and such work therefore represents a grounding in the operation of the EU. The reverse is also true; personnel of consultancy firms sometimes include those who have worked in the European institutions, although these are often regarded with suspicion by present-day EU officials.

Lobbyists perform roles ranging from information collection through to case presentation with officials and politicians from the European institutions, and assistance provided to interest groups and networks in their day-to-day operations, such as writing newsletters and, in a few cases, providing secretariat facilities. The best are held in high regard by those with whom they come in contact in the institutions. However, the influence of professional lobbyists as a whole has sometimes been overestimated. On the whole, European institutions prefer to deal with interests direct rather than interme-diaries. Lobbyists don't provide any of the benefits of democratic contact with interests in the member states, or the ability to encou-rage the transfer of competencies from the member states to the European-level. They are often less useful to the Commission than are experts in sectoral fields, because their knowledge often extends to no more than their brief, and they are unable to provide technical assistance to the Commission in formulating public policies. One Commission official reflected that

> in most cases, lobbyists come ill-prepared for their discussion and in general the quality of their presentations is low . . . where good lobbying takes place, it is the exception and it tends to stand out very clearly . . . public-relations firms on the whole are not well regarded. They tend to be perceived as glib purveyors of a tale which they have prepared for a particular meeting. They are normally unable to get involved in any kind of detailed discussion of an issue because they do not understand it fully once the discussion strays outside their brief (Hull, 1993, pp. 82 and 86).

The best professional lobbyists tend to be those who have come to this conclusion for themselves, and who concentrate on advising clients as to how best to exert influence in European public affairs. The worst are those who lack real expertise in the way the EU operates, and who lack appreciation of the limits of what lobbying can achieve. Both types can be found throughout the lobbying community, although the most professional are undoubtedly those of long standing in Brussels itself. Despite working for rival firms, the old hands, particularly in public affairs firms, have formed a close network between themselves, not least because they move in the same circles. As is described in Chapter 4, this inner circle have also created a code of conduct for lobbyists. However, instances of undue influence are only rarely evident, and researchers seeking stories of bribery and corruption might find their time better spent in Palermo than in Brussels, Luxembourg and Strasbourg.

Commerical lobbyists tend to be used by clients as supplements to other means of pursuing interests in Europe. Use of lobbyists might be involved where a public-affairs specialist firm has particular issue strengths, or strengths in contacts with one of the institutions, or even where a dedicated Brussels presence is out of the question on resource grounds. Further occasions to use a commerical lobbyist might include dedicated intelligence-gathering needs, or when it would be unwise to expect an interest group to act effectively. This latter type of event might occur when the collective representative is weak, either in general terms or when it is faced with divisions among its members over a particular issue, or if an issue is likely to affect the interests of a particular firm more than others. The pharmaceutical firm Fisons, for instance, used a commercial lobbyist when a draft directive on animal laboratory tests seemed likely to affect their interests more than those of others in the industry.

One of the more unusual uses of a European public-affairs consultancy firm is that by the UK Environment Agency. Although part of central government machinery through its parent Department of the Environment, the Agency takes the view that it is able to secure better representation in Brussels by paying a retainer than it can do by relying on the normal UK government channels. Certainly, the Agency is likely to get a much better service by paying for dedicated service in Brussels than it might by mixing its interests with those of other sections of central government machinery. This situation is an excellent caution against analysts who tend to see member states, and their machinery of government, as unitary actors in European public affairs. The example is indicative of significant tensions and divisions which exist within domestic governments, including those such as the UK where co-ordination for European representation is generally thought to be among the best in Europe (Stow, 1991). In order to secure its interests in Brussels the Agency would have to first approach its parent department, which might even, for the Agency, be part of the problem it is seeking to address. The use of a Brussels consultancy firm by parts of central government machinery may not be unique, particularly in the recent climate of decentralisation in the member states.

There is no shortage of advice on how to lobby in the European Union (see, for instance, Gardner, 1991; Andersen, 1992; Stern, 1994). These sources contain informative and detailed insights into interest representation in Brussels, of which lobbying is one part. Distilled advice for a lobbyist from these sources might include the following:

1. Have a clear strategy.
2. Develop long-term, even permanent, relations with authorities. Establish a track record as a provider of useful, accurate, well-researched information. If you need to start forming a relationship when a problem arises it is probably too late.
3. Find out who is drafting an item and make your representations early. If you have not been able to influence the Commission draft proposal you have probably lost the case.
4. Prepare well for meetings. Beware of using hired hands to present cases where their knowledge of your issue will inevitably be limited. Leave a position paper behind.
5. Present with brevity and clarity.
6. Be aware of all sides of the argument. Keep it low-key; do not over-lobby. Appreciate the limits of what can be achieved.
7. Keep all viable channels of communication open.
8. Know the system, and get to know the points of entry to the decision-making process.
9. Remain vigilant.
10. Be clear about the differences in culture between Brussels and Washington.

Such advice would be helpful to any interest in presenting a case at the European-level, particularly as murmurs of criticism, of both lobbying standards and the crowding of the so-called lobby environment, are now audible around the European institutions (Chapter 4).

Despite the widespread attention given to the work of lobbyists, they are on the whole a seductive red herring for the student of European public policy. A focus on tactical operations by lobbyists is an insufficient basis for attempting to understand the impact of private interests on public policy outputs and outcomes. Instead, emphasis is given in what follows to the exchange of resources between private and public actors which determines access to public policy-making and implementation, where these parties become dependent upon one other. One of these factors concerns the importance of a coherent and well-resourced Brussels-based European group.

The operational resources of groups

An important distinction is that between organisations which represent themselves (e.g. firms) or other organisations (such as trade associations representing firms) and organisations which represent individuals (such as consumers or workers). Coherence is clearly (though not exclusively) much easier to achieve in organising a handful of firms, for instance, than it is when organising a diverse constituency of individuals. The exception to this is when a group represents a constituency so diverse (such as European citizens) that consultation among members would be impossible, offering the prospect of speedy platform-building. Such a potential advantage can also be illusory, because there are often democratic demands upon the European organisation concerned from a number of national organisations claiming representative status; such is the case, for instance, with consumer interests. Nevertheless, there remain greater difficulties in representing a constituency base of individuals than one of organisations such as firms.

A first and basic step researchers take when assessing the involvement of a particular kind of interest in European public affairs is to establish whether such an interest has a base within easy reach of Brussels. Such a detail might reveal important information about the influence an interest exerts upon European public affairs, and the extent to which it is affected by them.

A Brussels base is a prerequisite for any interest seeking a role in the EU, and/or for whom the stakes involved in European public affairs are significant. In addition to the 700-plus groups at European and/or international level, and other types of fora, 135 territorial authorities have opened representative bureaux in Brussels, while the majority of the world's largest firms have a public-affairs office within easy reach of the European institutions. In broad terms, the greater the degree of competence the EU enjoys in a functional domain, the higher the stakes are likely to be, and the more likely it is that an interest has invested resources in organising in Brussels. High-technology businesses, for instance, invest considerable resources in the European-level of organisation, because the Union, and the Commission in particular, places considerable importance on the industrial application of 'super technologies'.

Setting up an office in Brussels is expensive, with floor-space alone typically costing 7500 to 10 000 Belgian francs per square metre (Stern, 1994). This factor helps explain why over two-thirds of all groups based in Brussels are business groups, although also important to this imbalance has been the historic focus of the EU as an economic community centred on a business agenda. Office space is more expensive the closer one gets to the Brussels 1040/1049 postal district, where the Commission, the Council, the national delegations, the alternative Parliament chamber and the offices of the Members of the European Parliament (MEPs) are mostly based. In these districts can be found the European-level trade associations of the wealthiest business sectors.

The Commission recognises the importance of cost as a barrier to certain types of interests locating in Brussels, and therefore provides resources, financial and otherwise, to assist a range of non-business groups to operate from the Belgian capital. In a recent (autumn 1995) representative survey sample of Euro groups by postal questionnaire in which the author has been involved,[*] involving the responses of 405 (58 per cent) groups, over one-fifth (88 or 21.7 per cent) claimed receipt of EU funding, while around 5 per cent stated that this was their main source of funding (Greenwood and Aspinwall, 1997). Where Commission finance is not available to set up an essential Brussels base, an option for a cash-strapped interest is to locate the European association within the premises of the Belgian national association, or a kindred interest. Indeed, many interests find themselves sharing office space for their public-affairs base with others on cost grounds. For those whose interests are less affected by the competencies of the EU, apart from the option of retaining the services of a commerical lobbyist, an alternative is to operate a so-called European association based elsewhere in the member states,

---

[*] Afterwards referred to as 'authors survey' for shorthand, although this survey involved a team of four researchers from the Robert Gordon University, Aberdeen. In addition to the author, they included Linda Strangward, Lara Stancich and Mark Aspinwall. The full results of this survey are reported in Greenwood and Aspinwall (1997).

often located in the offices of a member national association. In particular, those interests less affected by the EU often choose to host the European association wherever organisational resources are strongest; for instance, the European Federation of Camping Site Organisations and the European Tour Operators' Association, both operate from suburban UK addresses.

What is at stake in Europe?

For the plethora of interests the stakes to play for at the European-level can be vast. Present European competencies in public policy decisions could, at their most dramatic, threaten the living standards of whole communities, such as those who fish the sea or farm the land for a livelihood; threaten access to customers for an entire industry (such as the tobacco industry with smokers); provide opportunities for consumers to enjoy safer, cheaper, better quality products; equip workers with the means to achieve better working conditions, particularly when faced with hostile domestic governments; provide regional solutions to global environmental problems; or make the difference between profit and loss for a manufacturing company in having to meet, for instance, environmental regulation. A large firm might waste millions of ecus and years in research effort trying to develop a new product only to have it made obsolete by a public policy decision. A region, and interests within it such as small businesses, could lose out on vital support funds for area projects by the withdrawal of funding initiatives. Set against this background, the increase in the number of Euro level groups – from 300 in 1970 (Butt Philip, 1985) to well over double that number today (Chapter 3) – should come as no surprise.

The competencies which interests at the European-level address can be grouped into five broad headings. These are: *regulation*, concerned with restriction and governance of activities, usually on public interest grounds; *promotion*, such as action designed to develop industrial application of key technologies or to support export campaigns; *integration*, such as measures to ensure free and fair competition between producers throughout the single market; *funding*, such as the structural funds for regional policy, or support under the EU research framework programmes; and *enablement*, where responses are made to pressing problems with support measures, such as measures designed to promote a cleaner environment which do not fall into the category of 'regulation'. These categories are not mutually exclusive, nor are they precise. Regulation and integration activities have clearly been interlinked in initiatives designed to achieve the single market. Public procurement regulations, for instance, insist that large public works and supplies contracts are advertised for tender throughout the EU. The purpose of this is to ensure value and quality for taxpayers, and the ability of firms to compete on the global market, through market competition, rather than permitting protected and cosy national and local 'champion' agreements with favoured suppliers which tend to inflate costs and make industry uncompetitive (Cecchini, 1988).

Despite interlinkages and overlap, the categories of regulation, integration, promotion, funding and enablement do have broad currency in covering the scope of issues facing interests operating at the European-level. Such categories include issues which have occurred, or which may arise, and the perspectives of interests who regard them, or who could potentially regard them as, opportunities and threats. Indeed, the entire single-market project represents both an opportunity and a threat for business: an opportunity in the sense of having over 370 million potential customers under conditions of similar market supply, rather than being excluded from foreign markets; and a threat in that one's traditional, and perhaps at one time protected, customer base is open to competition from other suppliers.

The logic of these forces is that large, mobile firms well able to compete outside their national markets would find the single market a glorious opportunity, whereas many smaller firms which had benefited from national rules, sometimes protectionist in nature, might struggle. In part for these reasons, the run up to the single market therefore saw a wave of mergers, acquisitions and strategic alliances as firms sought to make the most of the opportunities presented by the single market (Jacquemin and Wright, 1994). These conglomerations had a vested interest in a transnational, rather than series of national, set of rules governing market exchange. Besides the opportunities presented by, and need for, one single market, there was the chance to tear up the national rules and help create a whole new set, sometimes based around liberalisation. Indeed, the most competitive firms have been the loudest voices for liberalisation, whereas struggling rivals prefer more regulated systems; such a pattern is evident in the case of airlines, where British Airways is a strong supporter for liberalisation while many of its rivals oppose it (Young, 1995). As

Chapters 5–9 illustrate, market exchange arises within a framework of rules, and market building has brought with it not just deregulation of national rules but also re-regulation at the European-level. Business interests have therefore been active in the process of designing these rules. Unsurprisingly, large business interests have often encouraged the progressive transfer of competencies to the EU level, sometimes manipulated by a Commission anxious to transfer power from the member states to its own transnational power base. In such ways, business interest groups have become mechanisms of European integration. Chapter 10 examines in some detail the role of interests in European integration.

Low politics, high politics

A useful distinction to make for the purposes of identifying the sorts of issues to which interests respond is that between 'low' and 'high' politics (Hoffman, 1966). High politics involve the big, and generally highly politicised issues of European public affairs, such as monetary union or the balance of competencies between member states and the EU, where almost entire populations are affected. Because such issues are in the open political arena it is impossible for specialised interest groups to exert exclusive influence on them, although they can sometimes provide leadership by helping to structure debate in particular ways through the injection of ideas. Clearly, business interests can carry a significant weight in high politics issues, but to do so they need to see issues in the same way, organise themselves to influence public policies and have the significant actors speak with one voice. One such example concerned the role of the ERT as a catalyst for the single market (Chapter 5). Such influence over high politics issues is rare, but can partly be explained by the consensus which such an idea attracted, and because few in reality fully appreciated the consequences of signing up for the project. This partial exception apart, high politics tends to involve large and highly visible issues at the centre of public affairs to which no single interest has monopolistic access.

Low politics consists of the more routine, detailed and day-to-day issues which arise in public affairs. In general, these issues tend to be the less politicised ones, such as the technical details of product standards, and/or some of the measures taken to achieve the single market within an industrial sector. Low politics issues tend to intensely affect a relatively small set of interests; by nature, the sorts of issues involved are unlikely to attract wide political interest and demands for participation in the decision-making process. Highly specialised types of interests, such as sectoral business interest groups, may therefore be ideally placed to enjoy access to key public policy decisions which affect them without having to compete with other interests, by virtue of the monopolistic expertise they possess. Such groups are able to provide assistance in both formulating and implementing workable public policies. The single-market project was therefore an ideal stage for sectoral business to play on because of their ability to provide detailed, and sometimes unchallenged, input, from the crucial early stages of policy initiation (Chapter 2) through to policy implementation particularly in the circumstances of an overloaded Commission in need of expertise and co-operation from business interests. Indeed, some business interest groups have become full partners with the Commission in governance, and therefore essential mechanisms through which to achieve harmonisation and integration in the sectors in which they operate. Much of the responsibility for ensuring technical harmonisation and integration within a sector has been handed down to specialist interests, through the work of the European standards institutes (Chapter 2).

Now that measures to achieve the single market are largely in place it may well be that the role of Euro-level interest groups will undergo change. Indeed, there is evidence that business in Europe is weary from the pace of change and, given the choice, would like a period of assimilation (Jacquemin and Wright, 1994). Sectoral business groups, in particular, may therefore take a rather different role between now and the end of the century as the single market approaches completion in detail, and the EU returns to focus on broader political decisions involving high politics issues, such as the deepening of political and monetary union. These might demand an enhanced role for peak groups. However, precisely what is low and what is high politics is not straightforward. So, for example, for a country like Denmark with a large toy producer like Lego, the details of integration may represent a national interest and therefore become high politics, whereas for a country like Luxembourg, without a large producer in the sector, the issues remain very much in the low category. Similarly, issues such as competition policy can fall in the spectrum between high and low politics, and, depending upon the particular issue, can be more or less politicised. Consequently, it is doubtful whether firm predictions about the future role in the EU of cross sectoral, versus sectoral, groups could be offered, and, given the dynamic nature of EU politics, even more so whether they could be sustained. In any event, the processes of integration have meant that many business interest representatives have now become fully incorporated into the realms of sectoral governance with the Commission.

Insider groups and status

The relative lack of politicisation of many low politics issues makes the task of exerting influence altogether more manageable, because it involves a limited number of participants who have the opportunity to build semi-permanent, and often rather exclusive, relationships based on mutual dependencies. In these settings, political decision-making (and certain contexts of non-decision-making) typically arises in the first instance from the relationship between a small number of officials in the European Commission and representatives of private interests; that is, they become governing mechanisms for the domain in which they are involved. Richardson and Jordan (1979) have termed these 'policy communities'. Rhodes (1988) has updated this concept by use of the generic term 'policy network', under which lies a spectrum of more or less tightly integrated networks. At one end lies the tightly integrated policy community, which provides for a settled type of governance mechanism involving a limited number of participants who come to depend on each other over a long period of time. At the other lies the fragmented, thrown-together-by-the-circumstances, here-today-and-gone-tomorrow 'issue network', a label first used by Heclo (1978), often involving a large variety of participants who may not be very familiar with each other's perspectives.

It would doubtless be the ambition of any European interest group to limit the number of 'policy participants' (a term first coined by Jordan *et al.*, 1992) to themselves alone and a handful of Commission officials, in a settled policy community. At the European level it is possible to identify examples of arrangements throughout the entire spectrum of policy networks, ranging from the policy community to the issue network. Some policy networks are exclusive and organised around a limited number of participants. There are also examples of policy domains which have become increasingly crowded by the growing number of interests organising and seeking access, and/or through the complexity of public affairs which has necessitated policy co-ordination by a number of functional policy divisions within the Commission. In the more settled policy communities, business interests have been active to ensure co-ordination between these divisions, while the Commission has also been active to keep the number of interest organisations involved to manageable proportions. Policy communities provide a great many mutual benefits for both parties. For the Commission, they provide access to co-operation and a controlled environment with which to make their policies effective and workable, while for interests they provide an excellent way of exerting singular influence upon public policies.

Indispensability and insider status

Access to a policy community for an interest is dependent on how indispensable an interest can make itself to public policy-makers and implementers. This implies that interests can perform services in the broader public interest at the same time as promoting their own interests. Clearly, a successful company which brings in wealth to the European economy is also performing a public service; so too is a trade association which saves the taxpayer money by protecting the public through self-regulatory arrangements, such as travel agents affiliating to an insurance fund to protect holidaymakers if an operator goes into liquidation. Similarly, a consumer group might provide the Commission, which lacks resources to collect all the intelligence it needs, with invaluable information on which to make sound and workable policies to promote the public interest. Nevertheless, the overwhelming majority of all Euro groups are business groups, and these have been far more able to exert influence upon public policies because they have more of the resources which public authorities need. In short, the more bargaining chips an interest has in its possession, the greater is the influence it can exert upon public affairs, particularly on issues which do not attract widespread public debate.

For the private interest, the possession or absence of bargaining chips determines whether or not it enjoys 'insider' (Grant, 1978) status to policy-making and implementation and becomes a participant in policy communities. Interests which lack sufficient bargaining chips, or who shun 'insider' involvement are 'outsider groups' (Grant, 1978). The tactics an interest employs are symptomatic of its status. Crudely put, the less public an interest makes its affairs the more successful it tends to be, because it is able to get its needs met on the 'inside track' of public policy-making. Conversely, groups which need to appeal for public support for their concerns do so because they are unable to exert influence as an insider group. Increasing use of public appeal strategies may signify the erosion of insider status. For interests whose lack of resources, or whose wish not to compromise, makes them outsiders, a counter-resource is to attempt to politicise issues so that insiders lose their monopolistic, behind-closed-doors access to policy participation. Such a tactic is, however, an uncertain and long-term game, and one which is unattractive and unacceptable for some outsiders. For those who do not deliberately seek it, their outsider status makes the task of representing interests extremely difficult. For instance, COFACE, the family group, has complained that it is consulted by the Commission only after drafts have already been agreed.

Typically, business groups possess more resources of the type required for insider status than do non-business groups. However, the inability to organise such resources may mean that an otherwise resource-rich interest does not enjoy the privileged access which one might expect. For instance, firms within a sector which are unable to reach agreement on what to seek from public policies, and which speak with different voices to the Commission, would be unlikely to collectively achieve insider status.

There are different types of insider status. Thus, Maloney *et al.*, (1994) helpfully make the distinction between 'core' (always centrally involved in policy-making and implementation), 'specialist' (always centrally involved where technical issues are involved) and 'peripheral' (only sometimes involved) insider status. Here, the nature of insider status for peripheral and specialist interests thus changes with the type of issue involved. The dynamic nature of these categories is further emphasised by considering the case of public-interest environmental groups, whose status over time has shifted from outsider to at least 'peripheral insider', as a result of the politicisation of environmental interests. Similarly, it would be possible for a business group which has achieved core insider status to find its position over time eroded by changes in market conditions, and politics. Nevertheless, resource-rich business interests which organise their interests well can find themselves so closely ingrained in public policy that it is sometimes difficult to make a distinction between private interests and public policies. For instance, case studies of consumer electronics (Cawson, 1995) and pharmaceuticals (Greenwood, 1995b) suggest that public policies have adopted the character of business interests in these domains.

Types of bargaining chips

Bargaining chips with which to enter public policy arenas at the European level include the following:

1. *Information and expertise*   Public policies are often shaped around specialist information brought by private interests. Hull (1993, p. 83) has characterised a drafting official in the Commission as 'a very lonely [person] with a blank piece of paper in front of him, wondering what to put on it'. Firms, industrial associations and, increasingly, some public-interest groups, may well have greater collective expertise than the Commission official(s). Commission reports often contain statistics given by such sources. Sometimes, the Commission asks an interest group to prepare a report on its behalf, which it then uses as the basis for policy initiatives.

2. *Economic muscle*:   Some companies have greater resources at their disposal than do certain member states. They are therefore bound to be significant political actors. Public policy-makers are dependent upon businesses to perform; key factors such as employment, balance of trade and wealth creation, and indeed the popularity of public institutions, including ruling parties, count on business activities. The European pharmaceutical industry, for instance, has a net positive balance of trade with the rest of the world of plus 12 per cent, compared with a net deficit for all sectors of minus 0.67 per cent (Greenwood, 1995b). It represents a key player with which to compete with the rest of the world today and tomorrow, and European public policy-makers cannot afford to ignore it. Crudely put, the possession of powerful economic resources puts an interest in a strong position to be able to influence public policies, because such resources are indispensable to the welfare of Europe.

3. *Status*:   Status resources also influence access to public policies. The Commission, for instance, is particularly keen on high-prestige, high-technology industrial domains which promise to be key players tomorrow. In this way, domains such as consumer electronics, information technology, biotechnology and pharmaceuticals perhaps reflect to the Commission a desired self-image. Outside of producer domains, however, the impact of status is uncertain. On the one hand, many of the Commission's activities concerned with the free movement of workers have been directed at high-status professional groups like doctors, not least because of the role of medics in taking test cases to the European Court of Justice (ECJ). On the other, the

organisation of professional groups in Europe is on the whole weak; this goes even for those whose high status has commanded them an important role in public affairs in member states, such as the medical profession (Chapter 6).

4. *Power in implementation*: Groups such as farmers are powerful actors because they own significant land resources. It would be inconceivable for the Commission to develop a policy on, say, retaining hedgerows, without consulting with farmers first, because farmers have the ability to make or break such a policy in that they would be the key actors responsible for implementation. If the farmers refused such a policy it would undoubtedly fail.

5. *The organisation of the interest into a non-competitive format*: Interests organised into groupings who compete find interest intermediation difficult, because public policies either are unable to arbitrate between the factions or else favour one type of interest at the expense of others. Any bureaucracy finds it extremely difficult to deal with competitive groupings, and indeed the Commission has devoted considerable efforts, fiscal and otherwise, to assist with the organisation of interests into single formats. For instance, the Biotechnology Coordinating Committee (BCC), located within DG XII (Science, Research and Development), once publicly criticised industrial interests for their fragmented organisation, and in doing so caused the collapse of one forum, and was the catalyst for a more encompassing format to arise (Greenwood and Ronit, 1994). Such efforts indicate just how important it is to the Commission to have a 'one-stop-shop' European group based in Brussels representing all the interests within a category, because such groups are able to make life considerably easier for an overloaded bureaucracy. Issues concerning group coherence, and intergroup relations, are considered in detail in Chapter 3.

6. *Coherent organisation with representative outlets able to make decisions with ease and alacrity*: These properties include the capacity for speedy decision-making, which requires the delegation of powers to a group secretariat to take action without the need for constant prior referral to the membership constituency beforehand. Also important in achieving coherent policy statements is the weighting of influence towards the most important interests (Chapter 3). Effective collective action is a precondition for effective patterns of interest representation, while effective interest representation through a particular organisation acts as a membership incentive.

7. *The ability to help the overloaded Commission with carrying out policies*: An interest can make itself extremely attractive to the

Commission if it helps with the overload problem by acting as an agency of policy implementation. At the same time, considerable influences can be exerted upon the impact a policy has during its implementation. One way to do this is through self-regulation. Hence, the European Federation of Pharmaceutical Industry Associations (EFPIA) successfully offered itself as the means through which standards of medical selling to medical practitioners could be regulated through the provision of a code of practice, established and implemented by EFPIA, as an alternative to more statutory forms of regulation which had been proposed. Such schemes do, however, require strong associational capacities to ensure member compliance (Chapter 4). As is described in some of the chapters of this book which examine particular types of interests, apart from self-regulation, a variety of private actors across a number of domains are in some way involved in policy delivery mechanisms.

8.   *The ability of an interest group to influence its members*:   An interest group which entered into agreement with the Commission and which failed to make the agreement stick with its members would be of little use to the Commission. Conversely, one which can deliver authoritative opinion and carry its members, such as EFPIA's role in delivering self-regulation, is likely to be invaluable.

Models of resource exchange

Interests holding sufficient strength in the types of resources which have just been identified are likely to be insiders in European public policies, and those without are likely to be outsiders. If interests have certain types or combinations of resources which make them useful at particular times or over particular issues, such as expertise, then they may achieve specialist, or perhaps peripheral, insider status. Resource-rich interests become institutionally involved in European public policies because of their indispensability to a section of the Commission with functional competencies, on whom they depend to prosper.

EU competencies, in their broadest categories, include the ability to regulate, promote, distribute and redistribute resources. The Commission, as the permanent bureaucracy with capacities for initiation and executive decision-making in regulation, promotion, enablement, funding and certain integration measures, forms the

natural arena for private interests to engage. When sufficient resources are exchanged between policy participants, power depen-
dency relationships arise. Each party becomes dependent on the
resources of the other. Sections of the Commission holding the
relevant policy competencies, and the interest concerned, may thus
become power-dependent, and in so doing they develop a symbiotic
relationship through which public policies arise and are implemented. These arrangements thus become mechanisms of governance.
Colebatch (1991) therefore suggests that we think more in terms of
public policy-making capacities as arenas in which policy-making
and implementation arise, rather than to make the formal and
sometimes misleading distinction between public and private interests. The term 'interest intermediation' seems to capture these
realities rather better than does the term 'lobbying', which conjures
images of smooth-talking hired hands showing up one day offering
dinner and persuasion and clearing off the next.

Extreme institutionalisation of private interests into public policy-
making appears to occur in the case of interests whose indispensability is primarily by nature of the strength of economic bargaining
chips. When some firms have more resources at their disposal than
certain member states, their indispensability in public policy-making
and implementation means that they become institutionalised far
more than other types of interests whose access is based on different
types of resources. This level of indispensability provides access to
further tiers of involvement in governance, such as policy implementation. These intensely institutionalised arrangements, based upon
resource exchange with a high degreee of interdependence, are of a
specific character and require recognition in a category apart from
the broader concept of a 'policy community'. Recognition of the
distinctiveness of such arrangements has been provided by writers in
the meso (sectoral) tradition of corporatism, such as Cawson (1985)
and Grant (1985).

The distinctive features of neo corporatism at the sectoral level are
the organisation of an interest by a group to such effect that the group
is able to make binding agreements on behalf of its members with
government, and make these agreements stick with its members; that
the interest is in the economic division of labour; and that the interest
has become so institutionalised in public policies that it has 'crossed
the boundary' and become part of the arena of the state itself,
perhaps by taking on mechanisms of public policy delivery through
self-regulatory arrangements. EFPIA's performance of a public

protection function on behalf of the Commission through the operation of a self-regulatory code makes the organisation a full mechanism of governance. Whereas 'policy community' is descriptive, 'neo corporatism' is a refinement which seems to offer the advantage of explanatory capacities, in that ownership of particular types of resources predicts access to particular types of governance mechanisms.

Streeck and Schmitter (1991) had a different variant of corporatism in mind when they famously proclaimed the absence of corporatism at the European level, and indeed that the European level of operation would be disruptive to national corporatisms. What they had in mind was macro-corporatism, involving peak exchange over high politics issues between business, labour and a bureaucracy with state-like properties, whereas they had little to say about meso (sectoral) corporatism. Indisputably, the conditions for macro corporatism are not present at the European level, because of the absence of anything like a state. However, some (Hix, 1994; Lewin, 1994; Hayward, 1995) have over-generalised Streeck and Schmitter's arguments to suggest that corporatist arrangements *per se* are not present in Europe, or that it somehow is characteristic of a pluralist environment. In fact, Schmitter has more recently explicitly identified the presence of 'islands' (i.e. sectors) of corporatism at the European level, and has acknowledged, in a study of Austria with Franz Traxler, that the European level need not be disruptive to national corporatisms (Traxler and Schmitter, 1994). Indeed, as Falkner (1996) remarks, the predicted fade out of corporatism in Europe has failed to materialise.

There are cases where the relationship between private interests and public agencies become so one-sided that the agency is 'captured' by the interest; indeed, Mitnick has used the term 'regulatory capture' to describe such arrangements (Mitnick, 1980). Promotion may beckon for a relatively junior Commission official who has pleased one of the major European firms to such an extent that a favourable report is filed back to superiors. Regulatory capture, however, is rather different from neo corporatism, which is predicated on the idea of a more even exchange of resources between the Commission and private interests. On the Commission's side, regulatory and promotional competencies are significant capacities, and few interests can expect to routinely dominate a Commission unit; the resource-rich EFPIA, for instance, has on occasion lost an issue in public affairs.

Indeed, public policy outputs and outcomes are not as predictable as models of resource exchange and indispensability might at first glance suggest, because of the dynamic nature of politics. The strategy of excluded groups with interests in the field is to seek access by politicising issues. As issues become politicised, they disrupt the exclusive relationships between public agencies and insider interests. A recent example concerns the six-year passage of a directive on patenting of genetic modifications for commercial exploitation. Public-interest groups succeeded in watering down the directive to such an extent that it became unattractive to industrial biotechnology interests who had sought the measure, and, finally, ensuring the rejection of the watered-down version by the European Parliament (EP). What is all the more remarkable is that one of the key sponsoring interests for the measure was the Senior Advisory Group Biotechnology (SAGB), an industry Euro group comprising mainly large firms with interests in applications of biotechnology, which has been described by past Commission President Delors as the most effective group of the industry sector type.

'Policies make politics'

The dynamic nature of European public policies, the differential resources exchanged between the different actors involved, and of power itself, suggests that we must expect to find differences in public policy outputs. In a classic contribution to political science, Lowi suggested that the type of policy under consideration influences the underlying politics; thus, the type of politics underlying redistributive policies is quite different from those underlying distributive or regulatory issues (Lowi, 1964). Although these categories are not easy to apply to the European context with precision because of the partial nature of Euro competencies *vis-à-vis* the national level (Chapter 8), it is still possible to apply Lowi's ideas in a generalised sense. Thus, policies aimed at protecting Europe's steel industries as a whole are likely to result in collaborative politics between the different producers, whereas an impending Commission decision between rival technologies is likely to produce underlying competitive politics between firms in the respective camps. The entire logic of 'policies makes politics' is that generalised theories of politics, such as system theories of power offered by classic pluralism, are unlikely to match the diversity of empirical reality we find on the ground.

Indeed, the very basis of power-dependent resource exchanges is that there will be significant differences in public policy outputs, according to the players involved and resources exchanged between them. There is, therefore, considerable unevenness by sector, and issue, and it is not possible to characterise European public policy processes as a whole, as for instance, as either pluralist or corporatist in character. Readers should therefore treat with some degree of scepticism those accounts of European public policy-making which seek to demonstrate the validity of something as broad as a theory of power.

The methods which inform a generalised 'policies make politics' approach are often inductive, where the influences at stake are examined through careful case study research. Case studies have for some years been regarded as the Cinderella of methodologies because of a lack of rigour in, and familiarity with, ways of selecting cases and conducting enquiry. However, where cases are selected strategically enough (Eckstein, 1979; Lijphart, 1971), and enquiry is conducted with rigour (Yin, 1994), they can permit a degree of generalisability; that is, it is possible to generalise to a category of ideas from a single case. Outputs from public policies can be explained by studying the circumstances surrounding an issue, and by identifying the exchange of power-dependent resources. However, using the behaviour and perspectives of public and private actors is problematic, for two main reasons. First, self-perceptions and information gleaned from interviews need to be confirmed by evidence from other sources. Second, models of power have long been in existence which tell us that power cannot be studied by examining behaviour, because it can also be covert, or even latent (Lukes, 1974). Here, ideas such as power dependence help because they afford analysts the ability to model outputs without having access to seeing what goes on behind closed doors.

Ideas, norms, and socialisation

To understand policy outputs and outcomes fully, however, it is necessary to study more than power. The role of ideas, norms and socialisation is also important. Actors entering policy arenas are socialised by, and contribute to, a series of often unwritten rules governing exchange. These rules and ideas can have powerful effects. The relationship between the construction and dissemination of norms, and power, is a dialectic one, because ideas do not emerge and gain currency in a power vacuum, and nor do power constructs operate without consensus and dispute (Chapter 10).

Ideas and power interact to produce policy outputs at the European level. The European Commission, interested in the progressive transfer of competencies from the member state to European levels, will often do the groundwork to create an agenda of consensus whereby actors are talking its language. Private interests are essential mechanisms in this process. Sometimes, the Commission will leak information on its intentions to a large firm in the knowledge that businesses will inform national governments of the forthcoming agenda. Anxious to keep up with the pace of European public affairs, member states start espousing these ideas themselves, and contemplate ways in which they can respond to, or even drive, the agenda. The language becomes the same, and mutually reinforcing. Ideas become norms. Often, influence exerted by powerful private interests in favour of a measure will enlist the support of 'their' national government. In these ways, the Commission has significant 'hard' powers (in its formal initiation and executive roles) and 'soft' powers (through its ability to set the agenda of ideas which socialise others). Rhetoric expands, and interests seek to ensure that rhetoric is not empty. As Cram (1994) suggests, there is no such thing as cheap talk. However, ideas are capable are taking on a life and logic of their own, and are not somehow a tool to be manipulated at will by powerful interests.

Groups perform key roles in these socialisation processes. They are themselves socialised by their particpation in European public affairs, they act as bearers of ideas in the manner described, and they socialise their members to the norms operating at the European level. Groups can play a key role in the development of European integration, because of the ways in which they socialise their members and other political actors, the practical measures they take to harmonise and integrate, and the ways in which they can encourage the progressive transfer of competencies to the European level.

Conclusions

Such forms of grassroots integration mean that it is often interests in the member states which become impatient for further integration, sometimes against the backdrop of politicians and bureaucrats reluctant to cede further competencies away from member states. Few private interests work collectively and cohesively to exert a significant brake upon integration. This is an interesting contrast to the birth of the EEC, where politicians led the way against a backdrop of reluctant producer and public interests. The role of interests in shaping public policy outputs and outcomes, and in acting as mechanisms of integration, means that the study of interest representation in the EU is thus far from a specialist pursuit best left to enthusiasts. Rather, as the chapters ahead show, it is a central task for any student interested in understanding how the EU really functions, gives rise to governance mechanisms and produces policy outputs, and is likely to develop in the future.

2

EU Decision-Making and Channels of Influence

Interest representation at the European level is conditioned by the unique multi-level character of EU decision-making and policy processes. Participating in European public affairs therefore involves addressing subnational, member state, and supranational tiers of authority, and the complex interplay between them. Figure 2.1 identifies the major points of access in EU decision-making and implementation throughout the formal stages of the policy process, from initiation through to implementation and adjudication.

The points of access to EU decision-making are multiple and complex. As is evident from the discussion of interest representation in relation to the individual institutions later in this chapter, the role of the Commission as the responsible agency for drafting legislation makes it the foremost institutional target for interest representation at the European level because it is in the early stages of initiatives that most influence can be exerted. In low-politics domains, both the need for, and the character of, particular policies can arise from shared belief systems which arise in exclusive types of policy network between the Commission and private interests (Chapter 1). Second in importance as an institutional target is the Parliament, arising principally from its ability to amend proposed legislation. Third comes the Council of Ministers, where its focus as the final point of decision-making makes it a target for last-minute interest representation; at this later point in the decision-making cycle, it becomes more difficult to exert influence because issues have already been shaped, and interventions may require seeking changes to entrenched positions rather than seeking to shape problems into policy initiatives.

While other European institutions also provide the opportunity to exert influence, an institutional and decision-making focus is however

27

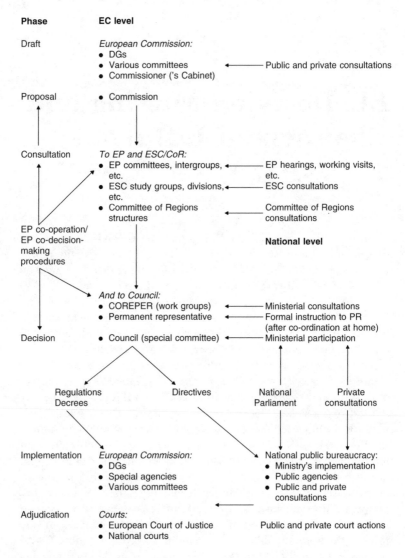

FIGURE 2.1 Formal decision-making linkages in the EU and its member states

Source: Adapted from van Schendelen (1993, p. 11). Reproduced by kind permission of Dartmouth Press.

an insufficient basis to analyse the ways in which interests contribute to the governance of the EU. Certainly, formal policy initiation can arise from the constitutional powers of the Council of Ministers and Parliament, who have the ability, albeit somewhat conditional in the case of the EP, to ask the Commission to bring forward initiatives. The rotating presidencies provide member states with considerable agenda setting powers. But perhaps more important than the possession of these constitutional powers, from the point of view of a discussion of interest representation, is that the preferences of actors who participate in institutionalised structures can be shaped considerably by interests who are, or who seek to become, policy participants. Formalised players such as MEPs, sub national tiers of authority, and in particular member states can and do propel issues on to the European policy agenda both within and outside of the institutional frameworks in which they operate. A good example of this is provided by the 1996 beef crisis, where decision-making became dominated by different member state positions, by their summitry and by bargaining between themselves and with the European Commission. This made the focus of European-level interest representation, in so far as actors are able to exert influence over high politics positions, arise principally at the national level. Indeed, as scholars of international relations contend, the starting point of the policy cycle for high politics issues is generally with the member states themselves, and these actors are without question a considerable force in the integration process (Chapter 10). Politicised issues such as fisheries quotas are by nature centred around the self-interest of member states. A common position between British and Spanish fishermen would clearly not be possible, making European-level collective interest representation on fisheries quotas through the fishing association, EUROPECHE, out of the question. Nevertheless, the role of the Commission, in partnership with corporate interests, in bringing forward the single-market programme demonstrates very clearly the way in which even very politicised issues can be developed by acting at the supranational level.

After policies are agreed at the Council of Ministers, a different balance of policy forces arises. Most European decisions are dependent upon national administrations for their implementation. Implementation represents an opportunity for private interests to exert influence, particularly where there are strong and relatively closed policy communities with government at the national level. In these circumstances, governments sometimes use self-regulation as a preferred mechanism to implement a directive, particularly where this suits preferences for parcelling out governmental functions, or where a private interest is in a position to offer itself as an agency capable of delivering it. As Sargent readily observes, 'corporatist agreements (such as those involving agreement on self-regulation) are sometimes promoted and defended by conservative governments which advocate a policy of minimal state intervention in the economy' (Sargent, 1985, p. 251). In the UK, for instance, self-regulation has been the preferred mechanism of implementing directives on financial services regulation, the energy labelling of domestic electrical appliances, and in a case where a draft directive on quickfrozen foods would have required costly re-equipping of freezer cabinets in retail stores. In this latter example, the government encouraged representatives of the retail trade, with the agreement of consumer organisations and food packagers, to establish guidelines concerning the handling of frozen foods in retail outlets (Sargent, 1985).

Despite the dominant role of member states in policy implementation, the European Commission has developed an increasing role in this part of the policy process. Significantly, in strengthening the role of the European institutions *vis-à-vis* the member states, the SEA provided the Commission with an increased sense of purpose and confidence in its role as guardian of the legal framework of the EU, for example as in the case of as competition policy (Chapter 5). Here, the Commission monitors non-compliance by member states, and the possibility of firms breaching EU law on restrictive practices, state aids and company mergers (Nugent, 1994). Partly because of its lack of resources, the Commission will be dependent upon public and private interests for monitoring the implementation of these through competitive 'whistle-blowing' activities, and, where necessary, in using this information to bring actions to the ECJ to uphold and assert the primacy of European law. While specific examples of this role can be found later on (see, in particular, Chapters 5 and 8), one which will suffice for illustrative purposes at this point concerns the proposed sale of the (then) British-government-owned Rover Group to British Aerospace in 1987. Belated attempts were made at a high level to secure Commission approval for the proposed terms of the sale. The conditions imposed by DG IV (competition policy) made the deal so unattractive to the parties involved that the British government had to offer a last minute package of financial inducements. When these were discovered by the Commission in 1993, British Aerospace was ordered to repay them, with interest accrued after further periods of delay arising from failed appeals (Greenwood and Jordan, 1993). As this example shows, notwithstanding some erosion of confidence in the 1990s as the supranational institutions went on the retreat after the Maastricht Treaty ratifications, the Commission has undoubtedly made itself a more important actor for interests to engage during the latter stages of the policy process.

The multi-level character of the European policy process means that actors seeking to participate in European public affairs therefore have a number of so-called 'routes' of influence. At its most simple level, the 'national route' refers to the use of national contacts and national governments to influence Brussels, whereas the 'European route', also known as the 'Brussels strategy', involves seeking to exert influence by representation direct to the European institutions them-selves. These two routes provide the focus for the rest of the chapter, with each identified and considered in turn ahead of a comparative discussion of them. The extent to which sub national domains are both a participant in, as well as a route of, European level interest representation, makes a separate chapter on the territorial domain (Chapter 9) more convenient. Although particular circumstances may dictate a greater use of one of the routes for certain issues and at points in time, they are seldom mutually exclusive. In practice, interests tend to use a combination of routes simultaneously as a means of accessing European public affairs.

European-level interest representation through the 'national route'

The use of the national route for interest representation at the European level is conditioned both by the role of the national level at different stages in the European policy process, including decision-making in the Council and in implementation, and by the extent to which it provides a convenient and familiar point of access for interests.

The main access to decision-making in the Council, the most important of the institutions for final agreement on legislation, is via the national route. Interests need to be plugged in both to their usual channels of national representation, but also to the ways in which national governments co-ordinate their machinery for working in Europe. More centralised member states tend to have better co-ordination of governmental machinery for handling European public affairs, whereas the more decentralised states sometimes find co-ordination more difficult. On the other hand, a strong degree of centralisation may mean that COREPER representatives from these countries are given very little room for bargaining in discussions at Council level, and such delegations may therefore be less available to direct interest representation from private interests than are some others (Nugent, 1994). Nevertheless, it is not uncommon to see Ministers hurry downstairs during breaks in Ministerial level discussions at the Council of Ministers to brief waiting lobbies in the Council ante-rooms.

Although policy officials in the European Commission are often easier to establish contact with than are those in some national administrations, the national route represents the tried and tested ground for many interests (Grant, 1995). It is where established policy networks operate which can equally well be used for the purposes of EU representation as they can for the governance of domestic affairs. Despite a number of single-market measures aimed at producing competition on equal terms and removing national favouritism in operating environments for firms, the interests of some large firms and domestic governments are so entwined that the former command the position of a 'national champion' in domestic politics. Citing an instance of this, Stern remarks dryly that 'the government of the Netherlands has displayed views on the issue of high-definition television (HDTV) that are remarkably similar to those of Philips' (Stern, 1994, p. 99). Interests can thus impact upon the preferences of state actors which are in turn reproduced in the transnational arena. In Chapter 5, an example of the reverse scenario is also provided whereby a member state influenced its national peak confederation to take up a particular position within UNICE, with important consequences.

Interests will be keen to enlist support for their cause from their own domestic government first. If this is not available, it may be more difficult, though not impossible, to further the cause concerned in Europe. In these circumstances, an interest may then have to seek the support of other governments if it wishes to continue using the national route. For most, however, the starting point is usually at home (Sargent, 1987; van Schendelen, 1993). Where the interest is without an identifiable host base in any of the member states, the choice of government to approach first may be determined by the significance of presence, the absence of competitor interests or the compatibility of ideology.

Representation at the national level is more available to those interests lacking the resources to take the Brussels strategy, such as small firms or some public interests which are more difficult to organise than are large corporate entities. National ruling political parties, and established political contacts at the national level, may be somewhat less remote than are European ones. Equally, national contacts who work in the European institutions may be well net-worked with national interests. Thus, the Brussels-based Scotland Europa publishes a book of Scots in Brussels, *Jock Tamson's Bairns*, while it is sometimes said that the best way for an Irish interest to network with Brussels-based officials in the institutions is to go to the Irish bar called Kitty O'Shea's adjacent to the Berlaymont building. National permanent delegations based in Brussels are likewise well networked with fellow nationals working in the European institutions. Sometimes, these latter figures can be national government experts on temporary outpost in the Commission, or even secondees of essentially national interests.

European-level interest representation through the Brussels strategy

Use of the Brussels strategy is essential for any interest whose affairs might be significantly influenced by European-level competencies. As is discussed in subsequent chapters, in some cases particular interests have invested resources in the Brussels strategy even though Euro competencies in their field have yet to fully develop, in part because a number of institutions have sought deliberately to develop European-level interest structures (Chapters 1, 8 and 10). The functioning of these institutions provide the starting point for most interests seeking to address the European level.

The role of the European Commission

The Commission's importance for interest representation stems from its almost exclusive right to initiate legislation, and, to a lesser extent, its role in policing European legislation. Although the powers of the Commission have been somewhat eroded in recent years, its role as the initiator of proposals means that interests seeking to exert influence in European public affairs need to build a relationship with it, thereby necessitating the use of the Brussels strategy.

Nugent has calculated that the EU institutions employ 0.8 staff for every 10 000 European citizens, set against 322 per 10 000 population in the member states (Nugent, 1994). The European Commission, accounting for two-thirds of total employment by the EU institutions, has a total staff of 12 183 (McGowan and Wilks, 1995), rather less than some large city administrations in member states. It remains chronically understaffed for the range of functions it undertakes, accounting for what Metcalfe has termed its 'management deficit', and thus its dependence upon outside interests (Metcalfe, 1992). However, this may also ultimately limit access by private interests as hard-pressed Commission officials find it difficult to cope with an increasing quantity of interest representation (Chapter 1).

The most prized contacts claimed by interests are invariably those of the Commission leadership. However, the power of the President derives more from the political leadership skills of the incumbent than from a constitutional position, since Commission decisions are taken by the College of Commissioners, if necessary by majority vote. In the Delors years it was evident that the President could use the position to shape the agenda of the Union, an observation which drove the UK government to exercise considerable influence in the choice of a successor. Other Commissioners are appointed individually by the member states. Although Commissioners forswear national allegiances in favour of their European-wide role, it has been claimed that they provide a channel of influence for some domestic interests (Collins, 1993). On the other hand, Commissioners also have a capacity to undermine the domestic government, particularly if the individual concerned is not from the party of government of the country of appointment. Such factors make the relationship between Commissioners and domestic politics somewhat difficult to estimate. Like the President, influence may depend upon the particular post-holder. Collins has suggested that 'a Commissioner, like a king, can be a lonely figure, adrift from executive personnel, cut off from domestic politics, having no popular constituency to provide a real power base. Their ability to exercise authority stems to a large degree from the force of their personalities' (Collins, 1993, p. 53).

Commissioners are often dependent upon the assistance provided to them by a 'cabinet', or private office of around six advisory staff (twelve in the case of the President), usually hand-picked individuals (often of the same nationality) who the Commissioner concerned has chosen to work with. Some are functional experts, while others might have a more wide-ranging role in keeping a Commissioner briefed on wider developments inside and outside the Commission. 'Chefs (heads) de Cabinet' meet once a week and prepare the agenda for the weekly meeting of Commissioners on Wednesdays, and filter the agenda by seeking to agree non-controversial proposals. They, and other members of a cabinet, are therefore much sought after as a target of interest representation, although these individuals are likely to move on when the Commissioner does.

Despite the importance of the cabinet and the possibilities which these can provide for domestic channels of interest representation, it is unwise to rely upon a Commissioner and her or his cabinet for representation for two main reasons, both of which emphasise the importance of addressing Commission-wide decision-making, rather than relying upon national contacts. The first of these is that a Commissioner will need to convince his/her colleagues of the merit of their proposal, while second, the all-important initial drafts of a proposal will be prepared within the permanent staff of a DG. These vary in size with the extent of Commission competencies in the field. Thus, DG XXIV (Consumer Policy) contains around 120 staff, while DG VI (Agriculture) employs 850 staff. Each DG is divided between functional directorates, usually from 4 to 6 in number, which in turn are divided into divisions, perhaps numbering 3 to 4 (Nugent, 1994). Heads of Divisions report to Directors, who report to a Director General, who in turn reports to a Commissioner. It is essential for private interests seeking to be proactive to develop relationships with the relevant personnel within the appropriate division, rather than seeking out these individuals when it is too late after a proposal has already emerged. In doing so, an interest will be able to effectively input the information it needs to, shape the thinking of those responsible for drafting initiatives, and perhaps even propose measures itself which might appear in an early draft.

A lower-level official within a division will usually be given responsibility for preparing the draft, operating within the broad parameters of EU policy. This is passed upwards through the cabinets of Commissioners to the weekly meeting of the Chefs de Cabinets, and from there to Commissioners. Relatively uncontentious proposals will be resolved at this level, and passed on up to Commissioners for rubber-stamping. Proposals which are more contentious are dealt with by the College of Commissioners. In general, the higher a proposal goes within the Commission, the more reduced is the capacity for interest representation because of its increasing politicisation, and the mechanics of seeking change. Engaging the

Commission proactively by developing relationships with responsible divisional officers requires a Brussels presence.

Hull has stated that much lobbying is of poor quality because it is conducted after policy initiatives have emerged from the Commission (Chapter 1). Once an issue has left the Commission and enters other decision taking arenas the chance of exerting influence is considerably reduced, and the interest is reduced to reactive 'fire fighting' rather than seeking to shape the agenda before, or while, it emerges (Hull, 1993). Indeed, he suggests that

> the individual who is responsible for the initial preparation process over a given period of time (first draft, consultations within the Commission, consultations with interested parties, subsequent drafts, navigation through the Commission) will find that when the final proposal is adopted by the Council it usually contains 80 per cent of his or her proposal (1993, p. 83).

Although the wisdom of attaching a figure to this process has been disputed (Peterson, 1995a), the more general point made by Hull is not contested, and interests who do not understand these realities risk incurring heavy losses. Commenting on the Commission's rejection (by one vote) of the Aerospatiale–Alenia bid for de Havilland, one lobbyist commented that

> Aerospatiale's leaders completely misunderstood the process. They didn't make a strong technical case early on when the civil servants were making all the crucial decisions. By the time they began lobbying the politicians, they were too late and presented the wrong arguments (Sasseen, 1992, p. 63).

It is therefore essential to seek to exert influence before the proposal has emerged in draft form. To do this, an interest needs to know that a proposal is being considered, and a first and basic step is therefore to locate the Commission agenda. While there are a variety of publicly available sources to do this (for an excellent review of these see Stern, 1994), notification through these channels may appear some time after agendas have been set and issues shaped. Those present in Brussels therefore make it their business to know the details in advance of clients or managers based in the member states, and of any potentially competing interest, as a strategy of being prepared to respond to the work of the EU. Interests which are actors in highly institutionalised relationships (Chapter 1) with the Commission, and well networked with a range of contacts on the Brussels circuit, will almost certainly obtain early warning of a proposal and have access to views and information which are likely to shape initiatives. This emphasises once again the status of Brussels as an 'insider's town', and particularly the advantages which resource-rich insiders enjoy over those without a Brussels presence (Chapter 1). In turn, this has inspired a series of recent initiatives from the Commission designed in part to address the imbalance which different interests enjoy in their European interface.

The 'openness initiatives' emerged from the European Commission in 1993 and 1994, and were entangled in a number of agenda issues surrounding European politics at the time. They responded to a series of a concerns about openness and transparency of decision-making first raised at the 1992 Birmingham and Edinburgh summits, and to extensive criticisms raised by the 1992 Sutherland report (Sutherland, 1992), which had found

> intermittent flows of useful information, inadequate prior consultation and the absence of information at each stage of the Community's legislative process . . . such shortcomings make the whole process unpredictable leaving the public confused, feeling excluded as to the need for and usefulness of Community legislation (Claveloux, 1993, p. 6).

The Sutherland report had recommended a complete overhaul of the way in which the Commission engaged with outside interests, including a systematic and co-ordinated way of establishing dialogue. It argued that

> wide and effective consultation on Commission proposals is essential. The Commission needs to introduce a better procedure for making people aware, at the earliest possible stage, of its intention to propose legislation (Sutherland, 1992, p. 30).

Following the problems of democratic deficit raised by attempts to ratify the Treaty on European Union (TEU), timely suggestions such as those from the Sutherland committee aimed at tackling the problem were likely to be well received by a Commission on the defensive for having sought to take Europe much further than some of its citizenry had apparently wished. Measures designed to achieve improved openness and transparency include:

- a greater use of Green (consultative) Papers, partly designed to engage the views of interests outside of Brussels;

- a commitment to ensure that target groups are aware of any new policy initiatives which are planned (hitherto, the Commission has had a reputation for consulting only those interest groups with which it is familiar);
- changes to the style of information provided so as to make it more user-friendly;
- the creation of 'Info Point Europe' offices in the member states;
- measures to increase the exchange of information between different Commission services;
- the publication of a database of interest groups as a means of ensuring that all the relevant groups get consulted during policy initiation stages;
- the creation of 'information plans' by each DG to cover every major proposal, including the establishment of a contact point;
- the creation of a Users' Advisory Council, including representatives from European interest groups;
- the earlier publication of the Commission's legislative work programme, in October of each year rather than in January;
- a more decentralised communication process, involving greater use of the existing relay networks;
- an increased role for audio-visual media;
- the much-heralded availability of the majority of Commission papers (i.e. excluding those where confidentiality is in the public interest or concerning individuals and commercial and industrial secrets as well as the Community's financial interests) for any enquirer on a cost-only basis within 28 days.

These initiatives have been promoted as a type of 'citizen's charter', forming part of the response to concerns about the remoteness of the EU from the everyday lives of its citizens. As such, they provided the opportunity for the then incumbent Commission President Jacques Delors to take the lead on an issue which portrayed the Council as a secretive and unresponsive institution, and it may be this which provides the best context for understanding what became known as the 'Pinheiro initiatives' (after the Portuguese Commissioner who, rather reluctantly in the first instance, first presented the schemes in February 1994). Indeed, the reality of the 'openness initiatives' is that they have fallen some way short of expectations. For instance, following Pinheiro's claim that around 99 per cent of documentation would be made accessible to the general public, some well-publicised journalistic investigations testing out the procedures revealed the continued lack of availability in this area, and in particular the outright refusal of the Council, confirmed in COR- EPER 1 (officials at deputy ambassadorial level) meetings, to supply documentation. Indeed, in the months following the initiatives only around two-thirds of document access requests were approved (European Roundtable of Associations and Federations, 1994). Similarly, established European interest groups, together with journalists, form up to half the members of the Users' Advisory Council. In reality, measures such as these have done little more than reinforce the privileges of the already privileged, in that those best able to take advantage of the availability of documentation are those already established in Brussels. The advantages of resource-rich groups over others in gaining entry to public policies via the role of the Commission as policy initiator, and the extent of the institutionalisation of some interests in public policies, seem rather unlikely to be addressed by such initiatives; indeed it is somewhat ironic that some of the measures designed to tackle the problems seem likely to worsen them.

It may be in the future, however, that the tentative start thus made will have an impact on producing a 'level playing field', particularly because of the power of widespread concerns about a democratic deficit in Europe. Indeed, now that the issue has been raised on the agenda certain interests are likely to latch on to it in an attempt to promote it, as is evident from the behaviour of organisations such as the European Roundtable of Associations and Federations (ERAF), a Brussels-based umbrella group representing around eighty non-governmental organisations. ERAF has recently formed a declaration to achieve further openness in an attempt to take the issue forward, with detailed requests and ideas for making the European institutions and decision-making processes more open. Once an issue becomes talked about widely enough, an agenda for change through socialisation can sometimes develop. Certainly, the accession of Sweden, a country noted for open government, is likely to further develop openness in European decision-making; Sweden, Denmark, Finland and the Netherlands may well create a power bloc within the Council for such reform. There is also evidence of a change in culture in some of the services of the Commission, since there is now a determination to actively seek out the views of non-business groups, if necessary by going outside Brussels to do so. For instance, a recent newsletter of the Biotechnology unit in DG XII records its intention to actively seek out the views of public-interest groups whose voices might not otherwise be heard, and explicitly recognises the ease of access which business groups have enjoyed (EBIS, 1993). Similarly, the Commission recently funded a liaison conference with non-governmental organisations on openness and transparency, and sent a number of top officials to it. However, the important role of the Commission as a policy initiator always seems likely to benefit those best able to take advantage by locating themselves in Brussels and developing permanent relations with Commission officials. This role makes it essential that interests take the Brussels strategy.

The 'management deficit' of the Commission itself makes the influence of those who are located in Brussels that much greater. Apart from their ability to make themselves indispensable, interests in Brussels may be well networked with the range of consultancies the Commission uses. A consultancy used by the Commission may itself be a channel of representation for an interest, particularly if the consulting firm also undertakes work on behalf of that interest. Such realities mean that a level playing field between business and other interests is unlikely, and underlines the importance of being networked at the European level rather than relying on the national route.

A quite different starting point for an interest simply seeking good, advance intelligence about the Commission's intentions, is the extent to which private interests can help create the agenda in the first instance. Public policies (whether resulting in decisions or non-decisions) can arise, and/or are developed, in institutionalised policy networks of public and private interests based on the exchange of power-dependent resources between them (Chapter 1). Thus, Collins suggests that the ERT has virtually written EU information technology policy over the past decade (Collins, 1993). Settled policy networks are not simply vehicles for private interests to table their own needs, but are fora in which public policies arise between two parties with a common set of perceptions, with socialising effects on the parties involved, reinforcing the ways in which issues are defined and responded to and common interests identified.

Even where institutionalised policy networks are absent, Commission structures afford a route of entry into public policies through advisory committees and working parties. Some of these are very high-level working groups, such as that convened by Commissioner Bangemann to formulate recommendations to the European Council on 'Europe and the Global Information Society', involving members of the IT industry (Cram, 1995b). Apart from these high-level groups, the Commission has established two types of advisory committees, expert committees and consultative committees, totalling around a thousand in number. The first of these, the expert committees, consist of national officials and experts. Although their role is not to represent national interests, they do afford a means of interest representation through the national route, whereas the second type, the consultative committees, involve sectional interests invariably drawn from European-level aggregations of interests. Indeed, the Commission hands out membership of consultative committees to European groups first, making this a membership incentive for interests to ensure affiliation to Euro groups and thereby encouraging their development. Together, advisory committees involve 50 000 representatives from national administrations and the private sector (Commission of the European Communities, 1990), on almost every conceivable topic ranging from the Committee on Management of Bananas (Grote, 1989) to health and safety at work. The technical expertise offered by some of these committees provide for policies of a high technical standard, and a route of access for interest representation, particularly on low politics issues (Buitendijk and van Schendelen, 1995). Other committees however, are simply formal structures of little importance; in a recent period, for instance, the Tourism Advisory Committee failed to meet for over two years.

Further, semi-institutionalised structures are the committees on standardisation, present since 1961. These are established within the framework of: CEN, the Comité Européen de la Normalisation; CENELEC, for electrical products; and ETSI, the European Telecommunications Standards Institute. Although these are formally independent organisations, they are structures used for EU objectives of removing non-tariff barriers by developing harmonisation. One single market for goods, services, people and capital demands measures for standardisation across the European Economic Area (EEA). Much of the work on product standardisation is of a highly technical nature, and therefore sometimes inaccessible to public officials. Equally, the European institutions do not have the regulatory resources to devote to the volume of work required to harmonise standards, and consequently the work is devolved to the experts themselves on technical committees. Indeed, since 1985 the aim has been to establish a few Directives of the minimalist-framework type, with members of standards institutes drafting technical specifications. Thus, members of technical committees include, in total, 25 000 participants drawn from industry, science, trade unions and consumer interests, who, together with local and central government departments, resolve the details involved in standardisation issues among themselves (Egan, 1997). In some, the committee chairmanship is provided by a figure from industry. In this way, private interests contribute directly to public policy-making in their own fields. However, membership of each committee is not constitutionally determined by a general structure, and therefore some committees are over-dominated by industrial interests. In any event, some issues are so technical that it is not possible to find consumer interests to contribute. Where they do contribute they tend to do so usefully, and in some committees they provide a counterweight to the influence of business groups. Automobiles, for instance, has historically been one of the most contentious of technical committees, where business and consumer groups tend to conflict over safety standards. Conflicts also arise because technical committees are comprised of European interests, and there have been accusations that the rules they create are partly motivated by a desire to exclude American and Japanese competitors, although participation is possible for these where they are included in European trade associations.

Most interests seeking to influence European public affairs need to address a range of different policy competencies within the Commission. Typically, the affairs of a particular interest may be affected by a number of different functional units within the Commission. Many have quite different perspectives, and their functional competencies leads them into rivalry and conflict. DG III (Industry), for instance, is much less concerned with applying the letter of the law of competition policy than DG IV has been, and has taken decisions to permit particular cases involving industrial joint ventures against the wishes of DG IV. As is illustrated in the chapters which follow, although some degree of co-ordination is provided by inter-service committees, often the way in which services of the Commission work together is at best weak and at worst antagonistic; McLaughlin quotes one official as saying 'quite simply, it's war' (McLaughlin, 1995, p. 177). This means that groups seeking to minimise their surprises have to cultivate relationships with a number of different units spread across Commission services, and to manage the relationship between them (Chapter 3). It is just not possible to do this without a Brussels presence of some kind.

To a certain extent, the role of the Commission in policy initiation has come under threat in recent years from the Council, and to a lesser extent from the Parliament. Under Articles 152 (for the Council) and 138b (for the Parliament), these two institutions can ask the Commission to bring forward proposals, while the European Council, through summitry, can also prompt Commission initiatives. Yet, as Nugent (1994) remarks, the Council remains more suited to a reactive role, while the extent to which the Parliament is prepared to use these newly acquired powers is unclear. Similarly, the Commission has driven forward integration through initiatives it has taken through both high politics fields, such as the single market and the social dimension, while in low politics fields its role as the sole authority with the power to draft initiatives makes it ideally suited as an arena for interest representation. These roles makes it both a magnet and a development agency for interest representation, and only the more disorganised and marginal interests do not engage with it.

The European Parliament

The EP is perhaps the most open of all the European institutions, and has for some time been the natural target for the attentions of non-business interests.

The most important mechanisms in the Parliament for interests to engage are the committee systems, rapporteurs and intergroups. Proposals from the Commission, and initiatives from the EP itself, are considered first in the standing committees of the Parliament. Each committee has a secretariat of around five officials, who provide regular support to the work of the committee, and are therefore often sources of information for outside interests. Committees differ in their importance, both by nature of the domains they cover and the interests of the Parliament itself. Two of the most important, and largest, are the Committee on the Environment, Public Health and Consumer Affairs and the Committee on Economic and Monetary Affairs and Industrial Policy, and consequently it is these which have become the greatest focus for interest representation activities. The first of these often attracts competitive interest representation, because the domains in which it is involved, such as pollution, waste disposal, recycling and medicines, make it a prime target for producer and public-interest groups alike, and because the Parliament has traditionally been active in these areas. Indeed, the most lobbied parliamentarian is perhaps the Committee's current chairperson, Ken Collins, who has increasingly come to recognise the value of interest representation activities as bringing to the committee welcome information and expertise which MEPs might otherwise lack.

Rapporteurs are MEPs appointed by Committees to prepare the Parliament's response to Commission proposals, and to those measures taken within the Parliament itself. When an appointment is made, a shadow rapporteur is appointed by each political group to monitor the process on behalf of the interests of that party. Because of the centrality of their involvement with a particular initiative, they are therefore key targets for interest representation. Here, interests can make themselves indispensable by providing expert information, particularly where the rapporteur may be only a lay figure in the area concerned.

Intergroups of the European Parliament are unofficial (with one exception) groupings of MEPs clustered around particular areas where members have particular interests. They began to emerge after the first direct elections to the Parliament in 1979. Only one of the first, the Intergroup of Local and Regional Representatives, was given official status by the Parliament. When intergroups began to sprout, the College of Quaestors (a committee responsible for administrative and financial matters directly concerning members, and the management of the EP buildings) came to realise that it would not be possible for the Parliament to resource these, and consequently all other intergroups have to survive by their own means. This has provided an opportunity for some interest groups to provide the financial and secretariat resources for them to operate (Chapter 8). There is, however, now some concern, particularly among the Socialist members, that intergroups are too closely associated with particular lobbies, and in some instances that they are manipulated by them.

Because of their unofficial and sometimes rather fluid status, there is no list maintained of intergroups by any of the European institutions. Thus, no one seems clear precisely how many intergroups there are, although one recent estimate suggests that there were around 50 in existence after the most recent EP elections (Jacobs *et al.*, 1995). Based on their own knowledge, these authors have produced a list of those known to be in existence in the autumn of 1994 (see Table 2.1).

The semi-anarchic existence of these groups means that they do quite different things and offer quite different avenues of influence to the European Parliament for outside interests. Some meet frequently and have a full-time secretariat, whereas others are little more than letterheads. Some restrict membership to MEPs, while others are open to a variety of outside interests. Some are highly specific, such as the High Speed Trains Intergroup, while others have more general

TABLE 2.1

Indicative list of intergroups

Name
Airport Regions
Atlantic
Automobile Users
Ageing
Ceramics
Cinema and Audio-visual
Conservation and Development
Commerce and Distribution
Children, Families, Partnership and Solidarity (CHIPS)
Consumer Affairs
Control at Frontiers
Cuba
EPIC (European Parliament and Industry Council)
Ethnic Minorities
Euro Arab
Forests
Français de la Mer
Friends of Music
Friends of Taiwan
Gene Splicing Technologies
GLOBE
Handicapped
Health
High-Speed Trains
Indian Peoples
Islands
Israel
Kangaroo
Local and Regional Representatives
Maritime
Mining Regions
Mediterranean
Minority Languages and Cultures
Mountain Park, Natural Reserves and Mountains
Prevention of Conflicts
Public Services
Peace and Disarmament
Rural Property
Rugby League
Saharaoui
Shipbuilding
Social Economy
Sports
Tibet

Table 2.1 (*cont.*)
Name

Tourism
Trade Union
Viticulture, Quality and Tradition
Welfare and Conservation of Animals

Source: Adapted from Jacobs *et al.* (1995, p. 172). Reproduced with kind permission of Cartermill.

to eliminate all barriers to the free movement of goods, services and people. Indeed, the Kangaroo group, with members ranging from former Commission presidents and heads of state to lobbyists and industrialists, was one of the support networks behind the 1985 White Paper on the single market. Stern has suggested that there is a natural affinity between the Kangaroo Group and lobbyists, not least because of the role of the latter in pursuing the goals of the group (Stern, 1994).

Jacobs *et al.* have suggested that the scale of intergroup activity has had a considerable effect on the working methods of the EP, and in particular during the plenary sessions in Strasbourg, where intergroup meetings are normally held:

> (intergroups) permit members to specialise, make contacts with outside interest groups on a more informal basis than in committee meetings, and last but not least to make close political contacts outside their own political groups. Intergroups thus not only help to form cross-group coalitions on specific issues, but to forge wider political friendships which can be useful in other circumstances, and can help to build that wider consensus which is essential in the European Parliament on certain issues (Jacobs *et al.*, 1995, p. 170).

For some interests, intergroups can represent a 'best chance' for interest representation in the EU, particularly for those who lack access elsewhere to institutional structures. Thus, the Tourism Intergroup provides an essential means of access for tourism interests which are on the whole poorly organised and poorly connected to the Tourism Unit inside DG XXIII (Enterprise Policy, Distributive Trades, Tourism and Co-operatives). Similarly, although consumers do have access elsewhere (Chapter 8), there is a natural affinity amongst parliamentarians for consumer affairs, and the Intergroup on Consumer Affairs, partly created by the efforts of a one-time chairman of the consumer organisation, BEUC, is one expression of this. Supported by secretariat resources provided by consumer organisations (Chapter 8), it has become one of the most active in the Parliament, examining a wide range of consumer related issues, and hosting speakers from among the ranks of Commissioners, Commission officials, and representatives of trade associations and public-interest groups. Indeed, although the impact of interest representation through intergroups remains an under-researched problem, it is likely that it has been underestimated and under-recognised as a channel of importance to date.

The development of intergroups is an indication of the growth in importance attached to the EP by public and private interests. This is undoubtedly a function of the enhanced role of the EP in European public affairs provided for by the SEA and TEU, in particular involving the co-operation and co-decision-making procedures. The co-operation procedure of decision-making between the Council and the Parliament was extended by the TEU to include a number of areas where the Parliament has traditionally been active, including the structural funds, the environment, development and co-operation, and the prohibition of discrimination on the grounds of nationality (Stern, 1994). However, of greater significance still is that co-decision-making procedures arising from the TEU provided the European Parliament for the first time with the power to veto a proposal. It also enabled the Council to use qualified majority voting (QMV) in cases where the Commission objects, provided the Parliament agrees to the proposal in question. Among the areas to which co-decision-making applies are included: internal market measures; the free movement of workers; consumer protection; public health; Trans-European Networks (TENs); and framework programmes on the environment. Under the co-decision-making procedure, the Parliament, acting by an absolute majority of its members, has the power to propose amendments to the Council's common position, or to reject it. Unlike the co-operation procedure, where the Council can reject the Parliament's objections if it acts by unanimity, co-decision-making procedures do enable Parliament to prevent a position of the Council from being adopted (Stern, 1994). Although the procedure is complex, and the difficulties of obtaining an absolute majority in the Parliament to defeat a Council position should not be underestimated, the powers provided to the Parliament under the co-decision procedure do force the Council to explain its position and to seek compromises with the Parliament, making the EP a powerful actor in the areas to which co-decision applies. Similarly, extensions to the number of areas covered by the assent procedures, requiring the Council to obtain the agreement of the Parliament, further enhance the importance of the EP.

The effect of all these changes means that outside interests now have to fully engage the Parliament, whereas at one time some paid little more than symbolic attention to it. The enhanced powers of the EP have particularly developed the landscape of European-level public-interest groups, because the concerns of these interests find a natural home in an arena with democratic credentials. Business interests, however, have experienced something of a learning curve in coming to terms with the Parliament's increasing status. The pharmaceutical industry, for instance, otherwise a sophisticated public-affairs actor on the European stage, has in the past caused considerable irritation by using its contacts to flood the EP with amendments, and there have been instances where committee rap-porteurs have refused to meet industry representatives (Sasseen, 1992). A number of firms and trade associations have filled the expertise gap by hiring lobbyists to handle relations with the Parlia-ment on their behalf, although this has brought its own problems, resulting in a series of initiatives to regulate the EP's relationship with lobbyists (Chapter 4). Young, however, notes that business interests are on the whole learning how to engage the Parliament, such that the special relationship between public-interest groups and the EP has been disrupted (Young, 1995). For instance, after losing a key debate in the Parliament on bio-patenting, the SAGB and EFPIA co-sponsored with the Parliament an EP/Industry Biotechnology Forum in April 1996 to help mutual understanding.

Other institutions

Apart from the Council, Commission and Parliament, some of the other institutions afford an access point for interest representation. It is a measure of the present lack of significance of the Economic and Social Committee (ESC) that some Brussels commentators suggest that it would be a waste of valuable InterGovernmental Conference (IGC) time to even discuss the question of whether it should be abolished. Nevertheless, the ESC does provide a point of contact with European public affairs for certain types of interests (Kirchner, 1977; Kirchner and Schwaiger, 1981).

The ESC is in theory an institutional structure designed solely for input by outside interests. Its 222 members are divided into three categories: group 1 (employers), group 2 (workers) and group 3 (other interests). Historically, it has been of most value to interests from trade unions, and the professions (Chapters 6 and 7). However, members are appointed in a personal capacity rather than as delegates of organisations. There are nine specialist sections, covering the functional range of EU competencies, with rapporteurs and plenary meetings. Categories of interests meet, rather like the parties in the EP, to seek to build common positions. The ESC acts in an advisory capacity only in relation to the other institutions, although it does have the right to issue opinions on matters for which it has not been consulted. Its influence upon EU policy is generally regarded as negligible, although it does provide a 'talking shop' forum for interests to come together, and the means to respond to proposals before they reach the Council of Ministers. At this stage there is therefore the opportunity to present issues or information which may have been overlooked.

Like the ESC, the Committee of the Regions (CoR) has only advisory powers. However, the CoR has the advantage of being a new institution in which hopes are invested for the future, particular as regional policy commands around thirty per cent of the budget. Some are of the view that it will eventually replace the ESC, and indeed it currently shares office space with it. However, as is described in Chapter 9, while the CoR may increasingly be a channel of representation for territorial interests in the future, it may be some time before it reaches maturity.

The European Investment Bank (EIB), providing loans and guarantees to co-finance medium- to large-scale investment in industry and infrastructure, has increasingly found itself a target of interest representation activities in recent years. The realisation of infrastructure projects between member states involving construction, transport, water, energy, telecommunications and finance interests depends upon the availability of secure, relatively low-cost finance. Increasingly, public interests such as environmental groups have been active in pressing the EIB to ensure compliance with strict environmental criteria for work involving large-scale TEN projects. Something similar also applies in the case of the Court of Auditors, which some public-interest groups have come to regard as a means of pursuing their interests (Chapter 8). A recent example of this concerns beef subsidies, where animal welfare groups submitted a complaint that money was being inadvertently used to subsidise the rearing of animals for bullfighting in Spain. Among the newest institutions established by the TEU, the European Environmental Agency (EEA), established to provide scientific and technical support in the field of environmental protection, and its network of national environmental monitoring agencies in the member states, as well as the European Agency on the Evaluation of Medicinal Products, are also likely to attract input from a variety of interests. However, the other institutions created by the TEU, such as the European Monetary Institute, the European System of Central Banks, the European Central Bank and EUROPOL, are by nature likely to be more insulated from the pressures of private-interest representation.

The national route and the Brussels strategy assessed

The ways in which interests are articulated at the European level can be categorised as a complex series of issues surrounding: aggregations of interests, through collective and independent action formats (considered in Chapter 3); the routes through which influence is exerted and voiced; and the institutional channel and point of entry within the institutional decision-making process. These are listed in Table 2.2.

Because one of the first rules of interest representation is to keep as many channels of communication available as possible, many issues will in practice be channelled through a number of the structures identified in Figure 2.1, sometimes at different points in the European policy cycle, sometimes simultaneously. The range of complexities involved makes it futile to seek to establish any hard-and-fast rules as to when a particular channel is operationalised. Indeed, the very idea of routes is complicated by the idea that member states and the supranational institutions are both objects and subjects of interest representation, i.e. they are participants as well as channels. There may be significant variations in the permutation of channels of influence used, depending upon a variety of circumstances, including the nature of the issue concerned, the type of interest affected, and prevailing circumstances. For instance, British trade unions are more likely to use the Brussels strategy as a result of their exclusion from domestic governance under recent Conservative administrations, while in southern Europe weak traditions of associability beyond the national level may mean a greater reliance upon national channels. Yet, while establishing patterns of usage of routes is fraught

TABLE 2.2

Representing interests in the European Union*

Aggregations of Interest	Route	Voice	Target
1. Individual (e.g. company)	Try to determine policy at local and/ or national levels	Self/collective representation	Commission and satellite structures;
2. Coalition (non-EU-level) (functional, territorial)			Council of Ministers; Parliament; Economic and Social
3. Formal (non EU level) interest group (functional, territorial)			Committee; Committee of the Regions; other EU
4. European office of local interest	Influence Europe via national		institutions and co-ordination structures
5. European-specific coalition (informal collective)	contacts	Commercial lobbyist	
6. Formal European-level interest group	Brussels strategy		Standards bodies and autonomous structures
7. European office of international association	External consultancy reports		Court actions

* The four columns of this table are independent entities.
Source: Adapted from Greenwood and Jordan (1993, p. 84). Reproduced with the kind permission of Dartmouth Press.

with difficulties, over a period of time it might be possible to detect a change in emphasis in use of national and European channels respectively.

In 1977, Averyt suggested that the orthodox strategy of interest representation to Europe would be through the Euro group. However, noting earlier criticisms of the capacities of Euro groups made by Caporaso (Caporaso, 1974), Averyt identified the persistence of the national route, where interests would seek to influence European public affairs through national contacts or through a national government. Although the Commission maintained a policy of talking only to Euro groups, in some sectors, Averyt suggested, these were either non-existent or so weak that they were unable to deliver meaningful, authoritative opinion. In consequence, if the Commission wanted coherent views it would have to trawl around the national capitals to obtain it. As is debated in Chapter 3, there is some evidence that the historic weakness of Euro groups has been rather exaggerated and, rather misleadingly, is a claim which has often been repeated, on the basis of rather sketchy evidence, during the 1980s and 1990s.

While the national route remains important, there can be little doubt that the Brussels strategy has developed considerably during these latter decades. Interests which have become over-reliant upon the national route take unnecessary risks of decisions bypassing them, or of becoming reactive to events rather than seeking to manage them in the first instance. Few interests whose concerns are significantly affected by the European level could afford to be without a Brussels presence. At its most simple level, a Brussels presence is required to manage the sheer complexity of today's European decision-making. For instance, the final decision on the Pregnant Women Directive was taken, of all places, at the Council of Fisheries Ministers. This was because the latter was the only Council meeting on the last possible day to meet the timetable for decision-making, and previous complexities in inter-institutional bargaining had used up the available time (Pedler, 1994). These circumstances are by no means extraordinary. The complexity illustrated by this example has, in turn, demanded a greater level of expertise by interests in managing European public affairs. In some instances this complexity has strengthened the position of insiders such as commercial lobbyists who are able to offer specialist advice to clients based on the detailed knowledge of the working of the systems they have acquired. It has also to some extent created a greater imbalance between business interests who can afford a well-staffed Brussels public-affairs base as a means of acquiring this expertise, and public interests from member states who have occasional needs to seek to exert influence over European public affairs. However, imbalances in the ability to manage such affairs are to some extent compensated for by ease of entry to the European policy process. One of the main differences actors find between some national experiences and engaging the European arena is just how easy the latter is to enter. Apart from the more secretive Council of Ministers, involving national actors, in most cases it is possible to simply pick up the phone and dial in order to speak to an official or parliamentarian, or even to call by on a passing visit to Brussels. Such ease of initial access has undoubtedly facilitated the development of the Brussels strategy.

The main factors which demand use of the more direct Brussels strategy concern: the role of the Commission in initiating policy, and in developing the landscape of Brussels-based European level interest groups (Chapters 5 to 9); the presence of formal, institutionalised structures of interest representation such as advisory committees; the need to influence Euro group strategies (Chapter 3); the need to network and to gather intelligence; the internationalisation of markets and politics; and the associated enhanced competence of the European Union, including, in particular, the increasing powers accorded to the Commission and Parliament.

The SEA ended the veto of member states on certain types of legislation operable since the de Gaulle crisis and the 'Luxembourg Compromise' of the mid-1960s. The SEA, and later the TEU, considerably extended the constitutional reach of the qualified majority system of voting. This meant that interests which had once been able to rely upon their national government as a last resort of protection at the Council of Ministers could no longer afford to do so, and instead had to invest resources in engaging the European level. Compromise has become the *modus operandi* of Council decision-making because of qualified majority voting. In a recent submission to the ECJ, the Council described its own decision-making processes in the following terms:

> The Council normally works through a process of negotiation and compromise, in the course of which its members freely express their national preoccupations and positions. If agreement is to be reached they will frequently be called upon to move from these positions, perhaps to the extent of abandoning their national instructions (cited in European Roundtable of Associations and Federations, 1994, p. 24).

In providing a quantum leap forward in the competencies of the EU, the SEA and TEU made it essential for a range of interests to engage further resources in addressing the European level. In establishing a basis for political and monetary union, the acquisition of new competencies to legislate in a number of fields (and particularly those where the Parliament has traditionally been active), and the creation of a number of new institutions, the TEU either brought a new set of political actors to the European level, or intensified the interests of others. Two further changes, relating to the Protocol on Social Policy, and changes to decision-making procedures, have particularly altered the structure of European level interest representation, and are therefore worth examining in some depth.

The Protocol on Social Policy as an annex to the TEU gave the Community the right to impose measures relating to health and safety at work, and, except in the UK, the ability to act in the field of social policy. All other member states can act by qualified majority voting in the fields of information and consultation of workers, sexual equality, and the integration of those excluded from the labour market. Unanimity among the participating member states is still required in fields of social security, equality within the labour market, redundancy and job creation schemes, and matters concerning the representation of workers' interests (Stern, 1994). Although issues of pay and labour disputes have been left out of the agreement, there is now an institutionalised form of social dialogue between employers' and workers' interests which in turn has strengthened the role of the peak confederations of business and labour, UNICE and ETUC (Chapters 5 and 7). Indeed, Article 3(1) of the Agreement on Social Policy gives employers' organisations and trade unions the right to be consulted by the Commission on both the content and direction of social policy (labour market issues) and in doing so, these organisations are provided with legitimacy as consultative partners in much the same way as is the EP in other fields (Obradovic, 1994). Member states are explicitly enabled to entrust employers' and workers' interests (the 'social partners') with implementation of functions arising from directives initiated under the social agreement, and, importantly, further rights are also provided, under the terms of Article 3(4), for the social partners to conclude agreements themselves. In this case, the interests are obliged to inform the Commission of their intention to embark upon an agreement, and, unless the Commission agrees to an extension, to reach an agreement within nine months. As Obradovic remarks, the enhanced powers envisaged for social partners has considerably expanded the agenda setting and implementation roles of EU-level employers' and workers' organisations, and provides private interests with an institutionalised public purpose (Obradovic, 1994). In Streeck and Schmitter's terms, it is a form, albeit a limited one, of private interest government (Streeck and Schmitter, 1985). The role of private interests in expanding the integration process in labour market fields arising from the protocol agreement of the TEU is examined in greater depth in Chapters 5 and 7.

In addition to certain social policy issues, the TEU introduced qualified majority voting (QMV) to a number of areas of legislation for the first time, including, among others those concerning consumer protection and environment measures (except fiscal, land use, water and energy, where the Council is enabled, by acting unanimously, to extend qualified majority voting). Interests affected by these areas have consequently had to make further investment in the Brussels strategy, although most were already well established in Brussels prior to the TEU (Chapter 8). Under QMV, a qualified majority of 62 out of the 87 votes is required, with a blocking minority thus set at 26 votes. According to the Ioannina compromise of 1994, however, where 23 to 25 votes against are mustered, the Council must seek at least 65 votes within a certain period of time, thereby putting further emphasis upon compromise setting and the need to take more direct European channels of interest representation.

Changes to the institutional balance of power under the SEA, and the TEU, mean that it is essential for an interest to engage all the institutions of the EU. The complexity which these changes have brought means that often the same proposal will be under consideration at the same point in time by the different institutions. The Council has to be addressed by using both the national route (for Ministerial level decisions) and the Brussels strategy (by engaging the national delegations, and locating sister interests to address their own member states), whereas the Commission and the Parliament have to be addressed by taking the Brussels strategy.

Conclusion

Recent years have seen a considerable growth in the Brussels strategy in response to the enhanced competence of the EU. It is now somewhat unwise to rely solely on the national route of interest representation. Changes to decision-making structures, including a much greater degree of complexity, new powers of the EP, new competencies, the role of the Commission in policy initiation, and the need for interests to gather information, mean that any organisation seeking to be effective in managing its European interface needs to secure representation in Brussels. Indeed, given the status of Brussels as an insider's town, those without a presence there are likely to be at a considerable disadvantage relative to those who do. The extent of growth in European-level public-interest groups who have overcome resourcing difficulties and managed to create a Brussels base (Chapter 8) is evidence that a wider range of organisations no longer find it possible to manage European public affairs from remote centres in the member states. For these organisations, attempts by the Commission to create a more open environment in which to operate, and the encouragement given by the Commission to such interests, make it likely that an increasingly wider range of groups will be found in Brussels in the years to come. Only the most resource-starved interests now manage their European interface from a domestic base alone. In turn, all these factors suggest rather that the balance of importance between the national and the European route of influence has now shifted in favour of the latter.

3

The Nature and Resources of Groups

Some accounts loosely treat interest representation as synonymous with formal interest groups. Although this text places some emphasis upon interest representation occurring through a variety of outlets, ranging from individual firms through to informal fora and formal groups, it is worth devoting special attention to formal groups because of the dominant position they occupy in European interest representation and intermediation. Indeed, the 200 firms with public affairs offices in Brussels may be set against a Commission estimate of 3000 groups (Chapter 1) interacting on the Brussels environment (Commission of the European Communities, 1992a). These estimates should, however, be approached with some degree of caution, because, as Grant illustrates, a variety of different figures have been produced from a number of different sources and authors (Grant, 1995). No one knows yet with any certainty what the exact figures are, although the impending publication of a Commission database of groups should go a long way to resolving the problem. Similarly, the popularity of the estimate of 10 000 individuals working in the interest representation sector (Chapter 1) seems to arise more from the frequency with which this figure is cited than from any solid foundations for such a claim.

Defining the boundaries of an interest group is notoriously problematic, involving a whole range of issues surrounding aims, scope, degrees of organisation, affinity and membership. For reasons of space the range and intricacies of these cannot be debated here (for a review of the extensive literature on this topic see, for instance, Moran, 1985). These complexities are somewhat greater at the European level, where a tier of organisation beyond the national level, and a wider membership constituency, are present. Perhaps the greatest level of complexity, however, concerns the boundaries to the collective action structures of interests, which range through the spectrum from formal groups, to more informal types of gatherings where the limits of collective action is harder to distinguish. While there is a considerable and well-established (mainly American) literature on different types of group membership incentives (see, for instance, Clark and Wilson, 1960; Moe, 1980) and mechanisms of associability (Olson, 1965; and collections by Mundo, 1992; Petracca, 1992; Cigler and Loomis, 1995), there is a marked lack of research on the boundaries of collective action structures. The boundary point at the informal end of the scale is seen as including contact between interests with common intent for collective action; it excludes, however, simple meetings between different types of interests called in response to external stimuli where prior patterns of collective action are not present, such as for example a meeting between car manufacturers and consumer groups called to discuss entrenched differences concerning car safety standards.

A distinct marker of formality in group structure is provided by the presence of a secretariat attached to the activities of a group. Progressively more informal types of structure range from semi-permanent 'clubs' with regular gatherings of similar personnel, through the transient issue networks described in Chapter 1, to gatherings arranged between parties with the intent of pursuing collective action on issues and thence to bodies with a greater degree of permanence. Any type of forum may begin quite informally, or it may start right away with a more formal type of group. Of the formal groups, two-thirds of European-level associations are primarily federations of national organisations; the remainder are either direct-membership structures without intervening levels of organisation, or else a combination of the two types where, for instance, the membership is made up of both national associations (and even other European associations) and individual firms. As is evident later, even these distinctions are complicated by differing levels of membership, such as full and associate status.

An impression of the totality of formal European-level groups is provided by Table 3.1, which indicates the constitution of European interest groups by domain and by geographical base of headquarters. Business groups predominate, accounting for over two-thirds of all those composited from the two directories. Public-interest groups and professional groups account for one-fifth and one-tenth respectively of all groups, a considerably higher proportion than was evident at the

TABLE 3.1

European-level groups by type and location, taken from two directory sources (1992–4)

	B	CH	D	DK	E	EIR	F	GB	I	L	NL	P	Total	%
Consumer	4						2						6	0.9
Business	218	10	63	2	1		80	33	11	3	26		447	67
Professions	25	3	7	1		1	9	17	3	1		2	69	10
Union	13	2	1				2						18	3
Public Interest	110		1			2	7	9	1		4		134	20
Miscellaneous	6		1				4	1		1	1		14	2
Total	376	15	73	3	1	3	104	60	15	5	31	2	688	
%	55	2	11	0.4	0.1	0.4	15	9	2	0.7	4.7	0.3		

Sources: Commission of the European Community (1992b); Landmarks Publications (1994).

time of the launch of the single-market project. This phenomenon can be attributed both to the enhanced competencies of the EU described in Chapter 2 and to the activities of the European institutions themselves in developing such networks (Chapters 8 and 10). Interests of other types account for a very small proportion of the total.

Of all groups 55 per cent are based in Belgium, almost exclusively in the Brussels region, although some with a base elsewhere also retain a Brussels presence. Of interest however is the extent of dispersal of bases throughout member states as a whole, and for particular categories of activity. Between them, Germany and France are home to more than a quarter of all Euro groups, and, when Britain is added, these three are home to over a third. France alone accounts for 15 per cent of all European groups, possibly reflecting an earlier tendency for some international organisations to establish themselves in Paris. In turn, some of these spawned organisations dedicated to the European level of organisation.

Also of interest in Table 3.1 is that the proportion of business groups based in Brussels, as opposed to elsewhere, is smaller than the average for groups as a whole, although it is these which are most likely to be in a position to afford a secondary Brussels base. Surprising perhaps is that some 82 per cent of all European-level public-interest groups are based in Brussels. By comparison, only a third of groups organising professional types of interests are based in Brussels, suggesting that some national organisations have doubled up functions as European organisations. These differences are partly explained by the availability of funding from the European institutions. Survey results drawn from a sample of 405 Euro groups (Chapter 1) indicate that whereas 59 per cent of public-interest groups are in receipt of Euro funds, only 4 per cent of groups representing the professions obtain such help (Aspinwall and Greenwood, 1997). The Commission provides 4 million ECU to ETUC, the European Trade Union Confederation, and around one million ECU to the wider structures of BEUC, the consumers' organisation. These funds enable such organisations to rank among the better-staffed Euro organisations, with 49 (ETUC) and 13 (BEUC) workers respectively. In addition to funds, the Commission also provides these types of interests with resources and structures through which to operate. Examples of these include linguistic services to ETUC, and, in 1993, setting up a General Consultative Forum on the Environment in order to bring together representatives from the variety of actors with interests in the environmental domain. Where the Commission provides funding for public-interest groups, and structures to represent them, however, there remains a question of the extent to which such finance in any way compromises their independence, and whether groups perceive obligations in return. Greenpeace, for instance, fiercely guards its independence, and therefore neither receives nor seeks funds from the EU.

The immediate personnel resources which groups draw on range from the services of a spare-time enthusiast to those such as CEFIC, the chemicals association, 'with a staff of 80 and 4000 company representatives involved in its committee work' (Grant, 1995, p. 119). In the sample of 405 Euro groups, 22 per cent have more than five executives (i.e. not including secretaries). These larger, producer groups can spend upwards of 2 million ECU per year. Over half of the sample of Euro groups had a turnover exceeding 100 000 ECU, indicating some degree of strength. It should also be taken into account that groups may also be able to draw upon the resources of members or associational structures elsewhere in the world. Thus, if needs be, CEFIC can draw on the resources of national and international associations, and firms, and, often, the support of other business interests in related fields. Public-interest organisations such as Greenpeace, Amnesty International, the World Wide Fund for Nature and Friends of the Earth can each supplement the resources of their Brussels policy offices from other centres. Although these are not typical of public-interest organisations in Brussels, each of them employs well in excess of one hundred staff world-wide. Thus, although business interests do have superior resources to public-interest groups when taken as a whole (Chapter 5; Chapter 8), the assets of some non-producer interests do enable them to engage in European public affairs from a solid resource base.

In relatively politicised domains, a source of power for public-interest groups concerns their ability to attract producer interests to issue alliances. Thus, manufacturers and retailers, for instance, are keen to attract product endorsement from consumer and environmental interests. Nothing is likely to impress the Commission more than an alliance of producer and public-interests which can produce a high level of agreement. These types of alliances are particularly visible in the environmental domain, where the European Energy from Waste Coalition, and the European Partners for the Environment, both with formal premises and a full-time secretariat, look set to become significant forces in the future. Increasingly, European sectoral business groups are having to pool their resources to respond to the politicisation of the environmental domain and to form structures such as the Packaging Chain Forum (PCF), a coalition of organisations representing different elements in the packaging chain from raw-materials suppliers to packers, fillers and retailers. In turn, the resources of such organisations are strengthened by overlapping memberships with other organisations, for example that between a key organisation in the PCF, EUROPEN (European Organisation for Packaging and the Environment) and the European Recovery and Recycling Association (ERRA). Coalitions between public-interest groups in the environmental domain are also strong, assisting groups to enter arenas which might not otherwise be possible without sharing resources, and generating membership incentives (Chapter 8).

Weak Euro groups?

The centrality of European-level groups to neofunctionalist accounts of integration has ensured that an examination of their effectiveness has to some extent dominated the literature in recent years. In 1974 Caporaso noted the stunted development of European-level groups, which resulted in interests using primarily national channels of communication as a means of engaging the EEC. A similar observation was made in 1985 by George, again by Grant in 1990 and 1993, and, in a more qualified way in 1995 (Grant, 1990; 1993a; 1995), and has been periodically asserted by a clutch of authors (such as Sargent, 1987; Arp, 1991; McLaughlin, 1992; McLaughlin *et al.*, 1993; Lewin, 1994; Coen, 1995; Hayward, 1995). Citing Sidjanski's study of COPA (Committee of Agricultural Organisations in the EC) in the 1960s (Sidjanski, 1967), McLaughlin *et al.* argue that

> in practice, Euro groups, far from being dynamic agents of integration, have tended to be rather ineffective bodies unable to engage in constructive policy dialogue with the Commission (1993, p. 192).

Given the lack of development of the EU during the 1970s and the first part of the 1980s, observations made in 1974 and 1985 concerning the lack of resources of Euro groups and the continued use of national channels of interest representation may perhaps not surprise the reader. However, whether the 'weak Euro groups' thesis is even generalisable during this period is itself questionable. Indeed, as Altenstetter shows, effective European-level federations of national federations in some business sectors have been in operation since as early as 1960 (Altenstetter, 1994), while groups such as EFPIA and EUROFER, the European Confederation of Iron and Steel Industries, have developed a reputation since the 1970s for their strength and effectiveness, and through self-regulatory arrangements have both become ingrained within structures of policy implementation. Certainly, results from the recent survey of Euro groups (Chapter 1) indicates that around two-thirds of Euro groups were established before 1980 (Greenwood and Aspinwall, 1997). But the persistence of the 'weak Euro groups' claims long after the single market had gathered pace demands close examination.

Federations of national associations

The most sustained criticisms of the capacities of Euro groups have been delivered by Grant (1990; 1993a; and, significantly, to a much more qualified extent, in 1995), who has suggested they are often inadequately resourced, weak and incoherent in building common platforms between members, and therefore of value mainly for fraternal contact. Grant had in mind mainly federations of national associations of (producer) interests, accounting for two-thirds of all Euro groups. Such formats do tend to find it more·difficult to operate effectively than do, for instance, direct firm membership formats. He has recently summarised these weaknesses:

> First, the problem of reconciling the interests of the different member states under what are often unanimity rules of decision-making means that the groups tend to produce 'lowest common denominator' policies which are unlikely to have an effective impact on decision-makers. Second, given that they are funded by national associations who want to retain a large proportion of their income for their own purposes, the associations often have insufficient resources to deal with the large range of issues that impact on the sectors. Third, whereas an effective association will be guided by the knowledge of its officials about what is and is not achievable in the decision-making process, too many of the organisations are membership led: the logic of membership predominates over the logic of influence. European level officials have insufficient autonomy in relation to either national level associations or multinational companies who may regard them as middle ranking bureaucrats (Grant, 1995, p. 106).

As is evident in subsequent chapters, 'peak' confederations of national confederations are particularly prone to these difficulties. UNICE (Chapter 5), SEPLIS (Chapter 6), ETUC (Chapter 7), EEB and CEDAG (Chapter 8) all find meaningful platform building extremely difficult. Some European confederations can take more than six months to reach platforms which are highly generalised, lowest-common-denominator position statements. They are by structure somewhat removed (as organisations representing organisations which represent, again, organisations of direct member interests) from the 'street level' of the interests they represent. Such a highly confederated structure makes these organisations reproduce several generations of compromise positions. Some of them (most notably UNICE, described in Chapter 5, and ETUC, described in Chapter 7) have recently taken steps to establish a more direct relationship with their members, although, as is described in subsequent chapters, these measures have by no means resolved the inherent problems of these organisations. Some of the national confederations maintain their own offices in Brussels, not least because of the ways in which interests are aggregated in Euro confederations, although such a presence is often required for a range of other reasons, including the need to interface with their domestic government structures in Europe. Because of such a parallel presence, however, the reliance upon the

European-level confederation is correspondingly reduced. As Sidenius argues, a dual presence alters the structure of membership incentives, because national confederations can often satisfy their own formal information needs through their own Brussels office. Membership of the Euro confederation provides the opportunity to influence potentially damaging proposals (Sidenius, 1994). However, the Euro confederation still provides the opportunity to obtain benefits through networking, including informal information. Such a range of benefits still pushes the logic in favour of participation in the Euro confederation.

Difficulties in platform-building are also a frequent problem for sectoral federations of national associations. The Confederation of Food and Drink Industries of the EEC (CIAA), for instance, encompasses not only each of the national associations, but forty associations representing particular sectors of the food and drink industries. Platform-building is thus highly prone to compromises. As with peak confederations, such weaknesses have been addressed by national association members operating a parallel presence in Brussels; thus, the British Bankers Association maintains an office in Brussels despite affiliation to the Banking Federation of the European Community (Claveloux, 1993), while something similar occurs in the case of the Law Societies of England, Wales and Scotland (Chapter 6) sharing a joint Brussels office. Some federations have collapsed on grounds of coherence. Examples which have been given of these include COCCEE, the distributive trades organisation, the Committee of Common Market Automobile Constructors (CCMC)/Liaison Committee of the Automobile Industry of the Countries of the European Communities (CLEA) for automobiles, and the European Biotechnology Co-ordinating Group (EBCG), in the case of Biotechnology. However, COCCEE came to its end in the 1970s, and was subsequently replaced by a successor organisation, the European confederation for retailing; CCMC/CLEA was restructured rather than spontaneously folding on coherence grounds, while EBCG folded in the early stages of interest representation in the biotechnology domain, when the landscape of groups was highly unstable and fluid. It is therefore important not to over generalise selectively from a limited number of examples. Indeed, Grant's most recent work acknowledges the presence of effective federations of national federations (Grant, 1995). As was described earlier, a number of Euro federations have developed reputations as well resourced and highly effective operators. Among the most frequently cited examples of these are the European Confederation of Iron and Steel Industries (EUROFER) and the European Federation of Pharmaceutical Industry Associations (EFPIA), each employing around twenty staff members in their Brussels secretariats, the European Insurance Committee (CEA) and the Association of the Chocolate, Biscuit and Confectionery Industries of the EEC (CAOBISCO), all widely credited with influencing significantly European public policies in the domains in which they operate (Gardner, 1991; Stern, 1994; Greenwood, 1995b; Camerra-Rowe, 1996). EUROFER is large enough to house five departments within its organisational structure, and like EFPIA is so deeply ingrained in governance mechanisms that its involvement bears the hallmarks of neo-corporatism.

It is also important not to over-generalise the difficulties common to a limited number of a certain type of Euro group to the entire population of Euro groups. Authors have rightly drawn attention to the declining effectiveness of COPA in recent years (Grant, 1990; 1993a; 1995), and to the weakness of groups in the tourism (Greenwood, 1995c) and consumer electronics (Cawson, 1992) domains. Yet it is important that these are not taken out of context. COPA's influence has declined as the share of the European budget devoted to agriculture has been reduced in the face of the high politics surrounding the common agricultural policy, and the tensions between northern and southern European countries; the European Association of Consumer Electronics Manufacturers (EACEM), simply satisfies the needs of Philips to be seen to be acting collectively in a sector so concentrated that there are only a handful of eligible firms; while in tourism the nature of the market, and sectoral characteristics, mean that collective action across a domain which lacks definition, and is characterised by fragmentation, is always likely to prove problematic. Even in this field, however, there have been recent (summer 1995) signs of effective co-ordination, with the formation of NET, the Network of European Private Entrepreneurs in the Tourism Sector, arising from a joint initiative of the hotel group, the Confederation of the National Hotel and Restaurant Associations in the European Community (HOTREC), and the travel agency association, the Group of National Travel Agents' and Tour Operators' Associations within the EEC (ECTAA). These partners have since been joined by the Tour Operators' Association (ETOA).

The bluntness of the 'weak Euro group' label also tends to hide differential circumstances facing groups. In some contexts, a group is able to respond effectively to issues in public affairs because its members are united, whereas in others divisions between its members make collective interest representation either difficult or impossible. Thus, in Chapter 5 an example is provided of a European directive on computer software which sharply divided members of sector-wide Euro groups in the information technology domain into two opposing camps. In this case, cohesive interest representation from the formal Euro groups concerned was simply impossible, although these groups have been able to act cohesively in other contexts.

The emphasis upon the weakness of Euro groups in some of the recent literature has to some extent masked the successes which some business sectors, in particular, have enjoyed from effective European-level representative organisations. It is true that some interests enjoy a token presence in Brussels, with an office perhaps staffed by as little as one executive, and which is reliant upon the resources of their members, such as firms, for effective interest representation. It is also a fact that where there is no financial support from the Commission, establishment costs represent a significant entry barrier for some interests. However, the difficulties of establishing a meaningful Brussels base should not be overemphasised, at least for a number of business sectors seeking to make an impact on European public affairs. Most recently, a collection of cases drawn from sixteen different business sectors found disabling problems arising from European-level groups in only one case (Greenwood, 1995a), while the overwhelming majority of these had demonstrated themselves to be highly effective collective actors. Indeed, most of the federated groups examined were institutionally involved in public policies and key agents in the public governance of their affairs.

The key to the effectiveness of federated structures appears to be the need to balance democracy with the capacity for effective decision-making; thus, EUROFER involves as many as 2000 specialists and experts in its work, yet still retains the capacity for speedy decision-making where necessary, which satisfies its constituency. The first important capacity for a Euro group to be effective is therefore for members to delegate considerable powers to its executive, its group secretariat, or even a single officer if circumstances demand, for independent decision-making, such that it is able to respond quickly to events without the need to consult its members on every issue. As Jordan and Wadsworth wryly comment, 'if asked, the members might disagree, but they might be prepared to live with a fast track decision' (1995, p. 119). A second key design factor for an effective group is that, in sectors with significant large-firm interests, decision-making in the groups needs to be weighted towards national associations with large interests, rather than split evenly between countries where industry sizes vary significantly. If a Euro group is unable to satisfy those members which comprise its most significant interests, then it is unlikely to survive.

In addition to possessing these characteristics, the success of EFPIA as a collective actor can be attributed partly to features of the pharmaceutical industry sector. First, the universe of firms is no larger than eighty, mostly multinational in character. Second, the experience of firms in operating throughout different markets make them an invaluable resource for the Commission to draw on when seeking information and advice. Third, common experiences in these different markets provided the basis for transnational collective action which predates the formation of EFPIA, such as the work of the industry through the International Federation of Pharmaceutical Manufacturers Associations' (IFPMA) in engaging the World Health Organization (WHO) in Geneva. This experience allowed EFPIA to imitate IFPMA's work in producing a self-regulatory code (Chapter 1) as a means of responding to attempts to regulate medicine-selling practices. Fourth, the relative success of the industry in Europe and its consequent popularity with member state governments, coupled with the high degree of regulation of arrangements for licensing, selling, producing and distributing medicines, means that these firms operate in broadly similar business environments throughout member states, and are familiarised with working together in responding to each of the national member state situations in which they operate. There is therefore a high degree of agreement between firms on the appropriate responses to make to regulatory issues, greatly easing common platform buildings. It has therefore not been difficult for the industry to work effectively at the European level (Greenwood, 1995b).

Outside business domains the picture is somewhat more mixed. As with business, around two-thirds of groups are federated structures. There are abiding problems of weakness in many of the groups representing the professions (Chapter 6), although this stems more from ambivalence among some professional interests to the European level itself and to the differential strengths of national state – social group relations than from the type of organisational structure. However, where only federated structures operate because direct membership structures for individual consumers would be almost impossible to sustain, European-level consumer organisations do not appear to experience difficulties which arise from the nature of the organisational format used. Similarly, sectoral trade union industry federations, which have developed in strength in recent years, do not experience problems arising from organisational design, while, for many groups in the social field, federated structures have proved the easiest way to organise sectoral interests.

Direct-membership associations

Public policy-making in Europe demands a speedier and more coherent response than a highly watered-down compromise statement which has taken six months to build, a problem which has beset some confederative Euro groups. If interests are to be able to exert significant influences upon European public policies they need to be able to respond more effectively. In a limited number of domains, this has meant building alternative structures which are direct representatives of particular interests. While the best known of these, and the easiest to conceptualise, are European associations representing firms directly, there are also a number of organisations in other fields without intervening tiers of organisation between a constituent interest in a member state and the European-level group. Thus, notable direct-membership associations operate within some public-interest domains (Chapter 8), and account for most European-level organisations representing subnational governmental interests (Chapter 9). With very few exceptions, however, such structures are largely absent in domains where the constituent interest is individuals (consumers and employees).

In business, direct-membership associations range from small and highly specialised subsectors to some of the most powerful cross sectoral organisations of firms. Thus, the European Vegetable Protein Association has 8 members, while the ERT (Chapter 5) represents over 40 chief executives of some of the largest multinational firms in the globe. At the sectoral level, direct-firm-membership types of structures may be most suitable: for subsectors so specialised that there is no comprehensive set of national associations to make up a federated structure, but where the firms concerned are significant enough to be able to fund their own dedicated Euro association; for sectors where most of the firms are so large that intervening organisations at the national level are either non-existent or insignificant; for sectors with a significant international orientation, with a relatively small number of multinational firms (Grant, 1995); where there are particular difficulties with the creation of a Euro group based on national association members; where there have been historic problems with federated structures; or where there are perceived advantages in terms of speed and coherence of decision-making, or the need for exclusivity of membership. However, the presence of one or some of these conditions does not itself predict the formation of direct-firm-membership structures, because there are examples of sectors, such as pharmaceuticals, which meet the criteria identified but whose members remain happy to work though federated structures which work well for them. In some business sectors, such as airlines, automobiles and plastics manufacturing, the direct-membership association is the only type of Euro group corresponding precisely with sectoral interests which is present. Elsewhere, direct membership associations of firms, such as those in information technology, and biotechnology, tend to exist alongside federated organisations. Business direct-membership Euro associations have been in existence since before 1950, but the peak period of their formation was during the 1970s, when, from an analysis of survey replies, 15 of 38 such associations were formed. On the whole, however, direct-firm-membership associations which are additional structures within a particular sector to a federation have emerged relatively recently.

Although direct-firm-membership associations have built excellent reputations as speedy decision-makers and effective representatives, those which exist alongside a sectoral federation suffer from the disadvantage of lacking constituency-wide representation in their membership because they tend to exclude small-firm interests. Such exclusion is often purposeful on the part of large firms. Indeed, one of the benefits of direct-firm-membership structures is that they are able to take decisions quickly, precisely because, in some cases, they represent limited numbers of firms which are large enough to be able to afford the fees; indeed, fee structures are sometimes set quite deliberately beyond the means of most small firms. Some direct-firm-membership organisations, such as the SAGB, quite deliberately set out in the first instance to be an exclusive rich-firm club, because of the relative ease of platform-building between a limited number of firms, which, by virtue of their size, are more likely to have homogenous interests than are associations representing mixed constituencies of firm sizes. So careful was SAGB to preserve this property that it started life as a 'by invitation only' forum. In domains less concentrated than biotechnology such arrangements can virtually prevent smaller firms from securing representation in Europe, because there are not enough of them to fund a Brussels-based association. Where a significant number of small firms do exist in a sector but are excluded, then, where resources permit, they tend to form their own associations which then compete with the rich-firm club, thus reducing the effectiveness of the latter. Although the direct-firm-membership format has become increasingly fashionable as the organisational structure through which to represent interests in Europe in recent years, its exclusivity of other interests, where these exist, is therefore an abiding weakness. This need not be a problem in wholly concentrated sectors such as automobiles, where the over-whelmingly majority of European production is concentrated in large firms, but it is a considerable problem in lesser concentrated domains. Here, as well as inviting competitive interest representation, the exclusivity of direct-firm organisations tends to be well recognised by the Commission, whose overriding concern, and need, is to be able to engage in dialogue with 'one-stop shops' where all interests are represented. Where direct-firm organisations are exclusive, the Commission will often go and seek out the types of interests which find themselves excluded as a means of obtaining wider opinion (Chapter 2).

One response to the relative disadvantages of federated and direct-membership structures has been to create associations which represent both firms and national associations together. Examples of these structures can be found in a number of business sectors, including chemicals, petroleum, polyolefins and cement, and in some non-business domains, such as public-sector employers. Such 'hybrid' organisations may effectively combine the capacity for speedy decision-making with a higher degree of inclusivity than is often present in direct-firm-membership formats. One effective variation on this is the European Federation of Retailing and Distribution (EuroCommerce). The full members of EuroCommerce are the national associations, and it is these which are allocated votes in decision-making, weighted in terms of importance. Firms can be affiliated members, however, provided they are also members of their national associations – thus ensuring the continued strength of these organisations, and ultimately of the federated type of structure. A final category of members are supporting members, which are those not directly in the commerce field themselves but who wish to support the activities of the group. Membership fees vary according to size and category of members, with the largest member paying around 125 000 ECU (Jordan and Wadsworth, 1995). The association provides a good example of how to manage the internal distribution of influence by balancing the weight and range of constituent interests. But the greatest collective action issues confronting a Euro group concern issues of associability in group formation and maintenance, and patterns of coalitions with other interests. These issues are considered in the sections which now follow.

Inter-group relations; federations and direct-member organisations

There are domains where federated and direct-firm-membership structures exist alongside one another, in such a way as not to be mutually exclusive. In information technology, both types of structures work comfortably alongside one another (Cram, 1995b), whereas in biotechnology the relationship has been more of a turbulent one, although there are now clear signs of a more harmonious relationship (Greenwood and Ronit, 1995b). This latter example suggests that there may be a logic of collaboration rather than of competition, a question recently explored by Greenwood and Cram (1996). First, for the Euro federations, collaboration may be a means of organisational survival. They cannot simply ignore direct-firm-membership fora and wish them away; instead, they need to adapt to the change in their environment which these structures represent, and seek to work with them to develop complementary roles rather than to see their own basis undermined as large firms seek to satisfy their representational needs elsewhere. Second, the Euro federation has properties which direct-firm-membership formats ignore at their peril. Euro federations tend to enjoy a greater degree of inclusivity than do direct-firm-membership associations, and therefore enjoy a special status with the Commission (Chapter 1). In consequence, they may possess information which is not easily accessible through other sources. For such reasons, large-firm interests with access to both types of collective fora may have a special role to play in fostering collaboration.

Exactly such a scenario has arisen in biotechnology, where firms such as Novo Nordisk have been instrumental in brokering co-operation talks between the federated European Secretariat of National Biotechnology Associations (ESNBA), and the direct-firm-membership SAGB. As has been discussed, SAGB's exclusivity laid the conditions for the formation and maintenance of ESNBA in organising smaller firms within the biotechnology domain, and for competing interest representation. Both parties suffered as a result. ESNBA's development was stunted through a lack of resources, and loss of clout, because it did not represent enough large firms, which lost it credibility in those sections of the Commission responsible for industrial policy development. Here, SAGB developed a close sym- biotic relationship with services such as DG III. In consequence, ESNBA developed a close relationship with DG XI (Environment, Nuclear Safety and Civil Protection), such that DG XI officials routinely attended board meetings of ESNBA. In turn, SAGB lost access to the environmental policy competencies of DG XI. In recognition of these respective strengths, a number of large firms kept a foot in both camps. Over time, these 'dual membership' firms helped ESNBA and SAGB develop progressively greater degrees of collaboration, leading finally to their merger on 27 September 1996 to form one organisation, EUROPABIO. However, it is possible that multi-representative formats can be more effective than singular ones, and there is evidence from the IT sector to show that overlapping membership can be advantageous. For instance, the relationship between the Liaison Organisation for the European Mechanical, Electrical and Electronic Engineering and Metalwork Industries (ORGALIME) and other sectoral bodies such as the Association of the European Telecommunications and Professional Electronics In- dustry (ECTEL) and the European Association of Manufacturers of Business Machines and Information Technology (EUROBIT) tends to work well and lead to mutually supportive policy positions (Greenwood and Cram, 1996).

The example of biotechnology identifies a further factor governing the relationship between multiple fora within the same domain. Biotechnology involves a number of Commission services with policy competencies, principally; DG III (Industry and Single Market), DG VI (Agriculture), DG XI (Environment, Nuclear Safety and Civil Protection), and DG XII (Research and Technological Devel- opment). Although these are co-ordinated by the inter-service Bio- technology Coordinating Committee, the relationship between them is characterised in the main by rivalry and competing perspectives, particularly centred on DG XI. This rivalry once provided a fertile breeding ground for competition between the respective interest groups. DG XI and ESNBA sought to strengthen their own positions *vis-à-vis* the organisations with which they competed by developing a mutually advantageous relationship, while the same was true of the relationship between DG III and SAGB. As McLaughlin's citation of a Commission official commenting on inter-service rivalry suggests (p. 42: 'quite simply, it's war'), this example is by no means unique. Sometimes, Commission services use interest groups and lobbyists as sources of intelligence for the activities, thinking and initiatives of other services.

Competition between Commission services seems likely to be a factor nourishing competition between interest groups in Brussels. Similarly, collaboration between services may have the opposite effect of fostering collaboration between groups by insisting on 'one-voice' fora. Equally, groups can themselves encourage inter-service collaboration, such as the role of SAGB in persuading the Commission to establish the BCC.

The issues of competition and collaboration between European interests have been at the centre of much of the recent debate about European interest groups, including Streeck and Schmitter's seminal contribution (1991) which foresaw Washington-like pluralistic competition between Euro groups (Chapter 1), and the debates reviewed in this chapter about the posited weakness of Euro groups. Yet, as Greenwood and Cram (1996) suggest, the issues of competition and collaboration between fora at the European level cannot be seen in straightforward terms, because examining the relationship between fora is likely to reveal the presence of behaviour which could be interpreted as evidence as both. Rather, they should be seen more as points along a continuum scale. The sheer range of informal patterns of collective action which exists alongside formal groups, both within and across domains, for example collaboration between firms, or between firms and public-interest groups, hints at the complexity involved in seeking to gauge patterns of competition and collaboration. Similarly, as firms participate in European public policy-making and implementation, so too do alliances form, and shift, and preferences become shaped. Thus, participation in a Commission advisory group can form the basis for interests represented by two individuals to work together. Thus, Greenwood and Cram comment that 'many of the critical contacts which IT firms have established with each other have been formed as a result of their participation in a whole range of EU research programmes or in the committees of standardisation bodies' (1996, p. 459).

Close contact with the Commission, in fora such as high-level EU working groups commonly found in high-technology domains, can inform decisions by firms and other interests as to which collective strategies are likely to be most fruitful for them. Public policy forums such as advisory groups might also help in producing common perceptions of problems and solutions which are then disseminated by members, and gain credence among the wider interest representation community concerned with the particular issues at stake. Equally, groups and fora can have similar 'socialisation' effects on their members; that is, they become mechanisms of agenda setting, and it is possible that initial collaboration between interests at the European level might lead in itself to further forms of collaboration.

New patterns of collaboration in Europe become evident to observers on a frequent basis, and in particular that involving less formal structures than groups. Research has by now challenged, dealt with and moved on from the misleading 'weak Euro groups' generalisations of the late 1980s and early 1990s, and has most recently questioned whether the development of multi-group structures implies competition. However, the development of different types of formal group structures still has some way to run, and analysis of the dynamic relationship between them will occupy contemporaneous research agendas.

The associability of interests at the European level

Apart from their resource base, organisational structures and capacities for coalition formation, the strength of Euro groups depends upon their ability to recruit and maintain a sufficient depth and breadth of membership to enable them to lay claim to the titles of authoritative and representative actors. The most original contribution to associability was undoubtedly that made by Mancur Olson (1965), who challenged dominant pluralist assumptions that interests would automatically associate in the pursuit of their interests. Rather, Olson suggested that the most rational behaviour for an interest would be to 'free ride' on the work of an association by obtaining its collective benefits without paying the membership fee. Associations would therefore have to develop a range of incentives which were only available by membership. 'Purposive' incentives, such as the ability to influence public policies, were benefits from which non-members could not be excluded. On the other hand, 'solidaristic' incentives, such as a sense of belonging derived from group membership, and 'material' incentives, such as access to goods on free or favourable terms, are excludable commodities. Group formation and maintenance, Olson argued, were dependent upon the ability of associations to develop excludable incentives. Membership decisions are thus characterised as rational, utility-maximising types of behaviour.

Olson's work profoundly challenged the most naïve versions of pluralism, and it is a testimony to his work that it remains, after more than three decades, the starting point of debate in collective-action theory. But Olson's work was not directed at the European level of organisation, where mechanisms of associability are not particularly complicated. More provocatively, a number of features about the European level seem to make mechanisms of associability almost automatic, particularly (though not exclusively) in the case of Euro groups representing business interests (the most prevalent category), where the stakes are so high. Indeed, responses drawn from 405 Euro groups indicate that the provision of 'hard', economically selective material incentives such as access to goods and services on favourable terms was virtually non-existent across the full range of Euro groups (Aspinwall and Greenwood, 1997). This means that rather than the extra services groups need to attract members, the basis of associability may be more the cost to the non-member of remaining outside membership (Jordan and McLaughlin, 1991). 'Non membership' costs are multifarious, but chief among them are the loss of information, and the ability to influence the behaviour of the group. In the case of the first of these factors, the European level represents a relatively uncertain information environment, particularly for business where non-membership of the group would mean a loss of vital market and political intelligence. In such an important yet uncertain environment as the single market, firms in particular need to 'minimise surprises' (Jordan and McLaughlin, 1991). Throughout Euro groups, information provision was ranked as 'important' by 84 per cent of groups themselves as a supply service influencing membership, being placed joint top alongside the more generalised 'representing members interests in Europe' (Aspinwall and Greenwood, 1997). In the case of the second factor, the loss of ability to influence group behaviour and positions caused the French car manufacturer PSA Peugeot to join the European automobile association, the Association of European Automobile Constructors (ACEA), after a period of determined resistance to membership caused by what it saw as ACEA's 'soft' position on membership by Japanese-dominated British car firms. Indeed, Camerra-Rowe (1996) suggests that firms which have developed alternative avenues of interest representation may work through Euro groups just as much to prevent a 'collective bad' than to pursue a collective good or to derive benefits from selective incentives. A further factor influencing membership of most Euro groups is the financial cost of membership, which may be relatively low for the potential member, fractional, or hidden by organisational budgetary and accounting devices. Set against the costs of maintaining a permanent presence in Brussels, the cost of joining a Euro group is almost negligible. The Commission's preference for engaging with European-level collective actors, and the disbursement of advisory committee places via Euro groups (Chapter 2), also means that to avoid paying the membership subscription is rarely a viable option.

The 'costs of non-membership' would seem therefore, to be the subject not so much of a full, rational, utility-maximising calculation on the part of the potential member or members, but rather of a bounded rationality, where the costs of not being in membership form more of a consideration than the carefully calculated the benefits of membership (Jordan and McLaughlin, 1991); that is, the focus is not so much on what may be gained by membership as on what may be lost through non-membership.

For the two-thirds of Euro groups which are federations of national associations, mechanisms of associability are almost automatic. Many Euro groups were founded from national associations in order to meet their own needs in engaging at the European level. Officials from national associations form a value and social network in favour of membership, a norm which sustains their own organisations; for some, the European association may even represent a career path which is important to keep open. Non-membership for a national association would almost be unthinkable, because it would mean that the association would be unable to service the needs of its own members, and, if members were not in receipt of vital European services from their own national association, the very credibility of, and the need for, the national association would be called into question by its own members. In any event, individual members of national associations would have to campaign very hard among other members if they wanted their national association to disaffiliate from the European association; such a Herculean effort would hardly seem worth the effort, particularly if the European association does not cause offence. Rather, the logic would seem to be to swim with the tide of membership. The rational calculation of membership benefits does not seem to apply significantly in the case of federated structures.

In the case of direct-firm-membership Euro groups, a rational calculus of membership might, in theory, be more likely to apply, with individual members working through cost–benefit considerations. Certainly, a slightly higher range of selective incentive provision is present among these Euro groups (Aspinwall and Greenwood, 1997). But even in direct-firm-membership structures the logic is still towards membership, particularly in the case of business. Most of these structures are 'rich-firm clubs', for whom the cost of affiliation is, once again, relatively low, fractional and/or hidden. Multinational firms are used to working together in different national environments, where they face shared challenges. As the example of EFPIA indicates, where these environments are similar, so transnational level collective action is eased, and the habits and benefits of collaboration can be learnt through participation in international associations and transnational structures at levels other than European. Market conditions may also create a pattern of large-firm collaboration. Indeed, some firms work so closely together that anti-trust legislation is needed to keep them apart. In the steel and cement sectors, competition from 'second-world' markets appears to have made enterprises see risks and opportunities in the same way (Aspinwall, 1995), which has led to large fines being levied upon European steel and cement producers for cartel-like behaviour (Chapter 5). A similar scenario may not be too distant in the case of freight shipping. At latter stages in the product cycle, in particular, firms need to collaborate as a defensive posture against cheap competition from second-world markets. Conversely, however, early stages in the product cycle may drive the logic towards competition, as firms cluster around competing technology standards (such as happened with VHS or Betamax in the video market), or significant market entry by new players arises. The latter scenario has occurred in biotechnology health care, with market concentration developing later in the product cycle as small firms which produced significant technologies were taken over or were the target of partnership initiatives with large pharmaceutical firms, or dropped out of the market altogether. In some new-technology markets, however, the cost of entry may create a barrier to new players.

Market conditions in Europe have already fostered large-firm collaboration through a wave of mergers, acquisitions, take-overs and strategic alliances in the run-up to the single market, either because the logic of the market construct in Europe dictates that large firms able to move across national boundaries will be most able to benefit, or because firms outside Europe need a market presence for a host of reasons. In any event, as firms began to find their 'national champion' status under threat, so the need for group membership of Euro structures intensified, either because of the uncertainties presented by the European market, or because of the need to seek 'Euro champion' status for particular industries at the European level. At a simpler level, direct-membership organisations, whether firms or local authorities or voluntary organisations, welcome opportunities to meet up for a range of reasons – status, social, career, interpersonal, learning-curve, information or reassurance. For instance, a Danish firm seeking to bid for a public procurement contract in Portugal for the first time needs some degree of intelligence about market and labour market conditions. While the Euro group may not be the principal source of its information, it does present the chance to network and gather impressions or points of view, and, once again, the cost of missing out on an item of information or rumour which could be vital to the chances of gaining a contract means that the cost of non-membership is too high to bear. Similarly, firms may be able to obtain reassurance for their market strategies by networking or witnessing the behaviour of other firms in Euro groups. Finally, as Olson anticipated, peer pressure between interests is likely to work in favour of group membership. For all these reasons, a firm or another type of individual interest may have to think harder about its reasons not to join a Euro group.

For most European business groups, potential collective action problems seem either to have been solved, or not to have arisen, by the time groups are formed. Because firms are the easiest units to conceptualise as direct member units, and because firms are the most numerous actors at the European level, the emphasis in the above sections has been on working through examples from the field of business. But even outside business, where direct-membership structures exist, many of the same pressures for group membership arise. In subnational government domains, for instance, where direct membership organisations predominate at the European level, a range of similar pressures may apply. Here, the impression of competition between regions and localities for structural-fund assistance is illusory because of the role of member states as 'gatekeepers' of applications, and the ability of member states to gain from their own regions receiving structural-fund award status (Chapter 9). Dense and varied networks of regional and local authorities at the European level can be observed, with high levels of collaboration, including arrangements between neighbouring authorities to pool resources by dividing membership of Euro groups and sharing the benefits between them (Chapter 9). In social fields, opportunities to obtain 'Euro gold', to swap know-how, to take advantage of new possibilities to network, and to respond to the Commission's attempts to build transnational networks (including the availability of expenses to attend meetings) may, once again, be irresistible factors making either the simple cost–benefit ratio extremely favourable, or the cost of non-participation too high.

In non-business fields, where patterns of collaboration are sometimes forming for the first time, the rationality of membership may be driven less by the perceived costs of non-membership, and more by the positive incentives of membership. Thus, Brussels territorial offices which allow direct affiliation from constituent interests often do need to recruit and retain members by the provision of a range of tailored services. However, here again some members, such as universities, interested in funding and information opportunities, may join a Brussels regional office more from concern about the potential costs of non-membership, including the presence of competitors in membership, than because of particular types of service provision, or because particular departments most in favour of membership do not have to pay the membership fee. In either the 'positive membership' or the 'cost of non-membership' scenario, the operation of dynamics exerted by the European level itself seems to ease the ability of interests to work collectively in Euro groups.

The review of evidence in this chapter suggests, either on grounds of resources or the ability to engage in collective action, that the 'weak Euro group' label is an unsustainable and unfounded caricature. This is a central issue in the study of European-level interest representation, because the ability of interests to contribute to the integration process depends upon their ability to work meaningfully through collective structures. It is therefore a debate which is revisited in Chapter 10, in which the circumstances under which the rather misleading 'weak Euro groups' label has emerged are considered, together with an assessment of the ways in which interests contribute to the integration process.

4

The Regulation of
Interest Representation

The fast growth of interest representation at the European level in recent years has brought its own problems. If the estimates that there is one person working in the Brussels interest representation environment for every Commission staff member (excluding translators and secretarial staff) are at all accurate (Chapters 1 and 3), there is now a danger of overcrowding.

Overcrowding brings with it a number of problems. One of these concerns the crowding of the information environment, where it becomes increasingly difficult to sift the useful from the less relevant. A second concerns the capacities of the European institutions to cope with the sheer volume of interest representation. An example of this concerns the five-person tourism unit within DG XXIII (Enterprise Policy, Distributive Trades, Tourism and Co-operatives), where hard-pressed officials do not have time to fully engage tourism interests. Another example involves incidents in the EP, where MEPs have arrived at meetings only to find them over-attended, with inadequate quantities of documentation because lobbyists who arrived earlier had exhausted the supply of English language documentation. Until very recently, access to the Parliament's buildings in Brussels were only moderately restricted, and, once in, lobbyists could gain easy access to members' offices, or, in the even less restricted environment of Strasbourg, seek MEPs outside the chamber. In response, some members complained that they felt under pressure from lobbyists.

A third type of problem associated with overcrowding concerns issues of disequilibria, where the increasing focus of public-interest groups on the European level raises questions about the relatively privileged access of business interests, the related issue of access to decision-making for European citizens, and the transparency of

decision-making procedures. Where the institutions have not managed their information strategies proactively, so as to easily engage a
wide range of outside interests, the system is loaded in favour of those
who know their way around it. A fourth issue concerns standards in
public life, where the growth of special interests raises questions about
undue influence exerted in public policies. Indeed, the issue of
standards in public life has manifested itself in a number of member
states recently, most notably in France, Italy, Portugal, Spain and
the UK (with the Nolan Committee). For all such reasons, the
regulation of interest representation has arrived on the European
agenda in recent years.

At the European level, the issue first surfaced in the European
Parliament in the shape of a written question in 1989 from the Dutch
Socialist MEP Alman Metten, ostensibly in response to a number of
abuses. The Parliament has only recently grown accustomed to being
the target of significant lobbying, and for both sides the relationship
has been a learning process. Some Parliamentarians naturally took
offence when they found multinational interests submitting mass
amendments to proposals through other sympathetic MEPs, sometimes with the company logo still on the amendment sheet submitted.
Both the Tobacco Advertising Directive and the Television without
Frontiers Directive attracted a quantity and intensity of interest
representation which caused a high degree of irritation in the
Parliament. One MEP was accused of being in the pay of the tobacco
industry (Claveloux, 1993). Public-interest lobbying has also caused
offence, with some of these groups accused of being over-aggressive in
the run-up to the vote on the bio-patenting directive. A number of
MEPs were overwhelmed by visitors from a political party in a third
country complaining of exclusion from domestic political life, while
'thank you' gifts of music recordings from a third-party government
following a particular vote caused offence. There were unsubstan-
tiated rumours of wider abuses, such as an MEP registering a number
of lobbyists as personal staff members, trespassing on Parliament
premises, stealing documents and mail intended for MEPs, selling
institutional documents for profit, and the invention of scare stories
by consultants to drum up business from clients. As was discussed in
Chapter 2, the Socialist group has also expressed concern at the way
in which a range of outside interests resource the work of some
intergroups. The Committee on Rules of Procedure and the Verification of Credentials and Immunities (CRP) therefore responded to the
climate of concern, and appointed the Belgian Socialist MEP Marc

Galle in May 1991 to 'submit proposals with a view to drawing up a code of conduct and a public register of lobbyists accredited by Parliament' (European Parliament, 1992, p. 1). At that time, the move reflected concerns which were mainly held by the Socialist group in the EP.

The Galle report

Taking on the special-interest community in the name of safeguarding the public interest was always likely to appeal to an EP in search of a populist image, and it is in this context that the role of the Parliament as the first institution to address the issue should be understood. Indeed, the immediate past President of the EP, Klaus Hansch, in office during the key point of decision-making for the regulation of lobbying, was particularly conscious of the image of the EP, and keen for it to take action on the issue.

Galle initiated a two-day public hearing as a means of collecting evidence and inviting views, and undertook research into lobbying regulations in Washington DC. Reporting in October 1992, he suggested: a code of conduct with minimalist standards aimed at preventing abuse (such as prohibiting selling on documents, and use of institutional premises); the establishment of 'no-go' areas in the Parliament's buildings including Members offices and library facilities; examination of the role of lobbying with intergroups; and, taking an idea from the United States, the registration of lobbyists on an annual basis, spelling out the rights and obligations of those on the register, and specifying penalties for failure to comply. A final, and contentious, proposal required MEPs to annually state their financial interests and those of their staff, on a separate register.

Galle's proposals were never put to the full EP plenary for a number of substantive and circumstantial reasons, including attempts by the Commission to pre-empt the proposals by seeking self-regulation by lobbyists, resistance from the College of Quaestors (p. 44), and the EP elections of June 1994 (McLaughlin and Greenwood, 1995). The most substantive problem, however, was that the Galle report became embroiled in definitional controversies as to what constituted a lobbyist. This problem has beset most attempts to regulate interest representation in the United States, including the 1938 Foreign Agents Registration Act, and the 1946 Federal Regulation of Lobbying Act. The latter act requires all interest groups, associations, consultants and lobbyists to register with the Code of Congress, respect a code of practice, and submit detailed accounts on their activities to the Congress every four months. However, the definition of what constitutes a lobbyist has proved virtually impossible to uphold in practice, and, consequently, the annual register of lobbyists, and of members' financial interests, has had relatively little impact, resulting in the Lobby Restrictions Act of 1996. Some US legislation requires a great deal of detail, and is widely regarded as excessively burdensome (Calamaro, 1992). In any event, the concept of 'policy borrowing' is notoriously difficult, and is unlikely to be successful when policies are taken out of context from their national settings and transposed into a completely different environment (Rose, 1993). Of interest, however, is that the Galle report was heavily influenced by American systems of regulating interest representation, and did not seek to draw from the experiences of other countries with schemes such as Canada, Germany, Australia and New Zealand, or other international institutions such as the United Nations.

Galle defined a lobbyist as 'anybody who acts on the instructions of a third party and sets out to defend the interests of that third party to the EP and other Community institutions' (European Parliament, 1992, p. 4). This definition appears to refer only to commercial lobbyists, thereby excluding those working for interest groups and public-affairs departments of firms. Indeed, finding a watertight definition of what constitutes the diverse range of interest representation activities represents a legislative challenge that has yet to be won. Not only would such a definition need to include private actors in producer and public-interest groups; it would also need to decide when activities by public-sector organisations, including Commission officials and territorial governmental bodies, constitute interest representation. The difficulty experienced right at the outset by the Galle report, however, was a lesson well learnt by the CRP, which was to make a second attempt at regulating interest representation in the subsequent Parliament.

The Commission initiatives and self-regulation

The debate surrounding the Galle proposals allowed the Commission time to attempt to find a solution. For its part, the Secretariat of the Commission was concerned by the Galle proposals because it interpreted them as a threat to the free flow of information on which the

Commission depends. At the outset, it specifically rejected the idea of regulating by providing controlled-access passes to buildings on the grounds that this would privilege certain types of interests above others. In its December 1992 publication, *An Open and Structured Dialogue Between the Commission and Special Interest Groups*, besides stating in its opening paragraph the value of interest representation to it (Chapter 1), the Commission reflected that, while no general problems existed with 'lobbying' *per se*, there had been instances of aggressive styles of lobbying, and misdemeanours such as lobbyists selling draft and official documents, and misrepresenting themselves to the public by the use of Commission symbols (Commission of the European Communities, 1992a). As a direct response to the Galle initiatives, the Secretariat therefore spent some time attempting to persuade the interest representation community to address the issues, and thereby to forestall regulation, by operating a self-regulatory code. Indeed, the December 1992 document specifically listed the principles on which such a code should be based, and invited public-affairs consultants to set up a representative organisation. The consultants initially gave a lukewarm response, partly on the grounds that to do so would be to invite future undesirable regulation, but as events unfolded and the Parliament became more determined to regulate, so a number of organisations, including the European Federation of Lobbyists (EFL) and the European Parliamentary Affairs Lobbyists (EPAL), were later (1996) established. A representative organisation has also recently been established in the public-relations sector. There are presently some signs of discussion between these organisations in an effort to establish a single organisation capable of representing the interest representation community to the European institutions.

In trying to encourage self-regulation, the Commission faced the difficulty of addressing an interest representation community of considerable diversity. While the EFL and EPAL each include members drawn from commercial lobbyists and interest groups, both organisations have started with modest membership numbers, and, because of the sheer problem of numbers and of diversity, it is unlikely that either will ever attract more than a fraction of the potential total constituency of members. Because these organisations seemed highly unlikely to emerge at the time the Commission had wanted them to, the Commission did not, initially at least, vigorously pursue the issue, yet at the same time it was not prepared to let the matter rest. The

Commission Secretariat sponsored, in partnership with AMCHAM-EU, ERT, UNICE and EUROCHAMBRES, a conference primarily aimed at commercial public-affairs organisations (Forum Europe, 1993). In July 1993, David Williamson, Secretary General of the Commission, called a round-table meeting with 200 members of the lobbying community, with the explicit aim of inviting them to draw up a self-regulatory code. When none was forthcoming, the Commission issued periodic warnings that the tardiness of the interest representation community might result in a worse fate of institutionally designed regulation, indicating that the Commission itself would take the initiative in elaborating minimum rules if self-regulation was not forthcoming (Agence Europe, 1994).

Throughout this period, a core group (initially 5, rising to 25) of public-affairs consultancy firms in Brussels had been informally discussing the issue among themselves. From this group emerged, in September 1994, a self-regulatory code which addressed the minimalist concerns of the Commission, with agreement among the parties to rotate its administration. It read:

In their dealings with EU institutions, public-affairs practitioners shall:

(a)   Identify themselves by name and company

(b)   Declare the interest represented

(c)   Neither intentionally misrepresent their status nor the nature of enquiries to officials of the EU institutions, nor create any false impression in relation thereto

(d)   Neither directly nor indirectly misrepresent links with EU institutions

(e)   Honour confidential information given to them

(f)   Not disseminate false or misleading information knowingly or recklessly and shall exercise proper care to avoid doing so inadvertently

(g)   Not sell for profit to third parties copies of documents obtained from EU institutions

(h)   Not obtain information from EU institutions by dishonest means

(i)   Avoid any professional conflicts of interest

(j)   Neither directly nor indirectly offer to give any financial inducement to any EU official

(k)   Neither propose nor undertake any action which would constitute an improper influence upon them

(l)   Only employ EU personnel subject to the rules and confidentiality requirements of the EU institutions (Reuters, 1994).

This code reflects very closely the principles which the Commission had spelt out almost two years earlier. Indeed, it had taken lobbyists this time to produce a code which the Commission had virtually written for them.

The code was quickly adapted by the College of Quaestors for use in the Parliament, changing its previous procedures by issuing passes to those willing to sign the code of conduct. The advantage of this approach is that it avoids the definitional problem of what constitutes a lobbyist. Nevertheless, the College provides for no enforcement of the code, leaving it completely to the conscience of the visitor. At present, any firm which signs up to the code is automatically entitled under the scheme to six annual transferable passes for its employees. This generous implementation makes it rather difficult for the Parliament to monitor entry. Indeed, to date only one pass has been withdrawn under this scheme. Of significance, perhaps, is that this scheme was devised and administered by one of the College of Quaestors, Richard Balfe, who is also a member of the CRP, and who is said by a number of lobby firms to prefer this more informal approach to stricter forms of regulation which have been proposed. Indeed, one member of the CRP has suggested that the Quaestors scheme was designed in part with the ambition of preventing more ambitious regulatory schemes from being introduced.

Although the public-affairs consultants have done everything asked of them by the Commission, and, as of December 1995, virtually all of the eligible constituency had signed up to its terms, it may have little more than symbolic value. As is evident from reading through its terms, it is somewhat minimalist in scope, and few public-affairs consultants had any trouble in agreeing to its measures. Not a single complaint has been filed under its terms. One public-affairs consultancy which signed the code described the scheme (during interviews conducted as part of the process of writing this chapter) as a 'fig-leaf', commenting that it was 'minimal, pointless and complete window-dressing'. The issue of applying sanctions is a highly delicate one among the lobbying community itself. As Claveloux pondered in briefing notes to the 1993 Forum Europe conference,

Could a lobbyist be struck off the list simply because he engages in what his colleagues consider uncompetitive practices? If a lobbyist is struck off the list would this bar him from ever approaching the EC institutions again? (Claveloux, 1993, p. 46).

Despite a number of reservations expressed about the code, its emergence did reveal some degree of demand among both public and private interests for it, in that the first secretariat received enquiries about the possibility of signing the provisions of the code from non-public-affairs consultancies, including industry associations, local governments, and lawyers. At least one key founding firm take the view that the code will have an impact beyond its signatories in standards setting, which in time might come to be seen as the norm. Yet the difficulties of catering for the diverse interest representation community were illustrated when the public-affairs consultants sought to strengthen the code in November 1995 directly in response to the issues being raised in Parliamentary debate at that time. It was proposed that condition (j) of the code (p. 85) be amended to include the prohibition of financial inducements to MEPs and their staff as well as EU officials. While all the public-affairs consultants were happy to sign up to this amendment, the only member of a trade association who had previously signed the code was not able to do so because of the activities of his organisation in funding an EP inter-group. These difficulties may also beset new codes which are presently being devised by EFL and EPAL, which seek to set standards across the interest representation community.

Self-regulatory codes can work in the interests of governmental authority, consumers and private interests alike under certain sets of circumstances. They are favoured by some private interests because of their ability to forestall governmental regulation, and in enabling the interest concerned to keep control over their own affairs. For governmental authorities, they can provide a zero-cost regulatory option, embody a spirit of self-discipline on the part of the regulated, provide a practical and ideological solution to overload, and can, in certain circumstances, protect the public interest. For consumers, they can provide a speedy and cheap form of redress, with flexibility provided by the interpretation of codes according to the spirit, rather than the letter, of the law. Although self-regulatory instruments have a chequered history, they can be successful under the following circumstances: when there is a direct relationship between the consumer and the producer; where they exist against a backdrop of reserve governmental legislation, provided the latter is not disabled by regulatory capture; and where they have proved responsive to turbulent regulatory issues over a period of time by improving the scope of provision. None of these favourable conditions apply to the code devised by the public-affairs consultants. Indeed, so weak were the initial 'industry' responses that they did not fulfil a basic condition of their success in forestalling regulation, in that the Parliament has since returned to the issue following a report from the CRP, devised by the rapporteur Glynn Ford.

Self-regulation of lobbying nevertheless continues to meet the requirements of the Commission, fitting comfortably with the Commission's own style and position, both because of its need to engage with the interest representation community and because it offers a solution to its overload problem. Indeed, in a related field the Commission relies upon the journalists association for vetting all journalist applications for accreditation, and has sought to use this mechanism to tighten up on abuses in recent years whereby lobbyists have obtained journalists passes. It has expressed its satisfaction with both the terms of the lobbyists code established from its own draft, and with the level of signatories. However, because, this code has gathered no supporters outside public affairs firms, the Commission has established a dialogue with public-relations firms, and non-governmental organisations, with the aim of encouraging each of these two groups to produce their own code. At present, a draft code for public relations firms is under discussion, while the Commission continues to seek a similar response from non-governmental organisations (NGOs). ERAF (Chapter 2) provides a means for dialogue between NGOs and the Commission for this purpose, and both organisations hosted a major conference on the subject in 1994. The conference established the clear position that any code, rather than being restrictive, should aim at achieving more transparency and openness in contacts with EU institutions and to promote a level playing field between business and NGO interests (ERAF, 1994).

For the Commission, the issue of regulating interest representation has always been embroiled in a much wider set of concerns about the openness and transparency of EU decision-making structures, a level playing field for access to EU decision-making and the way in which the EU engages in dialogue with outside interests (Chapter 2). Indeed, that the issues raised by the 1992 Sutherland report clearly struck a chord is well illustrated by the words of a Commission official who restated the problem at a 1993 conference with public-affairs practitioners on the regulation of interest representation:

There is no general scheme for talking to people representing different interests in the Community. As a result, the development of dialogue had been on an *ad hoc*, pragmatic basis and many different patterns of dialogue now exist depending on the people involved both inside and outside the Commission (Claveloux, in McLaughlin and Greenwood, 1995, p. 149).

There is some irony in that both the Parliament and the Commission have sought to regulate lobbying partly because of problems which their own lack of information strategies have caused. Although claims of abuses committed by lobbyists make good parliamentary debating material, it is somewhat unfair to blame faults in the system on those who seek to exploit them (McLaughlin and Greenwood, 1995). However, the Commission to some extent, has sought to use the issues raised by the Parliament as an opportunity to safeguard and strengthen its access to the information and views which special-interest groups bring, and to address the *ad hoc* way in which dialogue has developed. Nevertheless, neither the Commission, nor the Galle proposals, ever embraced producer associations, and in doing so missed around three-quarters of European-level interest groups.

The new Commission database of interest groups which interface with the European level, designed as part of the package of measures to improve openness and transparency (Chapter 2), will be made widely available during 1997; it will include not only European-level interest groups but also national-level groups which seek to engage Brussels from member states. It does not include profit-making hire-able lobbies, although the Commission has suggested that such firms draw up their own directory. Non-inclusion of these firms in the Commission directory emphasises the main purpose of the directory, which is to provide information to readers on who to consult over particular issues, thereby promoting equality of access to European policy-making for a wide variety of groups. Besides the name, contact details and date of foundation of the organisation concerned, each entry will include information on the names of senior officials and of member organisations, the principal objectives of the organisation, its legal status and its structure. Entry is voluntary, and does not confer or imply any official recognition by the Commission or access to any privileges. In part, the directory was conceived as a response to attempts by the Parliament to regulate, in that an open 'telephone directory', with access to any interest who wanted it, was an alternative to the Galle proposal to establish an official register of lobbyists, so that an entry would be part of a strategy to control these actors by making it conditional on good behaviour in return for access to the Parliament. Yet it is somewhat naïve to think that certain groups do not get consulted simply because Commission officials do not know who they are or inadvertently overlook them during early drafting stages (McLaughlin and Greenwood, 1995). However, it is likely to be an extremely useful tool for a wide variety of interests, and its publication is now keenly anticipated. For its part, once again in an attempt to promote openness, the Commission intends to actively market the database.

The extent to which issues surrounding the regulation of interest representation are part of a broader set of underlying concerns about equality, openness and transparency may partly help to explain why the Parliament returned to the issue after the failure of the Galle proposals to make any headway. Narrowly defined and rather symbolic self-regulation of lobbying standards completely failed to address these wider concerns. Some MEPs have also sought to link the regulation of lobbying as a precondition for the Parliament's campaign to obtain further powers. Consequently, the Parliament returned to the issue with some vigour after the June 1994 elections.

The Ford report

Almost immediately following the 1994 EP elections, the CRP requested authorisation to draw up a report on lobbying in the European Parliament. The President of the Parliament provided authorisation to do so, and the CRP appointed Glynn Ford, a British Socialist MEP, as rapporteur in November 1994. Ford's approach was markedly different from that of the Commission in that he started out with the view that self-regulation is a flawed instrument with which to achieve public goals, and in particular saw the self-regulatory code for lobbyists which had been devised as virtually worthless.

As part of his work, Ford embarked on a study of the rules governing lobbying in the national parliaments of the member states, thereby making the connection between his own work and issues of standards in public life which have arisen on the public agendas of many of the member countries of the EU in recent years (European

Parliament, 1995a). The report noted that in most member state parliaments there are no provisions governing the activities of interest groups or their representatives. However, formal regulation does exist in Germany, and several national parliaments issue access passes of variable duration. In the UK, the House of Commons Select Committee on Members' Interests did propose a register of lobbyists with an associated code of conduct. Although this has never been voted on by the House, two associations of Parliamentary lobbyists have launched self-regulatory codes. In other countries there is evidence that the registration of lobbyists has arisen on the agenda as a result of what has happened at the European level; for example, in Sweden, a private bill makes specific reference to the Ford scheme.

There is concern among some lobbyists that Ford did not embark on a systematic process of consultation with them. Beyond public-affairs consultancies, a number of the most established Brussels-based European-level trade associations interviewed for the purpose of writing this chapter had no knowledge whatsoever of the Ford scheme. This lack of systematic consultation has provided the opportunity for some lobbyists to express their reservations about the detail of the proposals. While welcoming the idea of a code of conduct, Elaine Cruickshanks, Managing Director of consultants Hill and Knowlton, focused in an interview with Reuters on Ford's plans to introduce a colour-coded badge system to identify categories of wearers, commenting that 'it's like in the time of the plague when people had to ring bells to designate they were ill' (Reuters, 1995).

Some lobbyists interpreted Ford's plan as a Socialist stick with which to beat Conservative politicians, viewing it as an extension of UK politics surrounding the Nolan report. There were predictions among some that the Ford report would find difficulty in passing through the Parliament, and claims that Ford was 'anti-lobbyist'. A common view among lobbyists has been to deny that a real problem exists, or that if one does exist then it is only the old one of the odd 'rotten apple in every barrel'. This was also a view to be found among leading industry associations. EFPIA, the pharmaceutical trade association, in a briefing to its members reporting on a meeting between the Commission and UNICE, CEFIC, COPA and itself, complained that it 'did not see why all "organised" and representative structures should be made to pay for the sins of the few, or for the failure of officials to abide by their own institutions' own rules of procedure' (EFPIA, 1994, p. 1). Instead, such groups have tended to stress the benefits which interest representation brings to the

European institutions, and to back self-regulation as well as the informal Balfe scheme in operation by the College of Quaestors.

Some public-affairs firms have been pointing out to interested observers some of the difficulties of regulating interest representation. These have included points about the difficulty of regulating practices such as the development of 'cyber-lobbying' through the information superhighway; the bureaucratisation of the work of MEPs by requiring them to record their relationships with lobbyists; and the administrative costs involved in receiving annual submissions from MEPs and lobbyists. However, it is of interest that there has in fact been little lobbying of Parliament over attempts to regulate interest representation.

Ford set out to avoid becoming embroiled in the definitional niceties of precisely what constitutes a lobbyist, which had so beset the Galle report. Instead, he proposed an ingenious scheme based on incentives, and one of great simplicity that would be likely to attract wide support within the Parliament in the first instance and which would not risk failing because it contained too many details to which parties could object. The scheme in its original form proposed the following:

> [T]he College of Quaestors shall issue permanent passes to persons who wish to enter Parliament frequently with a view to supplying information to members within the framework of their parliamentary mandate.
>
> In return, these persons shall be required to sign the register of the College of Quaestors, listing, in particular, their name and trade name and the nature of the activities which they wish to carry out in the Parliament.
>
> This register shall be made available to the public in all of Parliament's places of work and information offices in the Member States.
>
> The persons listed in the register shall draw up on a yearly basis a declaration of their activities, detailing, in particular, any benefits, subsidies, gifts or services of any nature rendered to Members, officials, or assistants.
>
> These declarations shall be set out in an annex to the register and shall be subject to the same conditions as regards public access.
>
> The provisions governing the application of this Rule shall be laid down in an annex to the Rules of Procedure (European Parliament, 1995b, p. 3).

The approach is therefore based on the idea of incentives, rather than defining what constitutes a lobbyist. Anyone who needed to visit the Parliament frequently would find their work made considerably easier by having one of the passes, which provides permanent access; the alternative would be to queue for one-day passes to the assembly. In return for receiving a pass of access, those benefiting would be obliged to sign a register and remit an administrative fee for doing so, and make an annual declaration of activities. The pass would be retained by the applicant as a guarantee of minimum standards of behaviour. Each year, provided no objections are raised and a declaration of activities made, the pass would be renewable by the College of Quaestors, who are to be responsible for implementing the scheme. As well as securing access to certain parts of the Parliament's buildings, the pass would also confer on the holder the right to secure documents from a special distribution counter. The annual declaration of activities would include all interventions aimed at the Parliament, and any gifts or services rendered to Members or others attached to the Parliament in some way, including MEPs' staff, and would be made public.

Ford's initial strategy was to keep his proposals simple by avoiding the complexities which had beset the Galle report. Because of the relatively greater difficulties involved for a new measure to be passed, Ford's original strategy was to reason that a simple measure would stand a better chance of being accepted at the first attempt, which could then be amended by later inserting further detail, and which would have the advantage of involving fewer complications because of its status as an amendment to existing legislation. In this sense, the important factor became not what would be included in the text to be presented to the plenary, but what was excluded. For some Members, the fear was that the devil would follow later in the detail, and this foreboding was to some extent realised, although not in the manner originally planned by Ford. However, at the early meetings of the CRP, the simplicity of Ford's proposals seemed likely to attract widespread support, and everything went smoothly right up to and including the meetings of the Committee until May 1995.

Ford's proposals were subject to comment from the Committees on the following: the Environment, Public Health and Consumer Protection; Civil Liberties and Internal Affairs; and Social Affairs and Employment. This last committee specifically called for a number of measures related to members' financial interests, and in particular close vetting of proposed donations of a significant size from lobby groups. Because of the sensitivity of the issue for lobbyists, the May meeting of the CRP, was unusually, held in private. From this meeting onwards, the Ford report became concerned not only with regulating the activities of lobbyists, but also with those of Parliamentarians, and the incremental extension of its scope during subsequent CRP committee meetings in 1995 into these areas was to prove its weakness in the months ahead. Crucially, the report also became linked, and ultimately embroiled with, the Nordmann report on members' interests, which meant that it was perceived as straying even further beyond its original remit into the behaviour of members themselves. Particularly controversial was a proposal in the Nordmann report requiring members to disclose assets of 'movable and immovable property'. In some member states where issues of standards in public life have recently been raised, ruling parties have resisted the imposition of certain standards upon parliamentarians, whereas parties recently in opposition, whether Conservative (for example Spain) or Socialist (for example Britain), have attempted to make political capital by polarising the debate and seeking imposition. In the EP, similarly, a number of Socialist members have seen the issue in terms of likely conflicts of interests between the work of Conservative members, as parliamentarians, and their interests and links with business and commerce. One senior Socialist MEP told his regional newspaper that he suspected certain right-wing members of the Strasbourg Parliament of taking inducements, and commented that

> [I]t's not just putting arguments and making representations. It's the financial inducements, direct and indirect, which I suspect some organisations give to members to pursue their case . . . I certainly suspect examples do exist where companies pay individuals to promote particular causes, and that might be in terms of letters to the Commission, amendments to reports or indeed raising points in the Chamber itself . . . it's actually against the institution's best interests to attempt either to sweep under the carpet or forget about practices which could be called into question (*Western Mail*, 1995, p. 1).

The text of the Ford report presented to the Parliament in plenary differed from its earlier drafts by including a much greater degree of detail on the following: the issues and amounts of gifts to be declared by lobbyists; the mechanisms of declaration and disclosure; the passes to be worn and the visibility of display; the limitations on the rights of passholders including access to parts of buildings; the process of annual renewal and the registration fee; the registration of assistants, and the requirement that these sign a statement to the effect that they neither represent nor defend any interest other than those concerned with their duties; and the powers given to the College of Quaestors in implementing the scheme. In doing so, it departed from the simplicity of earlier schemes and left itself open to dissent on a number of points of detail.

Although it is constitutionally possible that the Ford report (focusing on outsiders) and the Nordmann report (focusing on members) could have been passed independently, the two came to be thought of as a coherent package, both at CRP meetings and, finally, at the plenary debates in the chamber in January and July 1996. Thus, just as the Ford report proposed that lobbyists should declare all gifts or cash in kind provided to MEPs over 1000 ECU, so the Nordmann report stipulated that MEPs would make a similar declaration of all gifts received over this value, with a common mechanism so that, if necessary, the two could be matched by checks. Because the Nordmann report sought disclosure of all assets of members, including bank accounts, its passage in plenary session of the EP was always likely to be far more contentious than that of the Ford report. In the days prior to the debate, some of the non-Conservative elements in the Parliament joined members of the European People's Party in expressing reservations. Indeed, it was rumoured that Nordmann himself, a French Liberal who took over as Rapporteur from Yves Galland, had serious doubts about the scheme he proposed.

In the event, after an intense debate the January 1996 EP plenary meeting voted the Nordmann and the Ford reports, together, back to the Committee on Rules and Procedure for a rethink. Unsurprisingly, the basis of disagreement focused on the disclosure of assets and gifts, with members of the European People's Party submitting a number of blocking amendments. In the days of acrimony following the vote, Ford sought to define the issue not so much as a failure to endorse a scheme to regulate lobbying, but more one of failing to assure the public integrity of the Parliament because of the 'activities of perhaps a dirty dozen or so members [who] could bring the entire assembly into disrepute' (*Financial Times*, 1996a). He explicitly linked the ability of the Parliament to obtain further powers with the fate of proposals concerning disclosure of gifts and assets by members, and, while casting doubt over the future of the proposals, announced that the Socialist group would be introducing its own register of gifts and favours. Equally, he contrasted the Parliament's attempts to gain further transparency in the Council and the Commission with the vote it had just taken. This was a theme vigorously taken up by subsequent press comment.

In the final analysis, this climate proved the right one for the measures to be passed at the second attempt. Alarmed by the loss of credibility to the Parliament caused by the January vote, Hänsch urged the Conference of Presidents to establish a working group to propose new ideas. The respective rapporteurs largely took into account the suggestions produced in this way. Nordmann proposed, as the principal feature, a public register to be completed by each MEP and containing detailed information about professional activities, other remunerated activities, and financial or other support by third parties in respect of their political mandate. In respect of movable and immovable assets, MEPs were to follow their national practice of listing. The Ford report proposed as the principal features that lobbyists must: enter a register; sign a code of conduct (with details to be established later, although it was likely, ironically, that this would be based on the one established by public-affairs practitioners); and wear a pass within EP buildings. In June 1996, the revised versions of the Nordmann and Ford reports were adopted by the CRP, although not without dissent. Controversy remained among Conservative MEPs about the issue of declaring assets and gifts and the substantive threshold of these, and, because the vote required a majority of EP members, it came to depend upon the stance taken by Christian Democrats, while on the other hand a number of Green and left-leaning MEPs were critical of the measures for not going far enough. Hänsch forged agreement between the leaders of the main parties for the proposals, although the outcome of the vote remained in doubt until the debate itself with a number of amendments being circulated from the left and right of the political spectrum in the days beforehand, and the possibility of the debate being removed from the EP plenary agenda for July as a measure designed to protect it.

Finally, after seven years of inconclusive debate, the Parliament agreed a modified version of the Nordmann and Ford schemes on 17 July 1996. The main points agreed in respect of members were that each MEP must make a detailed declaration of professional activities and list all favours support received from third parties, whether financial or otherwise, and the source of such support; that declarations would be available for public scrutiny; that MEPs must refuse any gift, payment or benefit which might influence their vote, and that all such favours must be declared before any relevant debate; that no MEP may accept financial support or the provision of staff or material except those supplied by the European Parliament; and that a code of conduct for MEP's assistants is to be agreed in the future. Attempts to ban MEPs from accepting any gift worth more than 600 ECU had to replaced by a concession to register all 'significant' gifts, with the EP to work out exactly what this meant. As regards lobbyists, Quaestors were formally empowered to issue a pass in exchange for the acceptance of a code of conduct and the establishment of a register. A code for lobbyists, and for the conduct of intergroups, is to be established in the future, although now the Ford and Nordman schemes have been agreed after exhaustive debate there is little sign of urgency, and these codes may not appear for as long as two years hence. The code for lobbyists is likely to take as its starting point that agreed by public affairs consultants, although a number of rival versions are now in circulation from the plethora of representative organisations which have now sprung up. Ford is also anxious to insert further detail, such as procedures on access to MEP's offices. While Ford commented that 'we have taken a modest but an important step which will throw a powerful public light on the relations between MEPs and lobbyists' (*Guardian*, 1996), however, there is little doubt that if the report of the CRP had been presented in its original form then it would have been passed with rather less difficulty than was experienced after the summer of 1995, and may ultimately have been more effective at regulating lobbying. In the event, what started life as a debate about the regulation of lobbying in the Parliament ended as a highly politicised contest between party groupings over the declaration of members' assets and receipts of gifts. By its entry into the political arena, discussion about the management of interest representation had once again evoked popular images of lobbying as shady deals done in dark corners.

As for the issue of the regulation of interest representation, the CRP text continued to claim that the scheme would lead to greater transparency. However, one of the dangers of establishing a register system might be that it provides advantages to, and confers benefits upon, those who frequently engage the Parliament, while disadvantaging those such as citizens from the member states who would be unlikely to register but who also have a cause to pursue. Although an eleventh-hour change to the scheme was to define 'frequent contact' (and therefore the need for registration) as those wanting to enter the Parliament for more than five days a year, thus enabling infrequent and occasional citizen contact with the EP without the bar of prior registration, a register may also come to imply some status upon those who are on it, and a lack of accreditation status of those who are not. Those on the register may use their registration to claim a status of recognition by the EP, thereby gaining advantage over non-registered groups. Equally, registered groups would have privileged access to documentation under the proposals, which in turn may create a customer-orientated culture as a price transaction will be involved. A register may therefore further exaggerate the advantages of insider interests over outsiders. Something similar may have already happened with the United Nations, where registered groups acquire official consultative services. Indeed, a number of MEPs from the former East Germany have been expressing the view that the Ford report will legitimate interest representation into official status. Although none of the EU schemes currently in circulation seek to deliberately create an inner circle of insider groups with consultative circles, in practice such a status exists with resource-rich groups. The difference between the scheme put forward by the Commission and that advanced by the Parliament is that the former has sought means of ensuring wider-ranging consultation of proposals, whereas the latter may further privilege the already privileged. There are already some signs of this. For instance EFPIA has called for the institutions 'to grant facilities to "recognised" structures such as industry-specific professional groups, and vet the representativeness of other would-be lobbyists more carefully, to rationalise the scale and frequency of contacts' (EFPIA, 1994, p. 2). Some public-affairs consultants have latched on to this potential for the CRP schemes to create a two-tier structure, and one lobbyist interviewed for the purpose of this chapter suggested that the Parliament was attempting to privatise lobbying. Partly on these grounds, the Commission does not favour the idea of establishing a register to which certain rights are attached. Similarly, a senior Socialist MEP who chairs one of the Committees responding to the CRP is said to have come round to the view that self-regulation represents the most workable solution to the issue.

Some of these concerns have recently been raised within the formal structures of the EP. The Committee on Social Affairs and Employment, for instance, called for more (unspecified) measures to facilitate interest representation by public-interest concerns and to promote equal opportunities between business and non-business groups, and recommended that the register be split into different categories to recognise the different status of those representing different kinds of interests. Similarly, the Committee on Regional Policy stressed the need for equity in the fee system and other procedures, such as not to discriminate against non-producer groups. The Committee on the Environment, Public Health and Consumer Protection also had a level playing field in mind when they suggested a differential pricing structure for obtaining documents according to the ability of different types of interest groups to pay. Ultimately, however, these detailed ambitions were undermined by the linking of the regulation of lobbyists with the conduct of MEPs, thereby weakening a scheme specifically designed to improve upon lobbyists' self-regulation. In the final analysis, in its attempts to regulate the activities of lobbyists the Parliament has been unable to move much beyond the code of conduct devised by lobbyists themselves.

While broadly in favour of the Ford report, a Conservative member of the Committee on Rules and Procedures also pointed out in interview that, in focusing upon lobbying, the Ford and Nordmann schemes are unlikely to tackle ingrained forms of interest representation where some private interests are institutionally involved in European public policy-making. While this is clearer in the case of the permanent bureaucracy of the Commission, resource-rich private interests will be able to use their power to influence some parliamentarians. The Ford and Nordmann schemes are unlikely, therefore, to really address the differential types of insider and outsider status available to different types of interests on the basis of power-dependent resource exchange, not least because the European institutions, in view of their own lack of resources, have become dependent upon the assistance brought by outside interests. As McLaughlin and Greenwood have argued,

> Regulating 'lobbying' cannot restructure the complex patterns of interest intermediation in which the Commission is involved with private interests. Yet the Commission's 'management deficit' means that it is now impossible to undo the complexity of these arrangements (McLaughlin and Greenwood, 1995, p. 151).

Despite the claims made for them, the Ford/Nordmann schemes will do little to achieve a level playing field between producer and non-producer types of interests, or indeed to address some of the wider issues in the *ad hoc* basis of dialogue between the European institutions and outside interests identified by the 1992 Sutherland report (Chapter 2). They are not therefore primarily about issues of democratic deficit, although the appearance of these schemes should be viewed as part of the same underlying set of concerns. Instead, the Ford and Nordmann schemes should be seen in the more limited terms of what they can achieve by way of maintaining public confidence in the work of the Parliament and of putting its work with outside interests on a surer footing, provided that they do not in fact end up by achieving the opposite of what was intended in privileging certain types of interests at the expense of others. Nevertheless, an agenda has been set, and the initiatives reviewed in this chapter may signal the start of a restructuring of the relationships between outside interests and the European institutions. To date, regulatory initiatives from the institutions have resulted in the establishment of a cluster of commercial lobbyists with their own code, the emergence of a number of associations seeking to organise members of the European interest representation community, and the insertion of modules on 'ethics' in commercially run training courses on lobbying provided by Brussels consultancies, while the establishment of ERAF was directly related to the wider Pinheiro initiatives on transparency and openness (Chapter 2). Together with the Parliament's initiatives, these indicate that a start, at least, has been made in organising the role of European-level interest representation in European public affairs.

5

Business Interests

Historically, business interests have always dominated European-level interest representation, in part because of the history of the EU as an economic community. In a sample of business groups, over three-quarters had established themselves prior to the single-market initiative being conceived, while over half had established themselves in Brussels prior to the single-market project (Table 5.1).

Neofunctionalist accounts of European integration place business interests at the heart of explanations for the development of the EU (Chapter 10). Not only have business interests been attracted to Brussels because of increasing competencies in producer fields: such interests have themselves often sought and developed those competencies. Today, Cowles has estimated that some 60 per cent of all legislation directed at industry in Europe has a 'Made in Brussels' stamp on it (Cowles, 1995a). Policy outputs in some business sectors cannot be accounted for without acknowledging the extent of input from private interests. Indeed, some of the highpoints in European

TABLE 5.1

Periods of establishment of a sample of business Euro groups

Period	*Establishment*		*In Brussels*	
	N	*%*	*N*	*%*
Pre-ECSC (pre-1950)	7	3	3	2
ECSC to pre-Treaty of Rome (1950–55)	19	8	2	1
Rome to de Gaulle crisis (1956–65)	67	29	25	19
'Eurosclerosis' (1966–83)	82	36	43	32
Single market (1984–92)	43	19	47	35
1992–1995	11	5	15	11
Total	229	100	135	100

Source: survey by author, February 1996.

integration, such as the conception of the single market initiative, have been attributed to the impact of business interests, both in responding to, and helping to create, a climate designed to ensure that business could flourish (Cowles, 1995b). The 1980s represented a considerable sea change for the role of business in the European Community, not least because of the mutually supportive relationships developed between business and the Commission dating from the period of Etienne Davignon as DG III Commissioner (1981–5).

Business groups

Tables 5.2 and 5.3 identify some of the resources of European business groups. Over half of all business groups have three or more staff, while over one quarter have six or more. Some thirteen per cent are extremely well resourced, with more than ten staff. Table 5.3 shows that the majority of business groups have a turnover in excess of 100 000 ECU. However, over a third have a turnover less than 51 000 ECU, while a fifth have a turnover of 20 000 ECU or less.

Table 5.4 identifies the principal organisational formats of business groups. Thus in common with the totality of groups, two-thirds of business groups are federated structures, i.e. federations of associations, and one-third are direct-membership formats. Of these, a small proportion (11, or approximately 4 per cent) are groups which either

TABLE 5.2

Employment levels among a sample of Euro business groups

Number of staff	Business	
	N	%
0	15	7
1 or 1.5	20	9
2 or 2.5	66	29
3 or 3.5	27	12
4	27	12
5	10	4
6 to 10	29	13
11 +	30	13
Total	224	100

Source: survey by author, February 1996.

TABLE 5.3

Turnover of a sample of Euro business groups

Turnover (ECU)	N	%
0 to 20 000	30	20
20 001 to 50 000	21	14
50 001 to 100 000	18	12
Over 100 000	78	53
Total	147	100
No response	72	33

Source: survey by author, February 1996.

TABLE 5.4

Principal type of business Euro group: federated or direct-membership

Principal type of group	N	%
Federated	169	66
Direct-membership	88	34
Total	257	100

Source: survey by author, February 1996.

primarily organise individuals within business, or else organise individuals within business and firms equally. The implications of these
different types of organisational formats were discussed in Chapter 3.

Cross-sectoral organisation of business interests

Perhaps the most familiar aspects of European business interest
representation are the formal, cross sectoral groups. These include:

1. UNICE, the Union of Industrial and Employers' Confederations
   of Europe, the peak association of business.
2. EUROCHAMBRES, the Association of Chambers of Commerce
   and Industry.
3. ERT, the European Round Table of Industrialists, comprising
   the chief executives of some of the largest European firms.
4. AMCHAM-EU, the EU Committee of the American Chamber
   of Commerce, organising American firms in Europe.

5. A variety of organisations seeking to represent the interests of small firms in Europe, of which the most representative are UEAPME, the European Association of Craft, Small and Medium-sized Enterprises, and EUROPMI, the European Committee for Small and Medium-sized Independent Companies. These two organisations are scheduled for merger by the end of 1996.

UNICE and EUROCHAMBRES were formed in 1958 in direct response to the 1957 Treaty of Rome, and are both confederations of national associations. ERT and AMCHAM, on the other hand, were formed in the 1980s as direct-membership associations, partly because, as is explained below, confederated structures were seen as insufficiently dynamic to represent the strength of business interests in an era when the European Community needed to develop a strategic response to the growing internationalisation of markets and politics. ERT and AMCHAM are modern transnational interest groups geared to the needs and demands of European politics in the approaching twenty-first century. The great strength of UNICE and EUROCHAMBRES, however, is that they are encompassing organisations representing much of the constituency of business interests, whereas the ERT (and to a lesser extent AMCHAM) is more an exclusive club representing interests drawn from rich firms.

UNICE

UNICE was designed to represent the interests of industry as a whole. It is a confederation of 32 national federations of 'peak' business associations from 22 European (i.e. not simply EU) countries, of which the majority in turn comprise sectoral associations. It therefore represents members which themselves have a wide range of interests to represent. It has a staff of 30, including 14 executives, whose work is supported by 5 policy committees, 55 permanent working groups on which some 1200 individuals sit, and a commercial lobbyist specialising in relations with the Parliament. It is run by an executive committee, consisting of the director generals of member federations (Stern, 1994). It seeks

> to be seen as a positive organisation, helping the legislator to produce better legislation. It operates not just defensively, but proactively: opposing measures which it believes will do harm to the interests of its members, while making constructive suggestions

for amendments, as well as recommendations for new policies which can promote those interests (UNICE, cited in Stern, 1994, pp. 137–8).

Because of its mission to represent the interests of business taken as a whole, the formal position taken by UNICE is that it does not intervene in sector-specific affairs unless there are broader implications for the entire constituency of business, or where a sectoral interest group is not present. Sectoral business interests sometimes prefer to be left alone to address an issue, and try to prevent UNICE from over dominating business affairs. However, what constitutes a 'business-wide' and what a 'sector-specific' issue can often be a grey area. Stern, for instance, provides an example whereby UNICE took up a position on the draft Directive on Tobacco Advertising on the grounds that banning tobacco advertising constituted a threat to free speech (Stern, 1994), while UNICE has also lent its support to sectoral interests over a number of issues involving pharmaceuticals. Like many organisations, UNICE seeks opportunities to expand its sphere of influence.

UNICE plays an informal and a formal role in European public affairs. On an informal basis, it meets daily with Commission officials and gives unofficial views on proposals. On a formal basis, it is routinely asked by the institutions to give its opinion on issues. In order to arrive at 'an opinion' it has to seek to reflect the broad constituency of its members interests and positions, which are in turn very often the result of compromises made at the national level. To help it arrive at common positions, UNICE uses its network of permanent committee structures, which in turn heightens the tendency for compromise. Thus, the organisation is well recognised for providing generalised, 'lowest-common-denominator' positions which are not always very helpful in providing the institutions with a clear signal to act upon. Indeed, Commission officials generally have to read between the lines of UNICE position papers in order to establish the differences and basis for compromises between members. Given the nature of UNICE's remit to represent the broad constituency of business interests, this is somewhat inevitable, although it does question the extent to which such organisations can ever be of either significant value, or influence, over specific measures in public affairs. However, it does provide a means to institutionalise the interests which could not otherwise be ignored, and in a generalised sense can be used as a vehicle for progress. The most obvious illustration of this concerns the role of UNICE as a macroeconomic or first-level social partner, together with the trade union organisation ETUC and public-sector employers (CEEP), where there is the possibility of reaching agreement on employment-related issues and in so doing to progress the frontiers of European integration (Chapter 2; see also the ETUC perspective in Chapter 7). Thus, the long stalled issue of industrial democracy reached fruition with the September 1994 Directive on Information and Consultation (formerly the Works Council Directive) after initial discussion between the macroeconomic social partners and the subsequent initiatives of the Commission in progressing the issue (Chapter 7). At one point, indeed, the three macroeconomic partners seemed likely to reach agreement on a text of agreement for works councils, until an eleventh-hour intervention from the Confederation of British Industry, heavily influenced by the British government, prevented UNICE from doing so (Falkner, 1995). In the event, the Commission had to drive the issue through.

The works council affair does illustrate how far UNICE has come in participating in 'social Europe' after its refusal through much of the 1980s to engage in meaningful dialogue with ETUC. Significant sections of business have been generally more interested in non-decision-making in employment-related issues at the European level, and in ensuring that the wider business community was not drawn into dialogue with ETUC. A number of UNICE's members have therefore sought to prevent the organisation from developing the capacities to enter such a dialogue, and there is a suggestion that UNICE may historically have been deliberately under-resourced for this reason (Ebbinghaus and Visser, 1994). However, the progression of the single market exposed some clear divisions between the interests of different national business communities, with the extremes occupied at one end by a group of 'northern' countries clustered around Germany (Netherlands, Belgium, Denmark) at one end of the spectrum, with 'social market' type economies, and at the other the UK, following the Anglo-American model of free-market capitalism (Rhodes, 1995). Countries with high-wage, high-quality working conditions sought to 'export' their policies to the European level to ensure a level playing field in production conditions in the single market, while the UK, with low-wage, more insecure labour market conditions, sought to retain the competitive advantages of these through lower-cost production as a strategy of encouraging inward investment. The single market thus created some degree of 'functional spillover' into the labour market field (Chapter 10), with new patterns of demand for labour market integration. As is described in Chapter 7, until the TEU a number of countries in between the extremes represented by the northern group on the one hand and the UK on the other were able to espouse the rhetoric of the protection and improvement of working conditions to satisfy organised labour, safe in the knowledge that progression would be limited while the UK government was fundamentally opposed to re-regulation of labour market conditions. Their support was thus 'cheap talk' (Lange, 1992). However, the TEU was the decision point, when all countries with the exception of the UK signed up to the Social Protocol, and the possibility for 'cheap talk' among governments had ended.

UNICE's position became somewhat clearer as a consequence of business in the countries concerned having to come to terms with the Social Protocol signed at Maastricht, although the picture among European business is much less clearcut than that between member states in summitry. Thus, some British firms have implemented directly the provisions of the social charter, and/or established consultation mechanisms with workers while some non-British business interests ally with the majority British position inside UNICE, seeking to resist the expansion of business involvement in the development of a 'social dialogue' or have responded minimally to requirements for worker consultation and information. In this way, large firms such as Daimler Benz remain committed more to non-decision-making in social policy fields, and have warned about the consequences of creating too expensive production in Europe (Cowles, 1995b). Nevertheless, UNICE's own position has shifted with the tide of European politics following the development of the social market, and together with the other macroeconomic social partners it wrote the Social Protocol annexed to the TEU. As was described in Chapter 2, the legal powers this confers upon the social partners has considerably strengthened their role in European public affairs. UNICE now has a limited mandate from its members to bargain with ETUC, whereas previously it had none. UNICE, whose own role as the voice of business during the 1980s came under threat from the establishment of ERT and AMCHAM, has to some extent therefore developed an interest in the social dialogue mechanism. Without doubt, UNICE continues to act as a brake on the rapid expansion of social Europe. But what is important is that it has an institutionalised role through the social dialogue mechanism. It is now to some extent enmeshed within a structure from which it cannot escape. Tangible results have now emerged from the social dialogue beyond relatively uncontentious initiatives on education and training, and there is no turning back to the days when business refused to do anything other than talk to ETUC without commitment (Chapters 7 and 10).

The social partners' acquisition of new powers of agenda-setting and implementation, Obradovic suggests, 'enhances increasing and intense involvement of private interests in the European Community policy processes and promotes the structured representation of functional interests in the process of Community policy-making' (1994, p. 7). More controversially, she suggests that they 'represent a significant step toward corporatist practices in policy formulation and implementation within the Community' (ibid., p. 5). A similar interpretation has also been made by Falkner (1995). These interpretations may in one sense be somewhat over-optimistic, not least because European-level authority does not consist of anything like the capacity to engage in (macro) corporatist-style bargaining (Chapter 10). Equally, while there is some degree of functional spillover to labour market regulation from the single market, the principles of 'project Europe' remain deeply entrenched in neoliberalism. Indeed, the effective participation of French and Spanish interests since the 1980s depended upon a change in preference formation of the governments in those countries in following market solutions. Nevertheless, as was argued in Chapter 2, the TEU Social Protocol agreement resembles a limited form of private-interest government. As is evident later in this chapter, meso corporatist arrangements (Chapter 1) are certainly possible, and have developed at the European level in certain domains and under certain types of circumstances.

By participating in European public affairs since 1958, throughout the full range of formal structures of European policy-making, and with a number of long-serving executives (two have been on the staff for over thirty years), UNICE has to some extent 'gone native'. It cannot help but have been influenced by its own historic participation in all the structures of the European Community. To some extent, the institutionalisation of UNICE has also been a deliberate strategy by the European institutions with these outcomes in mind, and, as such, supports the emphasis in neofunctionalist accounts of the role of these institutions in developing European integration (Chapter 10).

UNICE has also sought to address the difficulties it faces as a result of its confederate design by establishing a more direct relationship with multinational firms, most notably through the creation in 1990 of an Advisory and Support Group, and by ensuring that committee chairs come from large firms. Although this cannot be said to have transformed the organisation (in turn the reforms have led to accusations of a large-firm bias, despite the advisory group lacking formal decision-making capacities), Grant (1995) notes something of a revival in UNICE's fortunes. Apart from establishing a more direct relationship with large firms, this appears to be for four main reasons. Firstly, the general secretary, Zygmunt Tyszkiewicz, has been extremely reform-minded. A second is the shot in the arm provided by UNICE's status as a first-level social partner. Thirdly, UNICE withdrew its power of veto to national associations in the early 1990s. A fourth factor is that arising from the stimulus of other, cross sectoral organisations with a direct-membership structure, such as AMCHAM-EU and ERT. Indeed, in part, the presence of ERT can be attributed to the frustration felt by multinational firms at the lack of effectiveness of UNICE and its inherently cumbersome nature, during the early 1980s, when an effective voice for big-business interests was urgently required.

EUROCHAMBRES

EUROCHAMBRES, like UNICE, is a confederation of federations, bringing together 32 national associations from EU, EFTA and other countries, which between them represent 1200 local chambers of commerce, and, through them, some 4 million enterprises (Eurochambres, 1996). Many of these businesses are SMEs operating at highly localised levels. Some of the national associations of chambers of commerce have their own offices in Brussels, or structures for members and policy officials to meet up, facilitate and forge contacts, and a social atmosphere for policy influence. These are independent of EUROCHAMBRES, but are, like the EU Committee of British Chambers of Commerce, becoming increasingly important as network organisations for their participants.

Like ERT, EUROCHAMBRES has substantial interpersonal contacts with Commissioners, as well as participating fully in a number of formal structures throughout the European institutions, including with Commission consultative committees, Parliamentary committees and the ESC. One example of its institutionalised links concerns an agreement with the Commission to locate European information centres (EICs), whose activities are partly aimed at business users, within the premises of chambers of commerce; indeed, some 35 per cent of all EICs are accounted for in this way (EURO-CHAMBRES, 1996). There are also collaborative structures and projects with the Commission in fields such as the impact of VAT on firms, training, transport policy and regional development, an issue of considerable interest to locally based chambers (Claveloux, 1993).

EUROCHAMBRES has intervened effectively in European public affairs on ⌐lective issues, such as the downgrading to the status of a non-binding recommendation of a Commission proposal for a directive requiring all firms to have vocational training programmes and to report on them on a biennial basis. A particular strength of EUROCHAMBRES is its international links, including member associations from outside Europe, as a means of promoting international trade issues. Like UNICE, its importance in the future seems to be guaranteed by its 'social partner' status, although it is a second-level organisation in the social dialogue, whereas UNICE has first-level status.

European Round Table

The European Round Table is altogether quite different from either UNICE or EUROCHAMBRES. Formed in 1983, it is a 'rich club', with membership by invitation only, of (in February 1996) forty-six chief executive officers (CEOs) of some of the largest European firms spanning key sectors of the European economy, and which are multinational in character and thoroughly global in outlook. The firms managed by ERT members have combined sales exceeding ECU 550 billion a year, and which employ in excess of 3 million workers world-wide (European Round Table of Industrialists, 1996). Its views therefore command considerable respect in European public affairs, while the high-profile nature of the individuals concerned make it a powerful voice. Its original members included such household names as John Harvey Jones (ICI), Wisse Dekker (Philips), Umberto Agnelli (Fiat) and Pehr Gyllenhammar (Volvo). A full list of members (as of June 1996) is given in Table 5.5.

The ERT is governed by a twice-yearly plenary meeting, and a small steering committee of up to 7 members. Their work is supported by 8 policy groups on topics such as competitiveness policy, labour markets and information highways, and watchdog groups on issues such as the environment, Europe–US relations and export controls. These draw upon the resources of CEOs firms, as well as those of the ERT secretariat itself.

TABLE 5.5

Members of the European Round Table of Industrialists

Helmut Maucher (Chair)	Nestlé (CH)
André Leysen (Vice-Chair)	Gevaert (B)
David Simon (Vice-Chair)	British Petroleum (UK)
Giovanni Agnelli	Fiat (I)
Américo Amorim	Amorim Group (P)
Percy Barnevik	ABB (UK)
Jean-Louis Beffa	Saint-Gobin (F)
Marcus Bierich	Robert Bosch (D)
Peter Bonfield	British Telecom (UK)
Cor Bounstra	Philips (NL)
Simon Cairns	BAT Industries (UK)
Bertrand Collomb	Lafarge Coppée (F)
François Cornélis	Petrofina (B)
Gerhard Cromme	Fried. Krupp (D)
Etienne Davignon	Société Générale de Belgique (B)
Carlo De Benedetti	Olivetti (I)
Casimir Ehrnooth	UPS-Kymmene (SF)
Jean-René Fourtou	Rhône-Poulenc (F)
José Antonio Garrido	Iberdrola (E)
Fritz Gerber	Hoffmann-La Roche (CH)
Ronald Hampel	ICI (UK)
Ulrich Hartmann	Veba (Germany)
Cor Herkströter	Royal Dutch/Shell (NL)
Daniel Janssen	Sovay (B)
Jak Kamhi	Profilo Holding (TUR)
David Lees	GKN (UK)
Pietro Marzotto	Marzotto (I)
Brian Moffat	British Steel (UK)
Jérôme Monod	Lyonnaise des Eaux-Dumez (F)
Egil Myklebust	Norsk Hydro (N)
Harald Norvik	Satoil (N)
Theodore Papalexopoulos	Titan Cement (H)
Heinrich von Pierer	Siemens (D)
Lars Ramqvist	Ericsson (S)
Edzard Reuter	Airbus Industrie (F)
Nigel Rudd	Pilkington (UK)
Richard Schenz	OMV (A)
Manfred Schneider	Bayer (D)
Jürgen Schrempp	Daimler Benz (D)
Louis Schweitzer	Renault (F)
Michael Smurfit	Jefferson Smurfit (UK)
Poul Svanholm	Carlsberg (DK)
Morris Tabaksblat	Unilever (UK/NI)
Serge Tchuruk	Alcatel Alsthom (F)
Marco Tronchetti Provera	Pirelli (I)
Mark Wössner	Bertelsmann (D)

Key: (A) Austria, (B) Belgium, (CH) Switzerland, (D) Germany, (DK) Denmark, (E) Spain, (F) France, (H) Greece, (I) Italy, (N) Norway, (NL) Netherlands, (P) Portugal, (S) Sweden, (SF) Finland, (TUR) Turkey, (UK) United Kingdom
Source: European Round Table of Industrialists, (1996).

Whereas UNICE is more of a workhorse, involved in the everyday business of European public affairs and in responding to Commission initiatives, ERT is more of a strategic player, geared more towards seeking to create the longer-term European agenda in the interests of its members, and, it would argue, for Europe as a whole. Indeed, Stern (1994, p. 144) has described it more as an 'elite think-tank' than a traditional interest group functioning at the operational level of political influence. Thus, it has been widely credited with providing the impetus and blueprint for the single-market project, whereby the largest firms in Europe sought a European response to wealth creation through the creation of one single market for business to exploit, in recognition of the need to provide European firms with a strategy for survival and growth in the next century in response to the development of trade blocks in Japan, the USA and the newly emerging economies of south-east Asia (Stern, 1994; Cowles, 1995b). However, its role has not been restricted to one of ideas generation. As Cowles comments, 'When member states wavered in implementing the single market programme, the ERT lobbied European heads of state and government directly with a simple message: support the single-market programme or European industry will move its investments out of Europe' (Cowles, 1995b, pp. 226–7). Most recently, its report *Beating the Crisis* was launched by the President of the Commission, Jacques Delors, not least because it demonstrated support for Delors's own White Paper on Growth, Competitiveness and Employment. Similarly, Commissioners sometimes seek out ERT members to help them present a report or issue at a press launch. The ERT also presents recommendations to EU Summit Meetings, and meets every six months with the Presidency of the Council of Ministers. Unsurprisingly, it is presently engaged in the big issues of today in European integration, the 1996 Intergovernmental Conference and in particular European Monetary Union.

Typically, therefore, the ERT has provided the lead in European public affairs on a range of high-politics issues. It is well suited to working on issues of strategic importance to wealth creation in the European Community, and its highly authoritative reports invariably make a major contribution to agenda setting the areas of concern. Thus, it has been active in fields such as the development of TENs (an initiative it has been widely credited with prompting), and information technology, where strategic concerns of European infrastructure are involved as a basis for economic development, and in

1994 created a dedicated think-tank, the European Centre for Infrastructure Studies, based in Rotterdam. The ERT has also been active in the highly politicised fields of environmental policy, employment and education policy, and competition policy, and has undertaken a number of own initiative projects in these fields.

As an organisation with a relatively small number of members, it does not suffer from the cumbersome problems of democratic overload which confront UNICE. UNICE is essentially a confederation of national associations of business, whereas ERT is a membership organisation of a select number of CEOs of some of Europe's largest companies. In style, therefore, the ERT is well suited to exerting influence through the most effective methods of interpersonal contacts with key figures in the European institutions, and through the status of their firms and CEOs in member states. When members leave their firms, or firms are taken over, so individuals lose their place on the ERT. Similarly, individuals who are not active in the organisation can be removed (Cowles, 1995b). This means that the ERT is regularly reorganised and restructured, as frequently as every three to six months, creating a dynamic organisation, membership of which is highly prized (Stern, 1994).

There can be little doubt that the ERT has been one of the most influential of all European interest groups. Cowles comments:

> President Delors himself publicly states that the industrialists were critical to the success of the single market programme. Perhaps the most important contribution of the ERT, however, has been its promotion of what one Commission official terms a 'new culture' within the Community regarding Europe and the global economy . . . the ERT also influences the member states . . . Michael Heseltine, head of the Department of Trade and Industry (DTI) in the UK, for example, returned a draft copy of the DTI's paper on competitiveness to the authors and asked that they incorporate the ideas of the ERT report, *Beating the Crisis* (1995b, p. 235).

In many respects, the ERT has provided to other Euro groups a role model of success. UNICE, for instance, has established its own think-tank in an effort to shape the European agenda after witnessing the success of ERT in this role, and a number of federated structures have sought to establish a more direct relationship with the CEOs of the firms in membership of national associations.

EU Committee of the American Chamber of Commerce

Like the ERT, AMCHAM-EU, created to represent the interests of European firms with American parentage, is one of the most effective and admired of all Euro groups. However, while the ERT focuses on strategic issues, AMCHAM-EU tends to focus more on specific legislation. Although the present structure was established in 1985, with a membership constituency of forty companies, AMCHAM has had a Belgian office since 1948 and a European-level interest representation mechanism since the foundation of the EEC. The organisation has grown rapidly in recent years to around 150 companies, including almost all of the largest American firms. This reflects the growing realisation among American firms of the impact, or potential impact, of the EU upon its interests. According to Stern, some of the public affairs issues which have most interested American firms include matters such as the second Banking Directive, environmental issues, and technical standards (Stern, 1994). Indeed, there is widespread concern among American firms that European standardisation structures such as CEN are being used by European firms as a means of erecting closet technical barriers to the entry of non-European products into the European economic area.

The example of the second Banking Directive provides an example of the effectiveness of AMCHAM-EU, in that it successfully proposed an amendment to the 'reciprocity clause' of this draft legislation. This clause would have required third-country banks to provide access to EU banks similar to that provided for their own banks in the EU, and would have effectively squeezed US banks out of opportunities presented by the single market. AMCHAM-EU was also extremely influential in some of the proposals of the Sutherland report on transparency and consultation of business interests (Chapters 2 and 4) (Claveloux, 1993).

AMCHAM-EU is less of an exclusive rich-firm club than is the ERT, because it speaks for the European Council of American Chambers of Commerce, an association of 14 American Chambers in Europe which together represent in excess of 18 000 firms (Jacek, 1995), and whose structures predate the formation of AMCHAM-EU. These firms are responsible for an estimated economic investment of $200 billion and 10 million employees in Europe, and it therefore has a powerful voice in European public affairs (Stern, 1994). These firms can sometimes also exert considerable influences upon member state governments. Indeed, there are examples of American trade associations intervening decisively (although sometimes clumsily, as is described later) in European public affairs. Thus, Jacek provides an example of how the Motion Picture Association of America, led in this instance by a Dutch lobbyist, was a significant influence on the decisions of the governments of Denmark, the Netherlands and Germany to vote against a directive requiring half of all television time to be occupied by shows made in Europe (Jacek, 1995).

American firms can also exert influence where they are incorporated as full members into European sectoral trade associations. Thus, American firms play a significant role in the Association of the British Pharmaceutical Industry, and, although excluded from some other national trade associations, this influence is in turn reflected in the European trade association, EFPIA. The US Pharmaceutical Manufacturers Associations is also one of the very few American trade associations to have opened a Brussels office, the Pharmaceutical Research and Manufacturers of America (PhRMA). However, the exclusion of American firms from some domestic trade associations has meant that they have either operated as troublesome 'free agents' in pursuing their interests on the European stage, working against collective agreements reached in European trade associations, or found an alternative voice within AMCHAM-EU. Indeed, exclusion from sectoral trade associations in Europe has if anything strengthened the collective identify of American firms in Europe, and in consequence the ability of AMCHAM-EU to organise its members to act collectively. The exclusion of American firms from trade associations in Europe, on the whole, has not helped the interests of European firms. American-owned firms may be more of a threat to the interests of European industry outside European trade associations than inside, and consequently there is now a tendency to include them, rather than to exclude them as was common in the 1970s and 1980s. However, Jacek still detects a hostility in the attitude of some European business associations towards American business in Europe, most notably, and significantly, from the ERT (Jacek, 1995).

AMCHAM-EU has a full-time staff of 17. It holds a monthly plenary session of members, with a supplementary structure of 12 active specialist subcommittees, which produce position papers and provide monitoring functions, each consisting of around 50 specialists and company representatives, and *ad hoc* task groups. It draws considerably upon the specialist resources and expertise of personnel in member firms in Europe for the collective benefit of American firms, and upon the plethora of American lawyers acting as commercial lobbyists. Although it has in its own history been accused of a somewhat aggressive style, its strategy has been to seek to play the European game, and to recognise that interest representation in Europe requires quiet diplomacy rather than the brash, direct methods which may work in Washington (Gardner, 1991). It has deliberately tried to play a positive role in European public affairs, both with enthusiastic rhetoric about the single market and in providing detailed support to EU officials in the preparation of drafts and in providing the information necessary throughout its work with the European institutions to ensure that European public policies are technically sound and workable. On the whole, it is regarded within the Commission as a supportive ally in favour of European integration. Without such a strategy on the part of AMCHAM-EU, it would be easy for the interests of American firms to be excluded from European public affairs. It is a measure of the success of AMCHAM-EU that this often happened in the years prior to its formation.

AMCHAM-EU has also sought to provide a European-interest perspective on issues which affect American firms, and, where possible, to use European figureheads in its campaigns, and to staff its offices with officials from a European background. Similarly, it has sought, with mixed success, to socialise American firms to adopt stances which better fit the continental European model of social-democratic capitalism, rather than US-style free market economics. On the whole, however, American firms have been the staunchest opponents of Commission measures for industrial democracy, and it is this lack of cultural affinity to European traditions which Jacek identifies as the biggest hurdle to American business influence in European public affairs (Jacek, 1995).

AMCHAM-EU is particularly noted for the high quality and thorough nature of its publications and reports, which have become sought after handbooks and 'guides to the European Union' among European firms, and which are often used by EU officials as the basis for drafting legislation (Jacek, 1995). But above all, the key to its effectiveness is its ability to reach meaningful collective positions quickly, facilitated by its role as a direct-membership-driven organisation. It has proved itself reform-minded to maintain capacities for speed and adaptability to changing circumstances (Jacek, 1995), including the recent creation of a structure for high-level executives to meet in, namely the European American Industrial Council, an idea partly inspired by the role model of ERT (Cowles, 1994). One high-ranking Commission official has commented that 'AMCHAM is fast and it establishes good positions – as a result its contributions are always well received by the Commission, even though it represents US rather than European companies' interests' (quoted in Stern, 1994, p. 144). This capacity is one of the major factors responsible for its effectiveness. Although its American basis prevents it from being incorporated too much within the formal structures of the European institutions, its *modus operandi* and culture make it a more effective general player on the European stage than are federated, peak structures such as EUROCOMMERCE and UNICE.

Despite such advantages, AMCHAM-EU does not have the institutionalised ability to exert influence in fields such as social policy, which UNICE does by virtue of its social partner status. This is an area where UNICE can, and does, broker and lead coalitions consisting of itself, ERT and AMCHAM, such as when these actors needed to act in concert to block Commission proposals on consultation of workers. Indeed, where these cross sectoral associations work together they can constitute an almost irresistible force in European public affairs. There is some degree of co-ordination between them, including an institutionalised structure where large firms and UNICE meet together. Thus, the European Enterprise Group (EEG) is an informal forum drawn from senior European-affairs executives from a number of large European companies. UNICE is invited to these meetings twice a year, and participates in the discussions.

Other cross-sectoral groups

Apart from informal fora, considered in greater depth later in this chapter, formal cross sectoral groups are present in issue-based arenas, such as the Paris-based Association for Monetary Union in Europe (AMUE). The association was created in 1987 by high-profile European industrialists, who agreed on the objectives of establishing monetary stability and a single currency for the success of the single market. Current board members include Etienne Davigon (President) and Giovanni Agnelli (Vice-President). Over 250 companies and 30 banks, employing between them more than 6 million workers, are members of the association, including some of Europe's largest firms such as BAT Industries, Bosch, Daimler Benz, Deutsche Bank, Eléctricité de France, Fiat, Guinness, ICI, Nokia, Novo Nordisk, Philips, Rhone-Poulenc, Siemens, Total and Volkswagen. Given such a constituency, unsurprisingly, the group works closely with the ERT, and a number of sectoral associations on an *ad hoc* basis. In addition to large firms, however, a number of national employers' confederations (France, Greece, Ireland, Italy, Spain) are also members, providing a further means of co-ordination between federated and large firm-member business structures. As a group operating in the high politics field, where it is one of a number of actors (including, of course, member states) and therefore lacks the opportunity for monopolistic access to (and influence on) public affairs characteristic of some low politics fields, the Association works mainly at the level of ideas generation. The association has held some 280 meetings throughout all European countries during the past four years, has conducted a number of working sessions with public officials for its members and has produced a number of important studies and publications, including *A Strategy for the ECU*, *How to Prepare Companies for European Monetary Union*, and *Preparing the Transition to the Single Currency*. Important studies have also been completed for the Commission and the Parliament.

Small and medium-sized enterprises

Although UNICE seeks to incorporate the interests of SMEs though its Committee for Small and Medium-sized Enterprises, there is a plethora of European-level interest groups dedicated to the representation of small firms (Table 5.6), which accurately conveys an impression of fragmentation in the landscape of organisation of SMEs. The Commission considers that the relationship between these peak organisations is marked by competition (Commission of the European Communities, 1993). Additionally, there are a number of sectoral associations whose members are almost exclusively small firms, particularly in the food and food-processing industry where there have been a number of EU directives. Other business sector associations, such as Eurocommerce, for the retail trades, have substantial SME membership. Some of the sector associations with exclusively small-firm membership seek to organise a very similar constituency of interests. Grote considers that this fragmentation is partly a result of fragmentation of policy competencies within the European institutions themselves, like that described in Chapter 3 (Grote, 1995). For their part, however, both the Council and the Commission are extremely concerned at the fragmentation of interest representation in the domain, and the Council has recently asked the

Commission to take measures to encourage a better consolidation of interest representation to ensure that the voice of SMEs is heard more clearly within the European institutions. Indeed, as Grote remarks, there is at present something of a 'demand underload' from SME associations for European public policies (Grote, 1995, p. 251). One of the initiatives with which the Commission has most recently (1996) responded is by working with some of the key actors to fund the creation of an 'SME Forum', linking the range of associations in the field.

Direct-membership structures tend to be impractical for SMEs, because the sheer numbers of enterprises involved would make it difficult for associations to be representative, and because many SMEs either could not afford the membership fees which would be necessary to resource a European-level association or would not regard membership as a priority when faced with day-to-day

TABLE 5.6

EU-level associations of small and medium-sized enterprises (1996)

Acronym	Name	C or D?[1]	Constituency
UEAPME	European Association of Craft, Small and Medium-sized Enterprises	C	Craft primarily, and SMEs
EUROPMI	European Committee for Small and Medium-sized Independent Companies	C	SME primarily, and craft
CEDI	European Confederation of Independents	C	Commerce, self-employed
EMSU	European Medium and Small Business Union	C	Small firms in professional practice
UEM	European Union of Small and Medium-sized Companies	C	Small firms in professional practice
YES	Young Entrepreneurs for Europe	D	Young managers
AECM	European Independent Business Confederation	D	SMEs
CPMECEE	Committee for Small and Medium Commercial Enterprises in the Countries of the EEC	D	SMEs

[1] Principally confederation (C) or direct membership (D).
Source: Grote (1995, p. 248–50), and survey by author, February 1996.

questions of survival. Confederative structures therefore dominate. However, this brings its own problems, in that one of the problems for SME associations has historically been their unevenness of development across member states, not least because of differences in firm size structures between countries. Craft associations, for instance, where UEAPME dominates, have been strongest in Germany, such that UEAPME, and its predecessor organisation (dating from 1959), were based in Bonn until as recently as 1990. Indeed, Germany, the country with the highest proportion of SMEs, has almost twice as many, as a proportion of total enterprises, as the UK, at the lower end of the spectrum.

UEAPME and EUROPMI are the most representative of all the SME European-level collective outlets, and both now have second-level social partner status, not least because they have developed a joint structure for the representation of employer-based interests. However, they are likely to lose these dual seats on merger later this year, while they bitterly resent not being included as first-level social partners, particularly as UNICE has this status. Although UNICE would claim that its remit and its SME Committee together mean that it also has the interests of small firms at heart, UEAPME regards it as an organisation dominated by the interests of large enterprises. Consideration has also been given by the Commission to including YES, CEDI, EMSU and AECM within the social dialogue.

UEAPME tends to be the lead SME organisation in the domain. It works most closely with DG XXIII, followed by DG XVI (Regional Policies and Cohesion), where there are a number of regional policy initiatives aimed at SMEs for the purpose of encouraging local economic development. At least in terms of rhetoric, SMEs are pushing at an open door with the Commission. Following the Delors White Paper on *Growth, Competitiveness and Employment*, where SMEs were identified as a major sector to target support at, the Commission adopted a major action programme for them, and specifically identified the importance of interaction with SME interest associations as a means to achieve the objectives of the programme. There is concern within the European institutions to achieve a thoroughly integrated programme for SMEs, and throughout the Commission desk officers seek to actively include SMEs in the programmes for which they are responsible. Indeed, most of these are quite well aware that they hear the voice of large-firm interests loud and clear, but that, particularly on a sectoral basis, the interests of SMEs go unheard. Some of them actively seek out the views of SMEs in response. As far as small and medium-sized enterprises are concerned, the only barrier to greater influence in European public affairs is their own degree of organisation at the European level. Clearly, the nature of SMEs themselves makes this a difficult goal to achieve.

Sectoral organisation of business interests

Business sector (or, where sectoral definition is difficult such as in tourism, domain) trade associations account for the overwhelming majority of Euro groups (Table 3.1, p. 59), reflecting the predominance of 'project Europe' with producer interests. The study field has been dominated by case studies, such that there is now a wealth of accounts identifying patterns of interest representation, investigating concepts of collective action, and examining the contribution of business interests to the integration process (see, for instance, the collection of contributor case studies on information technology, pharmaceuticals, consumer electronics and broadcasting, aerospace, bioindustry, cement, banking, retailing, tourism, water, textiles, automobiles, shipping, firms, and cross sectoral associations, in Greenwood, 1995a; and those on Philips, Airbus Industrie, fruit companies, Euro Disney, airlines, couriers, gas, automobiles, and information technology, in Pedler and van Schendelen, 1994). As has been shown by Tables 5.1 to 5.4, and the discussion in Chapter 3, there are a number of business groups (including most of those reviewed in the edited collections cited above) which are well resourced and which have proved effective collective actors and influential players in European public affairs.

In some policy fields, both the outputs and outcomes of European public affairs cannot be understood without reference to the behaviour, presence and stances of sectoral trade associations. The members of some business sector associations have more resources at their disposal than do some member states, and they are bound therefore to be significant political players. They are often incorporated fully within European policy-making structures right from the outset, sometimes by setting the agenda, sometimes in implementation at the European and national levels, and sometimes in influencing the draft which emerges from the Commission. As Claveloux comments,

The frequent contact between the Commission and sectoral interest groups means the outside association is allowed onto the inside track, so it knows what proposals are in the pipeline and which Commission official is drafting them. These single sector associations, particularly the European federations, are often asked to give line by line analysis of texts before they even become draft legislative proposals (Claveloux, 1993, p. 20).

Some are so deeply ingrained within the structures of the European institutions that it is difficult to draw a distinction between public and private interests (Chapter 1). Many have formal consultative status, and some form, with the relevant parts of the public institutions, a lasting and ingrained policy network which acts as a governance mechanism for the sector concerned. Some of the Commission services have become entirely dependent upon the information, expertise and other resources which these actors bring to European public affairs. DG XIII, for instance, contains many staff on secondment from the European consumer electronics firms, and the development of strategically important technologies, such as high-definition television broadcasting, would simply not be possible without the work of major firms such as Philips (Cawson, 1992; 1995).

Another example of ingrained interest intermediation was provided by the example of EFPIA, described in Chapter 1, where the association's involvement in the governance of selling standards in medicines at the European level bears all the hallmarks of neo-corporatism. EFPIA has been able to exert influence over other key issues significantly affecting its interests. It persuaded the Commission to take the governments of Belgium and Italy to court over pricing arrangements to which the industries in those countries had once been parties, indicating the extent to which the industry has been able to achieve more at the European level than once seemed possible at the national level. It turned a regulatory threat of a restricting directive on medicine prices into a directive requiring member states to produce transparent criteria for pricing decisions, and to provide detailed justification where price rises were refused. Similarly, EFPIA provided the blueprint for the extension of the patent period for medicines in Europe, when the Commission had initially been reluctant to do so. It also gave encouragement to the idea of the creation of a European Medicines Agency to ensure recognition of medicinal products throughout member states, and to ensure a faster process of pre-market product evaluation by regulatory authorities. Together with other business associations, it prevented insertion of a 'fourth-hurdle' criterion of 'social acceptability' in the registration of medicinal products. Through its position as one of Europe's major wealth creators, and its potential for wealth creation in the next century, the pharmaceutical industry has becoming the driving influence behind public policy outputs in the pharmaceutical sector. Indeed, the industry continues to improve its performance, set against a general loss of competitiveness and declining performance of European industry as a whole (Chapter 1).

It would clearly be naïve to draw a simple connection between the influence of EFPIA and policy outcomes in the field, and there are a number of examples where the organisation has been disappointed with public policy decisions. However, because EFPIA is a highly effective organiser of interests within the sector (Chapter 3), the organisation has, on the whole, become a centre stage player in issues affecting the industry. The Commission prefers actors who have the ability to provide it with authoritative collective opinion, and where interests are well organised groups can therefore be more effective than single-firm interests (Chapters 1 and 3). Although it would be wrong to claim that pharmaceutical firms never engage the Commission in deference to EFPIA – American firms are more prone to act outside EFPIA, particularly as they are excluded from some domestic associations – they have achieved striking successes by acting collectively.

As the cases in Greenwood *et al.* (1992), Pedler and van Schendelen (1994) and Greenwood (1995a) indicate, EFPIA is by no means an untypical case, although it is arguably perhaps the most influential of all sectoral interest groups in European public affairs. This 'crown' has also been awarded to the SAGB (Chapter 1), which was instrumental in setting the agenda for the framework of support for European bioindustry, and in the creation of structures within the Commission to co-ordinate the work of different services with competencies affecting the industrial domain (Chapter 1). As is described later in this chapter, particularly in cases where business groups are less effective than EFPIA, large firms can to some extent compensate by bringing essential resources to sectoral governance. Where sectors are characterised by small firms, interest representation is characteristically, although not exclusively, weak. Similarly, lack of sectoral definition tends to lead to the proliferation of representative groups, and to problems of co-ordination, or even competition, between them (Chapter 3); thus tourism interests, for example, exert very little influence upon European public affairs.

Prior to the single-market period, COPA/COGECA (Committee of Agricultural Organisations in the EC/General Committee of

Agricultural Co-operation in the EEC), in essence a confederation of national and regional level farmers' unions, was most frequently cited as the most powerful of all European-level interests (Averyt, 1977; National Consumer Council, 1988; Tsinisizelis, 1990; but see also Sidjanski, 1967, who somewhat dissents from this view). Some accounts continue to describe the agricultural sector as 'corporatised', on the basis of the input of COPA to agricultural policy-making and the role of DG VI (Agriculture) as the spokesperson for agricultural interests in the Commission (Gorges, 1993). Given the historic share of the Community budget devoted to agriculture, these descriptions are not surprising. COPA was founded in 1958, and merged with COGECA (founded in 1959) in 1962. It is an umbrella organisation of national farmers' unions and co-operatives. It has a total staff size approaching fifty, supplemented by the work of staff from many national associations with an office located in the same building, and a budget approaching 2.5 million ECU. It has good contacts throughout the European institutions, and often makes direct representations to the Council of Agricultural Ministers. Indeed, it has been a highly institutionalised actor in European agricultural affairs. There are no less than eighteen advisory committees associated with the CAP, and on all but one of these COPA/COGECA has half the number of places available (Tsinisizelis, 1990).

There is a consensus among authors that the influence of COPA/COGECA is somewhat on the wane. A recent (November 1996) internal consultancy report conducted for COPA/COGECA by a former Commission Director General was highly critical of its unwieldy structure, its proneness towards compromises and delays in decision-making, and the competitive nature of its relationship with a number of national members who have established their own Brussels offices (Mann, 1996). Some authors have identified a previous 'golden era' of influence, drawing the connection between the power of COPA and European policy outcomes. Stern has argued that

> In the 1960s and 1970s, COPA enjoyed unparalleled influence, reflected in the Community's ever increasing farm budgets, over production and a surplus of agricultural products. In its period of influence COPA was a well organised and well co-ordinated lobby, whose ascendance was aided by the fact that the food industry and consumer lobbies were poorly organised and ineffectual at this time . . . in the past, COPA/COGECA had enormous influence over farm prices, but in the past seven or eight years, the Council and

the Commission have given a decreasing level of attention to the organisations' views (Stern, 1994, p. 150).

Grant (1995), among others, has argued that the idea of a 'golden era' in the influence of the organisation may have been exaggerated, and that some accounts have drawn too simple a connection between a sophisticated and well-resourced group and a favourable common agricultural policy (CAP). Citing the work of Neville-Rolfe (1984), he draws attention to the fact that price increases have always been set some way below those sought by COPA/COGECA. Although these may have been tactically inflated demands, Grant draws attention to a variety of other influences upon European agricultural policy, including domestic pressures from farmers, and simple policy inertia, which may not be particularly related to the work of COPA/COGECA. Nello, meanwhile, draws attention to a declining frequency in meetings between the COPA presidium and European commissioners (Nello, 1989).

A number of factors explain the decline in influence of COPA/COGECA. Foremost among these are budgetary pressures on the Community. At times, CAP has commanded in excess of two-thirds of the EC budget. Although it is now down to something approaching one-half, CAP is still widely regarded as a nonsense in urgent need of further reform. Other factors explaining a decline in influence of COPA/COGECA include increasing organisation of consumers and other public interests, the growing prominence of countries within EU politics to whom agriculture is less important than elsewhere, and the organisation of COPA itself. Like some other confederations, it suffers chronically from lowest-common-denominator positions. Members from the southern countries, in particular, feel that insufficient weight is given to their views. Platform-building can be so difficult within COPA that it only rarely succeeds in publishing its forward look of annual demands ahead of the Commission's annual proposals for agriculture (Nello, 1989).

Large firms as single and coalition actors in European public affairs

Large firms provide the powerhouse for both cross sectoral and sectoral European-level business associations, providing resources, experience in political action, and status for collective structures.

Many large firms selectively share out responsibilities within groups for taking collective issues forward. As was discussed in Chapter 3, collective structures can offer the opportunity for large firms to achieve the cloak of collective identity; in the case of Philips, the EACEM is little more than a 'front' organisation for its interests (Cawson, 1992). Group participation is also a means of accessing the institutional structures of the EU, in that the Commission's preference for collective actors means that committee places are handed out through groups first.

Increasingly, structures less formal than the federated and direct-membership Euro groups reviewed in Chapter 3 have emerged in recent years, based primarily around large firms. These range on a spectrum from visible groups with a loose organisation through to privately organised occasional dining clubs. Some are issue-based, others are built around sectors, while others are cross sectoral. Some are open-membership structures, sometimes initiated by the European institutions, while others are more exclusive clusters of a select number of firms. Some are developing into more recognisable and formal Euro groups, whereas others are transient, or are likely to remain, by design, as informal meeting points. These more informal types of groups have become somewhat fashionable in recent years as the interests within them find such structures valuable; as Cram has suggested, co-operation in one type of structure can lead to collaboration elsewhere (Cram, 1995b). But equally, such structures can lead to the foundation of similar fora by outsiders who witness their effectiveness, or who seek to find ways of responding to their exclusion. In turn, this illustrates how the presence of collective structures, and participation within them, can influence the behaviour of private-interest actors themselves.

At the more visible end of the spectrum are an increasing number of 'round tables', such as those which have sprung up in information technology and banking. Some round tables have become formal groups, while others are a semi-permanent structure of dialogue between firms. Other visible structures include issue alliances, with the secretariat often provided by a public-affairs consultancy firm, such as the European Energy from Waste coalition. In the information technology domain, two issue alliances emerged in response to proposals which eventually became the 1991 Directive on the legal protection of computer software, representing competing positions on the desirability of allowing the retranslation of computer software. In turn, these organisations began to spawn further issue alliances, with slightly different configurations of interests. These structures emerged partly because of the inability of sector-wide groups to accommodate the competing interests (Pijnenburg, 1996). An example of another type of issue structure from the IT sector illustrates Cram's point about how participation in the structures of the European institutions can yield co-operation. Thus, collaboration within the CEN/CEN-ELEC framework facilitated the creation of the European Workshop for Open Systems (EWOS) in 1987 as a means of drafting standards (Greenwood and Cram, 1996).

Other visible groups have emerged along cross-sectoral, multi-issue lines. Thus, the European Business Agenda (formerly 'Business in Europe') group, a Brussels-based group comprising a handful of large British firms, has sought to influence the behaviour of the British government towards Europe and the present Intergovernmental conference by, among other activities, the production of papers for internal and external use. These papers are sent to UK Commissioners, UKREP, and to British interest groups with a Brussels presence. The organisation formed in 1994 from a dinner meeting among a circle of friends who were the European directors of their respective companies, including British Aerospace, British Gas, Guinness, ICL, Marks & Spencer, National Westminster Bank and Rolls-Royce. The group has no formal secretariat, is kept deliberately small and informal, and operates primarily through interpersonal exchanges between a group of friends based in Brussels. Such features mean that group members can talk freely about developments in Brussels without problems of accountability, and work very quickly together as issues demand. It is, however, not a splintergroup in any sense, and its presence is made quite open within UK Brussels circles. Collective tasks are divided between members, and information exchanged at monthly meetings held in the premises of a leading Brussels public-affairs consultancy. Because of the nature of the group and its focus upon high politics areas, it is not a lobbying organisation, but operates more at the level of ideas and information. Since the IGC commenced, the group has now switched its attention to other issues such as research and development, innovation, energy policy, the environment and social policy.

The less-visible groups also span the sectoral, and cross sectoral, dimensions. One example is provided by the 'Ravenstein group' (Cowles, 1994; Coen, 1995), an elite, unstructured dining club of government affairs directors operating from Brussels, who meet and talk informally. The membership list is strictly confidential. Executives from multinational firms from Europe and the USA, meet as a wholly private organisation without a formal structure or budget, and with a temporary rotating chair. Members are invited by a particular company to a lunch meeting at which a topic will be presented, followed by a discussion and the consideration of the latest rumours.

There is now a plethora of such structures encompassing a variety of interest domains. Some are caucuses of firms seeking to provide a particular direction to the activities of a particular interest group. They can provide important think-tank capacities and ideas leadership, as well as providing a 'short and unclogged' (Pijnenburg, 1996, p. 27) information channel and socialisation network for members. Their exclusive and informal nature, together with their roles as networking structures, mean that decision-making and collective action problems either do not arise or are relatively small in comparison to those of some formal groups. They provide flexible structures for firms to respond to the unpredictability of the European business environment, whether they act as issue networks, information and socialisation networks, forums for ideas or quick-response mechanisms. They can enhance identity and interest cohesion, and carry few risks of a loss of autonomy that might arise from compromising positions through Euro groups (Cram, 1995; Pijnenburg, 1996). As significant actors themselves, large firms have the ability, and sometimes the need, to act exclusively as a 'small club' with a handful of others, or alone, in seeking to influence public affairs. As was highlighted in Chapter 3, these structures can sit quite comfortably alongside formal group structures. The creation of super-firms through mergers, take-overs and alliances (sometimes prompted by the need to compete effectively in the single market) has created corporate actors which sometimes have more resources at their disposal than do some member states. Inevitably, these have become powerful political actors in their own right, sometimes becoming insider interests within the European institutions in ways most often associated with collective actors.

Firms with their own dedicated public affairs offices in Brussels may have as many as eight executives based in such offices (Stern, 1994). Those for whom resources rule out a Brussels presence tend to be restricted to collective structures, or to the hire of commercial lobbyists as necessary, unless other corporate functions are switched at the same time to the Belgian capital. Large firms' Brussels offices can however provide a means of interest representation for smaller, supplier firms, unable to fund their own Brussels presence (Coen,

1995). But for the largest firms, the stakes can be too high to risk not investing in a Brussels presence. From a Brussels base, a firm can satisfy its information needs, take advantage of the openness of the European institutions to make its voice heard, and seek to participate fully in the institutional structures surrounding the EU. For some large firms, therefore, the Euro group is just one of a variety of means of fulfilling its needs. For the range of reasons outlined in Chapter 3, a large firm can rarely, if ever, afford not to be a member of corresponding Euro groups. Formal and informal information needs, networking, the need to influence collective strategies, and the Commission preference for collective actors, among other factors, make participation essential. Many large firms have to maintain multiple membership of different groups to satisfy the range of product interests they might possess. But they can rarely satisfy their political and economic needs at the European level by acting through collective structures alone, and, where firms have their own dedicated structures, the incentives for group participation may be driven by the need to prevent a 'collective bad' (Camera-Rowe, 1996; see also Chapter 3).

Multinationals are undoubtedly valuable political actors to the European institutions. They bring with them to European politics experiences of operating in a wide variety of regulatory regimes around the globe. They provide the Commission with the means to develop key structures in European public affairs, from leading-edge new technologies as a basis for future wealth creation, to technical standard setting. Without their involvement, a real single market would not be possible.

Cowles traces the stimulus to the involvement of multinational firms, as single players in European Public Affairs, to the 1970s, when the Commission established programmes directed at multinationals, and the ECJ made a number of key rulings concerning competition policy. Also significant were the development of industrial policies by Commissioner Davignon, and the partly related establishment of the two cross sectoral (principally) large-firm representatives established in the 1980s, ERT and AMCHAM. The ERT provided large firms not previously involved in direct-membership structures with direct experience and involvement in political action at the European level, and a role model for them in inter-firm collaboration (Cowles, 1995a).

Direct actions by large firms at the European level are more than simply a fallback should they be unsuccessful in persuading representative groups to accept their position. For a very large firm, policy level issues of regulation, deregulation, integration, enablement and funding, operational issues in fields such as competition policy, and the need to obtain information in a less than certain economic and political environment, mean that a Brussels presence is often imperative. Firms need their own dedicated eyes, ears and response mechanisms in Brussels, but, as with Philips, also the capability to become routine players in European public affairs.

The role of large firms in European public affairs is not, of course, restricted to their activities in Brussels, Luxembourg and Strasbourg. Large firms exert significant influences upon member states, which is in turn reflected in influences upon EU politics, through the behaviour and stances which governments adopt in both low and high politics fields (Chapters 2 and 10). Britain's attitude towards the development of Community social policy is clearly influenced by its desire to encourage firms to go regime shopping for conditions offering the lowest production costs when making investment decisions. Similarly, a member state's attitude towards a competition policy issue (an example of the blur between high and low politics discussed in Chapter 1) may be driven by its perception of how it is likely to affect a key domestic firm. But a change in perceptions of actors is reflected in the activities of firms in the ERT in the early 1980s, which exerted significant influences upon the perceptions of member states that national protectionism would inevitably lead to the loss of ability of European firms to compete in international markets, and building a climate of support in favour of full implementation of a free and single market. The super-firms in this elite were multinationals which operated across national boundaries and did not depend for their survival upon the support of a single host government to protect their national market. Rather, the size of these firms meant that their interests lay more in opening up markets to transnational competition. Evidence such as that provided by the Cecchini report on the costs of 'non-Europe' (Cecchini, 1988) also provided essential rational information to help build a climate of support among national governments for the deconstruction of national protectionism, and the re-regulation of rules of market exchange at the European level to ensure free competition.

The basis of European competition policy is provided by Article 3(f) of the Treaty of Rome, which seeks to prevent the distortion of competition through national and local protectionism cartels, monopolies and mergers. DG IV did not make full use of the powers until the 1980s, when the relaunch of 'project Europe' by the transfer of authority to the transnational level led to a renewed confidence by the European institutions in exercising their authority (McGowan and Wilks, 1995). In doing so, these authors consider that DG IV transformed itself 'in the course of twenty years from an uninspiring and fringe directorate into one of the most prominent and important . . . the 1970s image contrasts sharply with the crusading spirit of the DG IV evangelists of the 1980s' (McGowan and Wilks, 1995, p. 151).

During the 1980s and early 1990s, DG IV took a number of landmark decisions in competition policy which signalled its new-found confidence. These include fines levied on firms such as Solvay and ICI; fines on the UK government for its package of 'sweeteners' given to British Aerospace for the take-over of Rover; and the refusal (albeit by a single vote) by the College of Commissioners to sanction the proposed take-over of de Havilland by Aerospatiale and Alenia (Chapter 2). McGowan and Wilks (1995) argue that industry, and most notably the ERT of Industrialists, were are the forefront in seeking this more active role in European competition policy. Although there has been a certain degree of retrenchment since the 1980s, partly arising from a lack of staff resources in DG IV and partly from the declining confidence of the European institutions as a whole following attempts to ratify the TEU, the service has continued to make a considerable impact upon the European business environment. In December 1994, it imposed the largest fine to date – almost 250 million ECU – on a group of cement producers for cartel behaviour. This fine came hard on the heels of the (then) record-breaking fines on steel beam, and carton board producers, and has been followed since by action against telecommunications, banking and airline industries, and football authorities. These anti-trust activities have partly come to light as a result of whistle-blowing by competitor firms; thus, British Airways has been at the forefront in encouraging DG IV to take action against state aids for Air France, and Renault has complained about regional aid provided to Ford and Volkswagen for a joint production facility in Portugal. Of interest, however, is that these last two complaints have to date been unsuccessful, which in turn draws attention to the limitations of single firms acting outside trade associations as political actors at the European level.

While individual firms can be powerful actors at the European level, they are unlikely to be so where their views differ from those of encompassing Euro groups. A firm consistently out of line with the collective position is likely to lose credibility. Of interest is that, while

American firms do have a reputation as freebooters, they have had to approach the European level by acting collectively, and in doing so they have formed one of the most powerful of all Euro groups (Jacek, 1995). Similarly, Japanese firms, aware that their views are likely to carry little weight if expressed as a single firm, are likely to adopt strategic alliances with European firms as a means of access to collective structures where they would otherwise be excluded, or to work through structures such as the Japanese external trade organisation, or to use their investment influence with member state governments. One advantage of this exclusion is that they have not had to compromise their views with those of other firms in trade associations. However, while Japanese strategies have been driven by their exclusion from European politics, their points of entry are mainly those of seeking interest representation through collective structures.

There are very few large firms able to sustain the costs of remaining outside of Euro groups (Chapter 3). The influence of collective business structures such as the ERT, AMCHAM and UNICE is testimony to the impact such actors can have upon European public affairs. Not only do these interests exert influence by reacting to the detail of proposals which are being considered, but they can also be considerable forces in shaping the European agenda in the first instance, in both low and high politics fields. As is discussed in Chapter 10, business interests have been major actors in European integration, both through the influences exerted at member state level and through their presence at the European level.

6

Professional Interests

Professional interests in Europe are organised at the peak and sectoral levels. Table 3.1 (p. 59) indicates that there are 69 European-level associations representing professions, although, as is indicated later (Table 6.1) this may be an underestimation, depending on the definition of a 'profession'. Of interest is that a much smaller proportion of these (25 or 36 per cent) are based in Brussels than is the case with other types of interest groups, indicating an earlier stage of development. Also of significance is that a higher proportion of European-level professional associations are based in Britain than are other types of associations, and that, after Brussels, Britain is the most important base for European-level professional associations, accounting for 17 (25 per cent) of all of these.

This is for two reasons. The first is the higher prevalence of professional workers in Britain than elsewhere (EUROCADRES, 1995), while the second is the much higher degree of organisation of professional interests in Britain, with many professional associations exercising monopoly powers through licensing and self-regulatory arrangements granted by state authority. Indeed, twice as many professionals are included within the UK interprofessional association than in any other member state. In turn, the difference in location maps between professional, and other, types of European-level associations is indicative of different degrees of developed competencies of the EU in different professional fields; the selective impact of European authority upon different types of professional associations; differences in national traditions of professional organisation and of state–society relations; and the relatively recent acquisition of generalised competencies towards the professions by the European institutions.

Peak associations claiming representation of professionals

At the peak level, there are no less than three European-level pan-sectoral groups which claim representation of general professional interests. Despite each of these containing quite separate membership constituencies, their interest domains overlap considerably. This architecture in turn reflects the fact that what constitutes a profession is highly contested. While early attempts at definition focused on the traits of professional groups versus non-professionals (Greenwood, 1965), including attributes such as systematic theory, authority, community sanction, an ethical code and a professional culture, later attempts have focused more on the processes of professionalisation. This has allocated social and economic power to such groups (Wilding, 1982; Friedson, 1986), and enables groups to define their own boundaries and exercise closure (Murphy, 1988). The criteria for definition used by such authors centres on the capacity to define and control their work, and thus on the political ability of these actors to exercise their knowledge in exclusive ways. Such a definition, however, only partially resolves questions such as whether occupations such as that of social worker should be viewed as professions, which their own representative organisations would claim, or more as semi-professions; or precisely which groups of engineers have professional status. Some groups which claim professional status might more accurately be described as trade unions, and indeed not a few of these groups are organised under the auspices of ETUC.

Further complications centre upon cultural issues, and questions of competence (Harris and Lavan, 1992). An interest may be seen within one particular country as having 'professional' status, while in another country such status is open to question. Related to such differences are the degrees of competence required to enter a profession and to practise, and the modus of regulation operational in different countries. There are also different national traditions of organising, with certain professional interests affiliated to wider units, or operating independently. In turn, these differences can be reproduced at the European level, with one branch of the profession from one country ultimately represented by a different European association to the same branch in another country. Thus, Italian civil engineers educate and license architects, who are organised separately elsewhere in Europe; British midwives provide family planning services, whereas those in Ireland do not, and Dutch midwives often operate as sole specialists at births. Dentistry in Italy is subsumed within general medicine; and there are no counterparts to British solicitors and barristers (Orzack, 1991). All this leads to a proliferation of national associations operating alongside European federations in Brussels.

From the review above, the Commission's definition of a profession comprising occupations with a high level of education (requiring a degree obtained after at least three years) encompassing a particular body of knowledge, and where some form of licence to practice is required, appears to be a rather limited one (Neale, 1994). However, this problematic debate cannot be resolved here; indeed, the theoretical and empirical boundary problem of precisely which groups are to be considered a profession is largely irresolvable. As will become clear below, these uncertainties mean that some of the associations representing professions have considerable difficulty in defining the parameters of their own membership constituency. However, the reader should be aware which groups are under discussion in this chapter, and which are the focus of Chapter 7 on labour interests. The focus in this chapter is upon both self-employed and salaried white-collar workers who are included within levels 1 and 2 of the International Standard Classification of Occupations (ISCO) (such as fully qualified doctors, lawyers, architects, vets, dentists, pharmacists, civil and electrical engineers, teachers, nurses and midwives, librarians, writers, artists, ministers of religion, and middle-ranking and senior corporate and public-sector managers), and not those included in levels 3 and 4 (Chapter 7), which cover occupational groups such as laboratory technicians, clerks, computer operators, safety inspectors, police officers, sales staff, and all 'para' professions, including those who are not fully qualified but who nevertheless operate in professional fields as ancillary workers. These constituencies of interests will become evident in examining the members of peak organisations of professional associations.

At the peak level, representation occurs through three organisations:

1. SEPLIS, representing the liberal professions, formed in 1974.
2. EUROCADRES, the Council of European Professional and Managerial Staff, which operates under the auspices of ETUC, and represents salaried, unionised professional and managerial staff. EUROCADRES was formed in 1993.
3. CEC, the Confederation Européenne des Cadres, representing independent organisations of managerial staff primarily in

industry and commerce. CEC is not affiliated to ETUC. It was created in 1989.

SEPLIS and its member interests

SEPLIS was formed in 1974 from the idea of a Commission official whose own department of liberal professions (as defined below) within the Commission was disbanded, and who therefore identified the need for the liberal professions to have a voice in European public affairs. Until 1989 it was the only European organisation representing cross-sectoral professional interests in Europe. Although it is a small organisation, with two part-time executives, a part-time secretary and a non-salaried president, it is somewhat larger than it was for most of the 1970s, when it struggled to mature beyond embryonic status. It is governed by an annual general meeting and a bi-monthly executive committee, whose work is supplemented by recently established (1995) specialist committees covering the social dialogue, continuous education, liaison between members, GATT issues and public relations.

SEPLIS is funded by its member organisations and, by choice of these members, has not sought funding from the European institutions in an effort to safeguard its independence. It is best conceived of as an umbrella organisation of professional associations, of which there are two broad types. The first of these consists of inter-professional associations from individual member states where such organisations exist, of which there are ten, while the second comprises European-level sectoral associations, of which twelve are SEPLIS members. Through these organisations SEPLIS claims to represent the interests of some 2.7 million liberal professionals in Europe, who are responsible for the employment of 9 million individuals. By far the most significant of its national member associations, in terms of numbers, is the British group, which, with over 1.1 million members, represents twice as many professionals as do the next largest associations, in Germany and France. Greece and Italy have no organisation, Luxembourg is not a member, while Switzerland has observer status, as do some members whose activities do not quite fit SEPLIS's own definition of what constitutes a liberal profession. Among other 'intermediate' criteria (high level of specific and intellectual training, personalised service, a relationship of trust, independence, and care with the client), the liberal professions are fundamentally seen as those which practice independently and require the backing of statute law (including licensed self-regulatory arrangements) relating to their profession (SEPLIS, 1996a). Groups such as the European Communities Biologists' Association therefore have observer status, while doctors and engineers, who are salaried state employees in some countries, are not members. However, some doctors are represented in SEPLIS via national inter-professional associations, and the non-participation of these two sectoral groups in SEPLIS at least via observer status is significant.

Sectoral members of SEPLIS have sought to limit its role to that of a listening post and information provider for its members, because they prefer to take the lead role on issues directly affecting them. Thus, in the passage of the recent Directive on Comparative Advertising, the role of SEPLIS was purely to provide information to its members, who then sought to exert influence over the content of this measure. The co-ordinating role performed by SEPLIS is strictly limited to where it is absolutely necessary to take cross-sectoral positions, and the provision of discussion seminars and events with speakers. This is in direct contrast to the approach taken by the Commission, which sought in the 1960s and 1970s to enable the free movement of professionals through sectoral directives, but because of the immense difficulties it encountered changed its strategy in the 1980s to pursue integration by means of general directives. One measure of the lack of influence of SEPLIS over European public affairs is that it was not consulted at all by the Commission during the draft and passage stages of these general directives, which date from 1988 (First General Systems Directive) and 1992 (Second General Systems Directive), even though they were the only European-level cross-sectoral professional interest organisation in existence in Brussels. Given that the directives were aimed right across the spectrum of professions, and taking into account the cross-sectoral remit of SEPLIS, this appears somewhat strange. However, as is evident later, part of the problem was that earlier sectoral initiatives had involved excessive consultation, resulting in considerable delays.

Another measure of the lack of influence of SEPLIS is that its best institutional contacts have historically been with the somewhat marginalised ESC, where it has been a full member, and opposite whose offices those of SEPLIS are situated. There has recently been an attempt by SEPLIS to strengthen contact with division E2 of DG XV (Internal Market and Financial Services), which contains twenty-two policy officials responsible for matters concerning the professions. There remains, however, little consultation of SEPLIS by

DG XV, and limited contacts with DG V (Employment, Industrial Relations and Social Affairs) and DG XXIV (Consumer Policy) have been initiated by SEPLIS. Indeed, the organisation has never been contacted by any of the Commission services seeking expertise or information, provision of which is one of the classic roles in public affairs performed by Euro groups. In common with a number of other groups, however, it will have a role in the Commission's 'Citizens First' campaign to explain to European citizens how the EU can benefit them, in that the Commission will use it to disseminate information through its member organisations on issues such as how to take advantage of worker mobility in the single market. The limitations placed on SEPLIS by its members, however, make it far more of an information processor than an organisation influencing, or seeking to influence, European public affairs. It has a largely reactive role, and indeed only intervenes in public affairs when specifically asked to do so by its members. Historically, its impact has been over-dependent upon the strength of the elected president. It is not recognised by the Commission as a social partner, because, as the Commission records in its communication to the Council and Parliament on social policy, 'its representativeness remains to be established' (Commission of the European Communities, 1993, p. 41).

Partly because it has failed to be recognised by the Commission as a Social Partner, SEPLIS is completely isolated from both EURO-CADRES and CEC, and has never once been in contact with these organisations. Its fraternal contacts concerning the social dialogue have been restricted to UEAPME, the SME/craft association, where, given the concentration of professionals in small practices, its most natural 'soul mate' may be, although even here contact has been highly infrequent and not at the decision-making level. Rather unsurprisingly, given these circumstances, it feels itself to be a loser on key decisions which have emerged from the social dialogue, such as the parental leave accord which permit leave of up to three months during the first eight years of the life of a child. Although there has been dialogue with the European consumers' organisation, BEUC, the relationship between the two organisations is best characterised as one of conflict, which has arisen from attempts to liberalise the services offered by independent professions, where each has broadly opposing interests. Indeed, in common with most interests, the single market represents a threat and an opportunity for the professions, particularly where the construction of a free market attacks the monopolies which professions have enjoyed on the supply of services. On balance, SEPLIS sees the single market as too consumer-oriented. Unlike business associations, which in the main established interest associations prior to the single market, the main period of growth of professional interest representation in Europe has occurred over the past ten years, largely in direct response to the single market. The majority of European-level sectoral professional associations now present in Brussels have established themselves during this period.

If there has been a high point in the work of SEPLIS, it came in the mid-1980s when it organised the professions within and beyond the EC to respond to the initiatives of the OECD (Organisation for Economic Co-operation and Development) aimed at encouraging governments to tackle barriers erected by professions against the competitive provision of services by new entrants to the market. It achieved agreement among the participants for a detailed resolution rebutting both the substance, methodology and procedure of the report from the OECD Committee of Experts on Restrictive Business Practice, and co-ordinated a campaign of national interest representation among the range of professional interests involved in opposition to the report (Orzack, 1992). This rather isolated outbreak of effective co-ordination of professional interests has not been repeated by SEPLIS at the European level, where it is dedicated to engage.

The issues on which SEPLIS has been working in recent years include: those arising from the social dialogue, such as the parental leave accord; mutual recognition of professional qualifications; comparative advertising; the provision of services by the professions to the general public, including the current passage of the legal services directive; the abandoned general directive on liability of service providers; the 'Citizens First' initiative; and the Defective Services Directive, on which its opposition departed from that of many of the sectoral professional groups, who took a more favourable view. As will be evident from the discussion below, the other peak professional associations have also been active on a number of these issues, yet, significantly, there is virtually no contact between these organisations.

EUROCADRES

EUROCADRES is a quite different type of organisation to SEPLIS. Formed in 1993 following a decision of the ETUC Executive in December 1992, EUROCADRES seeks to group together professional and managerial salaried staff in both western and eastern Europe who are organised in trade unions. This focus upon salaried, unionised staff is quite different from the focus of SEPLIS membership, which is on liberal, i.e. independent, professionals. The small degree of overlap of individual member constituency with SEPLIS is in practice negligible because of the type of organisations each association represents. EUROCADRES estimates that its membership constituency includes 4 million staff in International Standards Organisation (ISO) classifications 1 and 2, of whom 3 million are from the member states of the European Union. EUROCADRES's direct members are private- and public-sector unions from the national level (whether wholly or partly representing professional–managerial staff), and EU-level sectoral organisations of unionised professional and managerial staff in public- and private-sector organisations. These members provide the funding for EUROCADRES, together with ETUC and EUROFIET. Although EUROCADRES receives no core funding from the European institutions, it does draw upon the resources of ETUC, itself significantly financed by the Commission (Chapter 3).

EUROCADRES has a secretariat of two executives and a part-time secretary, with offices located in the Brussels premises of EURO-FIET, the European branch of the international trade union organisation of professional and managerial workers. It operates with an annual assembly, and an active steering committee of eighteen. It draws upon the resources of the organisations appointing members to the steering committee in its work. As part of the ETUC structure, its concerns are those of the trade union movement, and it takes the view that Europe should not be a deregulated market. Although it has virtually no links at all with SEPLIS (with whom it has never met), and only informal contacts with CEC, it has worked closely with the engineers' association, FEANI (Federation Européenne d'Associations Nationales d'Ingénieurs), where there is some degree of membership overlap in the field of electrical and telecommunication engineers. Apart from this, it has worked with few other sectoral professional associations. Like SEPLIS, it is therefore rather isolated in its work, at least outside the trade union movement. However, as will be evident from the discussion below, the issues on which it focuses are not dissimilar from those of SEPLIS.

The main strength of EUROCADRES is its trade union constituency, which has afforded it recognition as one of the second-level social partners and gives it excellent access to DG V, and to DG XXII (Education, Training and Youth). It is therefore an institutionalised actor for labour-market-related issues, and its status as a social partner provides it with the ability to influence key issues in European public affairs. It has been particularly active on core trade union type issues concerning unemployment among professional and managerial staff. Its contact with the other services which routinely affect its interests, such as DG XV, tends to be more issue specific, over concerns such as: the 'Citizens First' initiative; the mutual recognition of qualifications; obstacles to free circulation, including those presented by supplementary pension schemes; parental leave; and equal opportunities. Many of these issues also concern SEPLIS, CEC and sectoral professional groups, which makes the lack of contact between them all the more remarkable. On the whole, despite its relatively short existence, EUROCADRES appears to have a much greater degree of involvement in European public affairs than does SEPLIS. Thus, the majority of issues on which EUROCADRES has been active have involved the Commission initiating contact with it.

Confederation Européene des Cadres (CEC)

Formed in 1989 from the International Confederation of Professions, the CEC represents an estimated constituency of 1.5 million salaried managers in industry, the public sector, trade and commerce through national cross-sectoral associations of managers, and European-level (or international) sectoral associations. It has offices in Paris (inside the international association) and a dedicated office in Brussels. It is not affiliated to ETUC because it is dedicated to represent independent organisations of workers. It comprises 14 national cross-sectoral associations of managers (all member states with the exception of Finland, Greece and Ireland, and 2 for the United Kingdom, plus Norway), and 11 sectoral associations, ranging from bank to mining managers.

There is no membership overlap between SEPLIS and CEC. Although on paper there is a clear division between the three peak associations, with SEPLIS representing the liberal professions, CEC representing salaried managers and EUROCADRES representing unionised managers, in practice there is domain overlap, as all represent a constituency of professional interests as classified by the ISCO. As CEC records in its literature (Confederation Européene des Cadres, 1995, p. 1), its constituency includes national interprofessional (i.e. peak) associations, and its members include the words 'managers', 'professionals', and 'executives' within their titles. This broad constituency is also reflected in its objectives, which include the desires

> to ensure adequate representation of European managers and professionals within the European Union; to co-ordinate and provide guidance in the work of affiliated organisations in order to define harmonised solutions to problems affecting the whole sector (ibid.).

All three organisations represent similar concerns at the European level, all related to employment issues. All three organisations address DG XV. Thus, the list of issues CEC has been active on recently includes the Parental Leave Accord, the 'Citizens First' campaign, supplementary pensions, home working, and, to a slightly lesser extent, the mutual recognition of qualifications. Like EURO-CADRES, CEC has only experienced limited contact with other European-level sectoral organisations of professional interests outside its own membership. Like EUROCADRES, CEC is officially recognised as a (second-level) social partner, and both are therefore active on the same range of issues, including the social aspects of the 1996 IGC. Although both represent the interests of salaried employees, the limited contact between these two organisations can be explained partly because of the differences in perspective which unionisation and non-unionisation brings. While the relationship between the two is not problematic, EUROCADRES does make a point of claiming in publicly available documentation that it is a far more representative organisation than CEC (EUROCADRES, 1994). For its part, CEC has rather better contacts with business associations such as UNICE, UEAPME, and EUROCOMMERCE, with whom it has been active on high politics issues such as monetary union.

The three peak organisations representing professional interests to some extent defy expectations about issue network and coalition formation. Although they do have distinct membership constituencies with clear demarcation lines between them, all of these three associations are working on a very similar range of issues. This might otherwise predict either a good degree of contact between them, or at least a considered position among the actors on co-ordination, yet only two of them, EUROCADRES and CEC, have ever met deliberately. Indeed, one of the respondents from the three peak professional organisations interviewed had not heard of one of the other organisations. In turn, this also indicates the general immaturity of development of professional interest representation in the EU. Although EUROCADRES and CEC are fully recognised (second-level) social partners and therefore institutionalised actors in these spheres, their influence outside social dialogue issues, and the influence of SEPLIS, is not significant upon European public affairs affecting professional interests. A further indicator of adolescent development is that when the Commission was drafting the general system Directives of 1989 and 1992 concerning issues of free movement of professional workers, which are somewhat key issues affecting the professions, these organisations were either not in existence or not consulted. Nor were any of the European-level sectoral interests consulted.

European-level sectoral professional interests

Significantly, the majority of sectoral professional associations at the European level are not full members of SEPLIS, CEC or EUROCADRES. The range of functional interests (some subdivided by specialisms, some as alternative associations) are recorded in Table 6.1 overleaf.

Some of these associations (such as handwriting analysts) are highly specialised, sometimes located in far-flung corners of Europe (not necessarily even in the EU), and are in certain cases little more than letterhead associations, with 'care-of' addresses via a particular individual person, firm or international association, sometimes during a rotating secretariat. In some cases, there are no staff attached exclusively to European-level associations, but rather the secretariat is provided by a national member association. Some professions with considerable power at the national level, such as doctors, are not particularly well represented at the European level. Thus, despite the presence of a Euro association since 1959, the Comité Permanent des Médicins de la Communauté has had no permanent Brussels presence until very recently (Lovecy, 1996).

There appears to be a higher proportion of associations with similar characteristics in professional domains than in other domains. Similarly, there are more international associations representing

TABLE 6.1

Types of professional interests with European-level associations

Type of professional interest	Number of European-level associations within domain
Architecture	5
Property-related (surveyors, valuers, real estate)	13
Construction	2
Law	6
Dentistry	3
Nurses, midwives	3
Pharmacists and chemists	5
Opticians	2
Physiotherapists, occupational therapists	2
Other medical professions	9
Vets	2
Accountancy	6
Engineering	10
Financial services	3
Journalists	2
Designers	1
Scientists	3
Managers Associations not included above	5
Other miscellaneous (e.g. handwriting analysts, town planners, public-affairs practitioners, art restorers)	9

Source: Commission of the European Communities (1992b); Landmark Publications (1995); SEPLIS (1996b); survey by author, February 1996.

particular types of professional interests which have not yet spawned a dedicated European bureau than is evident in other interest domains. In other cases, there are multiple representatives of domain interests. Some of these are specialist, subsectoral functional divisions; in some cases, these are 'family associations' of specialities operating from the same premises, such as associations of notaries, while, in other sectors, associations are quite separate (such as accountants, and accountants serving SMEs). Although these divisions are based on clear functional lines, sometimes such specialisms do compete. For instance, the relationship between associations representing opticians, and ophthalmic opticians, has at least historically been highly conflictual, owing to the desire of the latter to exclude the former from the ability to provide certain types of services to the general public (Orzack, 1992).

Other domains simply have multiple representative outlets without clear functional lines, but where division arises more from tradition and preference. Thus, there is the European Lawyers Union (Luxembourg), and the Council of Bars and Law Societies of the European Community (CCBE) (Brussels); while in Germany we find the European Union of Dentists, and in Brussels the Liaison Committee for Dentistry in the EC (Brussels) (another subsector, dental hygienists, is based in Glasgow). Other European-level professional associations are joined in Brussels by national offices of their members, usually because of the inability of the European association to reach meaningful agreement among its members. Thus, the CCBE, dating from 1960, is now accompanied by a variety of national law associations in Brussels. While the presence of multi-representative formats does not in itself imply competition (Chapter 3), the extent of associational fragmentation, locations outside of Brussels, undivided (into European) international associations, sectoral associations not affiliated to peak associations, parallel national associations with Brussels offices, and 'empty-shell' groups, in professional interest fields, again indicates a degree of immaturity in development. So too, does the absence of groups with dedicated European-level associations, such as teachers. Of interest in the case of teachers is that issues of mobility have been resolved without special-interest representation, partly through common systems for exchange, such as the SOCRATES framework. The professions are one domain where the application of the label of 'weak Euro groups' may, at least historically speaking, have been justified.

Unlike business domains, it is not possible to find examples of European associations in the professions which are extremely well resourced and unequivocally influential in European public affairs. At the national level, such groups do exist, because the resources they bear have greater significance in national contexts. Thus, associations of lawyers, for instance, are extremely powerful actors in some member states. In part, this is because at the national level professional interests and processes of professional recognition are linked to wider issues of social and economic power, and partly because of the greater degree of competence hitherto existing over professional affairs at the national level. At the European level only competencies exist, and the degree of these competencies are partial, in that only a very limited transfer of competencies to the European level for the professions has occurred (Lovecy, 1993). Therefore, it is possible to find only a handful of even moderately developed and partially effective groups; those which do exist tend to suffer from classic lowest-common-denominator problems (Arnison, in Neale, 1994), and sometimes act more in the capacity of a listening post than in representative functions. In a survey of British professional groups, Neale found a marked preference for developing their own channels of interest representation to Europe, rather than using Euro groups (Neale, 1994). However, as Neale has pointed out, some European-level business associations do afford an avenue of representation for professional interests (Neale, 1994). Both CEFIC and EFPIA, for instance, have taken positions on core issues of interest to learned associations, such as wider European policy for science and technology funding (including the funding of higher education), while UEAPME has articulated concerns shared by professional interests in small enterprises.

The professional groups most organised at the European level are engineers, lawyers, certain interests allied to medicine, architects, surveyors and accountants. Among these only the European (general) engineers' association, FEANI, founded in 1951, predates the Treaty of Rome. Despite such an early presence, this association was unable to secure a sectoral directive for its members to be able to practice in other member states, an important issue for engineers who have a long tradition of occupational mobility. Other associations were formed later, often specifically achieve a sectoral directive aimed at the mutual recognition of qualifications within their field (Laslett, 1991). This has been the area where the EU has affected professional interests most, and has been the most important catalyst to the development of European-level professional associations.

As early as 1957, work commenced on developing systems for co-ordination and recognition of diplomas. In the period from 1963 to 1973, a number of directives sought mutual recognition of non-professional qualifications, in fields such as the retail trade, small crafts, hairdressing, insurance and travel agencies, and food manufacturing. These attempts were extended to cover particular sectors of professional groups thereafter, and directives were eventually passed to eliminate national legislation and procedures which discriminate against other qualified and licensed professionals in other member states. Thus, measures were passed to enable doctors, nurses, dental practitioners, veterinary surgeons, midwives, architects and pharmacists to practise in another member state, to offer temporary services in another country if requested to by a client, and to receive recognition of qualifications if migrating. A less encompassing directive aimed at enabling lawyers to practise in other member states was also passed, in 1977.

The process of establishing sectoral directives proved extremely tortuous and difficult to reach agreement. The first directive, aimed at doctors, was not agreed until 1977, while a directive aimed at pharmacists took sixteen years to achieve, and one for architects only achieved its final passage in 1985 after seventeen years. Another aimed at engineers dating from 1969 was completely abandoned, not least because of the inability of FEANI members to reach agreement on standards among themselves, and, despite later creation of a register aimed at producing a system of recognition, the influence of FEANI received a setback (Neale, 1994). Similarly, an ambitious set of directives aimed at opticians, concerning rights of establishment, to provide services, and mutual recognition of qualifications, was also abandoned largely because of the failure of the professional bodies concerned to reach agreement. This latter failure is somewhat symptomatic of the wider issues concerned, in that examining and dispensing opticians were involved in a turf fight over who should be allowed to provide certain services, which was complicated by national differences in patterns of service delivery (Orzack, 1992). Inter-sectoral competition between professions has also hampered the passage of integrative measures, such as disputes between lawyers and accountants over the provision of legal and financial advice services (Lovecy, 1993).

Where directives were successful, issues surrounding the unevenness of professional practice across the member states were considerable factors in their delay. Thus, for architects, disentanglement of qualifications allied to engineering in Italy were necessary, and special arrangements were needed for those who had taken three-year qualifications in architecture in a particular sector of German higher education (Laslett, 1991). As will be evident later, national interest associations, partly on these grounds of differences, were also significant factors in delays of passage of sectoral directives.

Other individual proposals aimed at physiotherapists, accountants, psychologists, librarians, tax consultants, journalists and surveyors have also been abandoned (Laslett, 1991; Orzack, 1992). This lack of progress on sectoral initiatives provided the basis for a sea change in approach. Considerable Commission resources had been tied up by sectoral initiatives, and a number of reorganisations within the Commission had failed to speed the process up. Following agreement at the 1984 Fontainebleau summit, as part of the drive towards a single market, the sectoral approach was abandoned in favour of outline generalised directives on the mutual recognition of qualifications aimed at the entire constituency of professions, and reliant upon the development of detailed arrangements at member state level (Orzack, 1991; Button and Fleming, 1992; Harris and Lavan, 1992). The first of these, the First General Systems Directive (FGSD) aimed at all professions not otherwise covered by sectoral directives, was agreed in 1988, and came into force in January 1991. The second, the Second General Systems Directive (SGSD), covering occupations requiring less than three years' qualification (and therefore beyond the scope of this chapter) was passed in 1992.

The passage of the sectoral directives attracted considerable interest representation. However, this arose mainly from the national capitals. Orzack records that

> The Community's Commission, and Council of Ministers, as well as its Parliament and Economic and Social Committee, laboured long and hard to prepare drafts of directives in a number of fields. Each draft was extensively scrutinized within these Community bodies but even more intensive reviews occurred in the separate countries. Governments for each member state examined and passed drafts and then negotiated bilaterally with other governments and at Community meetings . . . in some countries and for certain professions, governments sought out practitioner groups and educational bodies and solicited their views on these texts. Official personnel of the Community sometimes passed along drafts, often informally. Draft texts came under legal and professional microscopes. A great deal of lobbying occurred, both at national government levels and at the Community itself , as extensive delays characterised Community consideration of draft directives (Orzack, 1991, p. 143).

During the passage of these directives, then, interest representation occurred, on balance, mainly at the national level. At the European level, interest representation arose mainly in the implementation phase, through Committees established by Council decisions for each of the eight sectoral professions covered, to co-ordinate and review progress. Although these included places for representatives of the professions, Orzack has characterised what he terms these 'subbureaucracies' (Orzack, 1991; p. 143) as 'cumbersome and costly' (ibid.), and of limited effectiveness. Some interaction arose between European-level professional associations and the Commission, although the impact of this is inconclusive (such as the failure of the law association, the CCBE, to achieve anything more encompassing than the rather limited 1977 directive), and of less importance than interest representation through the national route. Throughout, the Commission had been careful to engage professional opinion, usually at a high level of detail, sometimes incorporating chunks of text written by professional associations. Yet the high degree of consultation was in turn largely responsible for the delayed passage of these directives. In consequence, the Commission decided upon its own course of action for the FGSD, and the passage of this involved almost no consultation whatsoever. Historically, if there ever was a high point of professional interest involvement in domain-based European public policies, the replacement of sectoral initiatives through the FGSD marked its end.

As for the FGSD itself , it is minimalist in scope, based not upon harmonisation of qualifications, but upon mutual recognition of them, the lowest-common-denominator form of European integration. Neither does it place a duty to encourage or facilitate freedom of movement; rather, it is concerned with ensuring that barriers to recognition are removed (Harris and Lavan, 1992). In Europe, 11 000 workers have received recognition of their diplomas to enable them to work in other member states. Of these 6000 are British. The UK also accounted for 400 of the 620 lawyers who had their qualifications recognised under the Directive (Commission Office London, 1996).

The FGSD is highly dependent for operationalisation upon the work of national governments to co-ordinate and oversee the work of licensing authorities for each profession, the source of a great deal of unevenness in implementation. In many cases, the competent authorities appointed by national administrations to oversee implementation are the national professional associations, which has in turn strengthened their role at the domestic level and *vis-à-vis* their European association counterparts.

The lack of consultation, and the style of the directive, led to frequent friction and complaints from the professional interests. SEPLIS expressed substantive reservations on a number of points of detail, and sought an extension period before the directive came into effect (Laslett, 1991). FEANI has for some time argued that it is set at an inappropriate level (Evetts, 1995). For the lawyers, the past president of the CCBE described it as a 'sudden and unwelcome . . . shortcut . . . greeted with considerable scepticism and opposition from most of the Bars of the Community. The proposal has all the hallmarks of a typical bureaucratic solution to a difficult problem' (Orzack, 1991, p. 148), and 'an element of danger . . . harmonization at any price . . . bogus equivalence based on the great fallacy of confusing unity with conformity' (ibid.).

Orzack has parodied opposition to integrationist measures among professional interests, which illustrates the degree to which these are still entrenched within their national capitals:

1. National insularity – 'We have the highest standards in Europe.'
2. Pure nationalism – 'Foreigners cannot understand local standards of practice and cannot tell us how to prepare specialists.'
3. Moral protectionism – 'Outsiders should not be able to compete against local professionals, threatening economic rewards merited by lengthy education and extensive experience.'
4. Educational imperialism – 'Different knowledge traditions can disrupt a country's profession, particularly where it doesn't match our own high standards.'
5. Turf protection – 'People with similar titles but different ranges and levels of skills should not be allowed to practice here.'
6. Services will be ruined – 'Migrants will flood in, increasing competition, reducing quality of services, and lowering income.'
7. Ethical considerations – 'Outsiders do not practice in accordance with local standards.'
8. Control of profession – 'Outsiders used to government controlled regulation of their profession will not be able to accept a culture of self-regulation by professional bodies.'
9. Modes of compensation – 'Outsiders will experience difficulties in adapting from schemes with different modes of recompense for service provision' (Orzack, 1991, pp. 148–9).

As with all characterisations, these generalisations mask considerable variations, and not all professional interests can be regarded as protectionist dinosaurs, hostile to liberalisation and integration measures. The European accountancy association, FEE (Federation of European Accountants), for instance, claims to have taken positions on a number of occasions broadly in favour of liberalisation (Orzack, 1992). Nevertheless, many of the professions have responded negatively to many of the implications of the single market, and Commissioners have complained of 'resistance' from them (Orzack,

1991). Often, they are quite happy with arrangements which they have negotiated and developed with domestic authorities over a number of years from a position of strength, with powerful intermediary associations which have acquired high degrees of competence in controlling entry to the profession, and in regulating service standards. Intrusion from the European level is therefore unwelcome. Although some associations have purposefully sought directives at the European level on helpful issues for their members, such as the mutual recognition of qualifications, on other issues such as deregulation of service provision they have been less than enthusiastic. In turn, this raises the interesting general question as to the ways in which perceptions of transnational authority conditions collective action questions. One hypothesis worth exploring further, for instance, concerns whether interests which respond negatively, and reactively, to the European agenda might tend to take the 'national route' of interest representation to Brussels and keep political resources invested largely at home, while those which see Europe more positively and in a more opportunistic sense might instead tend to work more at the European level.

For the professions, to whom on balance the European Community has been more of a threat than an opportunity, domestic associations remain strong while their transnational associations remain relatively weak. Even in the relatively better-organised European-level professional associations, such as the CCBE, contacts with the European Commission are insufficiently strong, and consequently the Commission still needs to turn to the national associations. National and sectoral differences remain so strong that groups have often found it very difficult to build agreement among members, and consequently interest representation is often dealt with on an issue-by-issue basis using different alliances of national associations. Indeed, the UK and the German bar associations have gone their own way in making representations on the December 1994 directive on the right of establishment for the legal profession. Historically, for many professional interests in the member states, the question has been why they should abandon their lucrative, comfortable and often protected territories at the national level, domains in which they have played no small part in creating, for a far less certain future in Europe. As was evident from comments obtained in interviews with sectoral associations, there is a lasting problem of national protectionism. Although a variety of changes are now disrupting professional power at the national level, in terms of neofunctionalist integration theory (Chapter 10), the way in which professions have sought the transfer of competencies from the national level to the European level has hardly been consistent.

Until very recently, European affairs directed at the professions have been dominated by the 1980's minimalist conception of 'social policy' in the EU as the elimination of barriers to labour mobility. Yet there is, in reality, limited demand among the professions for this, and the reason why such an outdated agenda remains is because of the lack of meaningful issues to address across professional domains. This helps explain the poor level of inter professional coordination.

The future of professional interest representation in Europe

As was discussed in Chapter 1, the European project involves the chance to be involved in designing a new set of rules. As the recent creation of some European-level professional associations attests, these interests can no longer afford to remain largely at the national level. Indeed, the relatively recent entry of peak associations such as the CEC and EUROCADRES, and the social partner status accorded to them, may signal the beginning of a new era of professional interest representation in the EU. From a case study article of the engineering profession in 1995, Evetts argues that 'international professional associations, such as FEANI, are becoming increasingly influential in the re-regulation process for service-providers in the single European Market' (Evetts, 1995, p. 770).

Evetts suggests that the Council of Ministers has now largely accepted the arguments of a number of sectoral associations that the FGSD is too blunt an instrument, and has identified a proposal for a more streamlined system of recognition. She documents the work of transnational associations in filling the gap in detail left by the FGSD by producing their own mechanisms of harmonisation. FEANI, for instance, has created a register of higher and lower qualifications, and the award of an international professional title to those who meet standards of seven years university engineering education plus professional experience. These systems are rapidly acquiring currency, in that some 8500 British civil engineers have been awarded the title. As has occurred at the national level with self-regulatory schemes, systems such as these are bound to develop significance for the associations which develop them. Indeed, FEANI has already progressed further, and since 1992 has been working to develop a pan-European system of accreditation and certification for engineers, and a new postgraduate qualification based on a credit transfer scheme (Evetts, 1995). Similarly, Lovecy draws attention to a common code of conduct prepared in 1989 by the CCBE for lawyer–client relations in the provision of cross-border services, which has now been adopted by its members (Lovecy, 1996). Further evidence of some growth in influence of professional interest groups at the European level is indicated by Preston, who considers that the accountancy profession has come to dominate the development of company law and taxation (Preston, 1995).

Professional interests operating at the European level have now become engaged in a much broader set of issues than simply those concerned with the mutual recognition of qualifications. Evetts provides two examples, concerning the proposed Directives on Liability of Providers of Service and on Joint Cross-Border Practice, where professional interests intervened in European public affairs. The first of these was withdrawn, and the second has been blocked. However, although she cites these two cases as evidence of the growing influence of transnational professional associations, some caution should be exercised, not least because the first of these involved considerable interest representation by business interests, and the second involved intervention primarily (but not solely) by the more powerful national professional associations. In the case of liability of service providers, some sector-specific directives are now under consideration, including one for lawyers which progressed from the Commission in December 1994, and which the European Bar association, the CCBE, has grave reservations about; indeed, its own draft text, submitted to the Commission, was largely excluded in the final draft. Since the withdrawal of the general draft directive on the liability of service providers, a number of replacements for it have been introduced, such as directives on distance selling, as well as measures on after-sales service and those providing much clearer rights for consumers of professional services. Together, these measures have, on the whole, been opposed by professionals selling services to the public. It is also worth pointing out that Evett's conclusions on the effectiveness of FEANI are not shared by most other analysts. As Millman (1994) points out, though the international professional title for engineers developed by FEANI has taken off in Britain, it has not done so elsewhere, and FEANI has been slow to establish itself. Neale (1994), meanwhile, argues that the influence of FEANI has been in steady decline since its failure to achieve a sectoral directive at the European level.

Recent scholarship indicating increasing influence is nevertheless an issue well worthy of debate, in that it at least questions an otherwise rather uniform characterisation of European professional associations as essentially weak. There are signs of change, at both the peak and sectoral levels of European-level interest organisation among the professions. Some of the sectoral associations are now beginning to develop, with the most organised having secretariats of half a dozen or so staff. Some previously conflicting interests, such as dispensing and examining opticians, now operate together. The present arenas in which professional associations are playing concern fundamental cross-sectoral issues, such as the social dialogue, a proposal for a third General Systems Directive on the mutual recognition of professional qualifications, the 'Citizens First' campaign and draft legislation on comparative advertising, as well as a number of important sector specific initiatives. Most recently, the Commission has published proposals to simplify EU rules for business and craft professionals wishing to work in other member states, which involved extensive consultations with European-level professional associations, as well as those at national level. If professional interests are to develop further, they will have to address the issue of cross-sectoral co-ordination. At present, there are no signs of inter-sectoral co-ordination arising. The peak associations which do exist lack the encompassing breadth of membership or the ability to initiate it, and, unlike business domains, there are no informal collectives of interests lurking behind the scenes. European-level interest representation for the professions has some way to go before it matches such sophisticated patterns.

7

Labour Interests

Labour interests throughout Europe have been heavily influenced by economic change. The increasing internationalisation of capital has posed considerable challenges to nationally based labour movements. In western Europe, labour markets have been transformed since oil price rises sent economies into free fall in the mid-1970s. These changes have led to a decline in the influence of organised labour. To a certain extent, the EU has until recently been part of the problem, although since the development of the social dialogue, and the TEU in particular, the EU level represents significant opportunities for labour interests.

The recession which followed the oil shock partly led to the renewed ability of capital to assert itself against organised labour weakened by mass unemployment (by 1993, 17 million in EU member states), and in consequence unions have enjoyed less of a central role in the operation of politics and markets than in the heyday of Keynesianism. Periods of mass unemployment do not favour union concerns with workers' rights, but rather place the emphasis on employment creation, often through the strategy of deregulation. As a strategy of recovery, political ideas and business interests have focused on economic restructuring which enabled capital to exert more control over labour market costs, and which has been directed at the reconstruction of European economies through their renewed integration based on market principles. The single market was part of the answer, and a market which therefore did not include collective bargaining and tripartism. At the European level, the desire to construct labour markets relatively free of intervention therefore precluded the involvement of labour interests, which have thus struggled to find a role in the EU.

The reconstruction of rules of market exchange has created the need to remove barriers to the free movement of workers, such as the obstacles presented by the lack of portability of pension schemes, and by the desire of some member states to 'export' their high-cost labour market regulation to ensure a level playing field in production. As is argued in this chapter, this process has to some extent developed its own momentum, such that 'social Europe' seems poised to develop beyond a simple role as an adjunct to labour market integration. For labour interests at the European level, the most positive part of rebuilding markets has been the development of a social dialogue, and it is this process which, more than anything, has led to an enhanced role for trade unions in the EU after several years in the doldrums. In consequence, the organisation of labour interests at the EU level now shows some degree of development.

The most important labour market changes since the oil crises have involved the decline in manufacturing and agricultural employment, and its partial replacement by service sector employment; and the reduction of full-time, permanent employment together with the rise of working patterns that are less secure, and typically, part-time and temporary. These changes have therefore brought a significant increase in both female employment and male unemployment (Rhodes, 1994). Service sector employment now accounts for nearly two-thirds of the European workforce. Mass postwar production with a mass, concentrated manual workforce and low unemployment had meant considerable power for labour. In consequence, therefore, a change throughout advanced economies, driven by economic, political, social and technological factors, to a more dispersed, flexible and service-based workforce, with a reserve army of the unemployed, considerably weakened the power of labour. Industrial concentration, partly driven by the single-market process itself, has also led to a loss of jobs. But at the same time, recognition of these labour market changes have helped to bring the need for regulation of them to the European level.

One set of concerns have been to ensure the harmonisation of labour conditions so that the single market operates on a level playing field, and that no country can gain advantage in seeking inward investment through cheaper labour costs. This outcome has been precisely what has happened (Chapter 5). Britain has attracted around 40 per cent of all Japanese investment in Europe by promoting itself as a cheap production centre and gateway to the single market. In 1992, advertisements in the German press advertising the virtues of Britain for industry as a low-cost production centre for location caused consternation. In contrast to the high-quality labour market conditions of the group of northern countries elsewhere round Germany (Chapter 5), in

Britain domestic politics in favour of the deregulation of production and labour market conditions have meant the removal of norms for minimum wages, attempts to deconstruct health and safety at work conditions, and resistance to a shorter working week.

British resistance to European-level labour market harmonisation has taken the form of: voting against measures or expressing reluctance through abstaining, depending upon the ability to exercise a veto; watering down Commission proposals at the Council of Ministers; questioning the legal basis of Community measures which have been proposed, to the extent of taking cases to the European Court of Justice; and, most obviously, in opting out from the Social Charter and the Social Protocol. Together, Anglo-American firms, European employers' organisations and the British government have either prevented, delayed, or significantly influenced by limiting: Commission proposals for a Fifth Company Law Directive on board-level employee participation; the 1980 Vredeling proposal on employees' rights to information; the extension of jurisdiction to cover non-EC firms; and the Directives on Working Time and on Pregnant Women (Rhodes, 1995). Perhaps most importantly from the point of view of these interests, for the reasons outlined in Chapter 5, there is only limited progress in collective bargaining at the European level, and most of the agreements made under the social dialogue to date have been voluntaristic and non-binding in nature.

A second set of concerns partly related to harmonisation have been politically driven by an interest in workers' rights and industrial democracy. Jacques Delors, the former Commission president, one time socialist minister in the French government, and trade union ally, was instrumental in the construction of social dialogue at the European level, from which there are now tangible results. Together, the conferral of macroeconomic social partner status on ETUC, the enhanced competence of the European Union in social affairs, the increased powers of the European Parliament, and the institutional relationship between the Commission, the Parliament, ECOSOC, and ETUC, have all significantly increased the effectiveness of trade union organisation and the impact of labour interests in the European Union over the past decade.

Although ETUC has largely been unable to achieve what it has sought from the European Union as a result of initiatives pursued by a combination of employers and the British government, by working together with some of its members in the member states it has been able to make a contribution to the wider European agenda in labour market fields, and, to a certain extent, to influence the character of measures which have been pursued. The tide may well be turning in its favour. Progress, albeit limited, has arisen under the social dialogue, and agreements have been concluded between the partners. The most recent of these concerned some agreement on parental leave, significantly, between all three of the first-level social partners, and seems to reflect an increasing acceptance of this channel by UNICE, which had at one time sought to prevent meaningful agreement under this mechanism. Further evidence of growing ETUC influence concerns its instrumental role in agenda setting the Pregnant Women Directive, even though it proved unable to influence its outcome. The Directive on European Information and Consultation (the European Works Council Directive), requiring the introduction of worker consultation procedures in large firms, has since (September 1994) been passed, where a predecessor initiative, the Vredeling proposals, was earlier (1980) defeated. Indeed, until a last-minute intervention by the Confederation of British Industry, agreement between the three macroeconomic partners for this scheme seemed likely (Chapter 5). The 1993 Working Time Directive (implemented in November 1996) is another which helps labour interests by providing most workers with a significant degree of protection on working hours, rest breaks and paid holidays. The passage of these illustrates that the capacity of the British government and employer interests to prevent such measures has diminished with the advent of qualified majority voting and its use in social policy fields. Indeed, previous resistance within UNICE towards bargaining now shows tangible signs of division.

The institutionalised involvement of producer interests in both the formulation and implementation of EC policy under the social dialogue (Chapter 2) has provided ETUC with a significant opportunity to expand the competence of the European Union in labour market fields. While only limited progress has arisen from agreement with UNICE (largely on uncontentious issues), ETUC's relationship with CEEP in the social dialogue has delivered more, and a number of agreements between these two have arisen. The first of these was signed in 1990. Although this was limited to sectoral training initiatives, the agenda of these have gradually expanded between the two partners. Writing in 1990, Peter Coldrick, confederal secretary of ETUC, described the relationship between the two as 'relaxed and progressing very well' (Coldrick, 1990, p. 59). Where UNICE has blocked agreement, the Commission has broken the impasse and taken measures forward, such as the Directive on Information and Consultation. Further initiatives are likely to arise from the social dialogue as a whole, which can only benefit ETUC's members.

In the northern group of countries, working conditions have on the whole been at least as good as, and sometimes better than, those proposed by Community measures. Consequently, labour interests in Germany have found little incentive to seek a transfer of competencies to the European level to improve domestic working conditions, whereas for British trade unionists the European level has been the main area within which to seek advancement of working conditions. However, the end of 'cheap talk' signalled by the TEU, and the introduction of QMV in some social fields, are important landmarks for European labour interests throughout Europe. The European Trade Union Confederation has not been a completely insignificant actor in these outcomes.

The European organisation of labour interests

Like other interests, labour concerns are represented in Europe through a number of channels. These include, where possible: domestic channels of influence where interests are incorporated into industrial and governmental decision-making; by national unions approaching the European institutions direct; and transnational channels, including cross-regional organisation of labour, and dedicated structures based in Brussels, in interaction with the supranational institutions of the Economic and Social Committee, the European Parliament and the Commission. Dedicated labour structures in Brussels include a small number of national unions with their own Brussels office; sixteen (although one is located in Geneva) sectoral transnational industry 'federations' (a name change to denote an enhanced role and status from their previous label as 'committees') and the most significant actor in European labour affairs, the ETUC.

Labour sectoral actors in Brussels

Unions with their own Brussels outreach offices include the UK Trades Union Congress, with two personnel operating from office space within ETUC, and the cross-sectoral General, Municipal and Boilermakers Union, with a one-person office. These are in no way rival structures to those of ETUC, which is, by design, by far the most important labour representative in Brussels. Neither are the sixteen industry federations. These differ vastly in their membership size, structure, strategy and potential (see Visser and Ebbinghaus, 1992). The largest have up to 130 union members (Ebbinghaus and Visser, 1996). Most have developed from structures of international sectoral unions, and/or located within these premises. Most have a very low level of resources in comparison to national sectoral unions. Typically, they have between 2 and 4 staff, although one of the better resourced organisations, the European Federation of Metalworkers, has 5 executives and 7 support staff, to take care of dedicated concerns in Europe, and for matters of participation and co-ordination with ETUC. Public-sector workers are also among the better-organised employee interests in Brussels.

Industry Federations are not designed to be self-sufficient labour representatives at the European level. Rather, they are supplementary structures to ETUC for sectoral organisations. They cannot be described as lobbying organisations, but act more as information posts, co-ordinators and structures for the Commission to consult and work with. A few have engaged in discussions, or even formed joint committees, with their sectoral industry counterpart, although these discussions have mainly been limited to the future prosperity of the sector rather than collective bargaining issues (Gorges, 1993; Cockburn, 1995). They have been most active in pursuing information and consultation rights for their members with multinational firms, where some agreements have been concluded with the industry federations as signatories, and in working with DG V, ETUC and the national unions, in the establishment of forerunner European Works Councils (Rath, 1994; Turner, 1995). Indeed, the role of the industry federations has been somewhat enhanced by the 1994 European Directive on Information and Consultation (implemented in September 1996), where they are ideally placed to co-ordinate the role of their members across countries to serve on works councils of firms who are often themselves multinationals. Some industry federations play such a central role that labour nominations for membership of works councils in some sectors have to be approved by the transnational organisation. At present more than half of all the agreements to establish works councils have been signed by trade unions, while two-thirds of all negotiated councils provide for trade unions to nominate employee representatives (*Financial Times*, 1996b).

As Lanzalaco and Schmitter (1992) predicted, works councils now offer significant prospects for developing transnationalism among labour interests because they involve 'grassroots' integration rather than relying upon top-down integration through conferring powers upon ETUC. Works councils have existed at firm level for some time prior to the 1994 directive, partly because of the strength of national unions in developing them (particularly in Germany and France), partly where national governments had supported them, and partly because the Commission has invested heavily in their establishment and development since 1991, originally through pilot schemes. Opposition from UNICE and the UK Government changed the scope of application and detail, rather than the thrust, of the draft Works Council Directive. Firms with 1000 or more employees, with plants of at least 150 workers in two or more member states or EEA countries, amounting to around 1200 companies in Europe (Marginson and Sysson, 1996) are now obliged to secure employee participation through the establishment of cross-national information committees. Typically, councils include around 25 workers, with a range from 7 to 70 (*Financial Times*, 1996b). Although experiences of the voluntary schemes prior to the directive has been mixed, the most successful examples, such as that at Volkswagen, established structures of cross-national labour organisation and dialogue with frequent meetings, ensured valuable information exchange on conditions and strategies in work plants in different countries, and produced tangible results for workers, such as shorter working hours at the SEAT plant in Spain (Turner, 1995). Ahead of the September 1996 deadline, one estimate indicated that more than 200 companies had concluded voluntary agreements to inform and consult with their employees (*Financial Times*, 1996b). Most allow for workers to meet without a management presence. A structure is now therefore in place for transnational labour activities which may well focus trade union organisation away from its largely national setting, and develop labour interest in the European level. European trade union leaders have not been slow to realise this and are now, targeting firms to monitor agreements through co-operative effort (ibid). Indeed, there is already evidence of cross-border regional co-operation in labour activities, through inter-regional trade union councils, focusing on employment-related issues concerning border areas (Rath, 1994). Around twenty of these have now emerged, and, while they presently have limited activities, they may emerge as more significant structures as European regional policy develops further, and as the Committee of the Regions finds a role (Ebbinghaus and Visser, 1994). These councils are partly integrated into ETUC's work through observer status and speaking rights at ETUC's congress meetings, held every four years. Like works councils, they offer prospects to develop grassroots integration among labour interests. Similar evidence of the development of union transnationalisation is provided by Rhodes, who found some unions developing strategic alliances across borders in Europe (Rhodes, 1991).

Although autonomous, industry federations are incorporated within the structure of ETUC. Each federation is entitled to one representative on the ETUC congress, and two where they have more than 4 million members. They have a seat, and voting rights, on all of ETUC's decision-making committees (except on financial matters, because they neither contribute to ETUC nor take funds from it). This reflects their growing importance in that, until ETUC reforms in 1991, industry federations had little more than information and consultation rights on the Executive of ETUC. In turn, their national members are also members of the national federations who constitute ETUC membership. This 'dual membership' structure has occasionally caused conflict through members being represented by different positions within their national federations, and the industry federations. Similarly, there have been tensions where ETUC has wanted to take the lead on sectoral issues. Indeed, although the relationship between the two groupings are now on the whole harmonious and resolved, the role of the industry federations within ETUC has historically been a contentious one, not least because of concern among some national confederations about the possibility of ceding some of their own power within ETUC. However, some confederations took the opposite view, and sought to incorporate them fully within ETUC structures rather than in a semi-detached role where they had become a source of criticism of ETUC, and where they might have developed into a parallel, and partly competitive, structure. This latter strategy has now been avoided by incorporation within ETUC, a move which has to some extent been a successful one for both sets, with the industry federations playing a complementary role. Both parties have agreed that in order for industry federations to be recognised by ETUC, their political and ideological standpoints must be consistent with that of ETUC. This move has suited both parties well. As the European industry federations have grown in importance, so it has been essential for ETUC not to lay down the conditions for the development of rival representative outlets in European-level labour affairs by failing to provide these organisations with enough influence in ETUC's internal structures. In turn, ETUC has become dependent upon the functional expertise of the federations (Visser and Ebbinghaus, 1992), and these organisations now have an effective voice within ETUC.

The European Trade Union Confederation

The history of European trade unionism provides some clues to its historic difficulties in collective action. Prior to the formation of ETUC in 1972, and indeed in its early years the European organisation was split between Socialist (International Confederation of Free Trade Unions – ICFTU), Christian Democratic (World Confederation of Labour – WCL), and Communist (World Federation of Trade Unions – WFTU) confederations. Thus, there are historic cleavages in European trade union organisation by function, by political affiliation and by religious orientation; indeed, there are national unions with, respectively, catholic and protestant orientations (Visser and Ebbinghaus, 1992). Further differences are between unions from different traditions, roughly split between the north and south of Europe; and between those in the member states, and those outside, including a transitional membership status for those from the former Soviet bloc. Although these cleavages have to some extent become less important within ETUC over time, they are nevertheless ever present in the background. Diversity is perhaps the most important issue in comprehending European trade union organisation. In the case of ETUC, its encompassing nature is by design rather than by default.

ETUC consists of two membership pillars. One concerns the sectoral European-level industry federations, while the second, and most important pillar, are the national federations of labour. Over time, cleverly, ETUC has incorporated the former while increasing the engagement of national confederations, partly because of the declining influence of some of these in domestic politics, and partly because some national trade union leaders have come to see the supranational level as offering a solution as social-level integration has advanced, and as labour interests have become more institutionalised in the structures of Europe. However, like UNICE, ETUC has a confederate structure, with its main membership pillar comprising national confederations who are themselves compromise-prone. Common platform building is therefore difficult because of the diversity of interests represented. The majority of ETUC's time is spent in seeking to overcome this problem, although a study of member positions and coalitions on key issues led Timmersfield to conclude that ETUC's collective action problems were insurmountable (in Turner, 1995). A further weakness it shares with UNICE is that it lacks a wide-ranging collective bargaining mandate from its members.

ETUC has 48 affiliates from 22 European countries, drawing members from a geographical area stretching from Iceland to Turkey, representing 85 per cent (46.5 million) of all unionised workers in western Europe (Leisink *et al.*, 1996). Approximately one-fifth of this membership are accounted for by the British TUC and the German DGB. With the exception only of the French Communist union, the Confédération Général du Travail (CGT), all major national labour federations in western Europe are now members of ETUC. The current position is that the CGT does not seek membership of ETUC, and nor does ETUC, or the French union federation Confédération Française Démocratique du Travail (CFDT), wish it to be a member. Some authors speculate that it cannot be long before the CGT ends its isolation and becomes a member of ETUC (Turner, 1995), because the CGT has broken its ties with the WFTU, because ETUC has accepted into membership two formerly Communist-led national federations (from Spain and Portugal) and because many delegates from industry federations work alongside CGT members on works councils. Others, however, remain sceptical, and point out that such speculation has existed since the turn of the decade (Roethig, 1995). The main sectoral absence in ETUC's membership are managerial, unionised workers who are in the main represented through CEC (Chapter 6), and CESI, the European Confederation of Independent Unions, which organises workers primarily in the public services. Although the latter has claims to represent all employees, it is around one-tenth of the size of ETUC (2 executives, 5 support staff), has no affiliates in Denmark, Greece or Ireland, and, in the words of the Commission, 'is not very significant in most other member states' in collective bargaining and formal consultation (Commission of the European Communities, 1993, annex 3, p. 5). Both CEC and CESI are 'second-level' social partners.

The size and diversity of ETUC's membership, together with its lack of a developed mandate for collective bargaining, the historic lack of pace of a social dimension in Europe, and the associated hostility of employer interests and the British government, have all combined to create a historic lack of effectiveness of ETUC in

Europe. In the early years of its formation, ETUC was only just more than a co-ordination centre for national trade union confederations to engage the European level, and it possessed nothing like the capacities of any of its members. One of its major affiliates, the British TUC, was largely opposed to European integration until as recently as 1987 (Gorges, 1996). Today, ETUC's largest affiliates still have the capacity to block major decisions proposed at congress. However, its foundation was a significant step forward, and it does represent an important structure for development. Unlike UNICE, where unanimity voting has dominated, it does possess supranational capacities through a qualified majority (two-thirds requirement) voting system. Stern has argued that 'in spite of its large membership, and to an extent because of it, ETUC has been an ineffectual organisation until quite recently. Now, however, its organisation has improved and its importance is increasing' (Stern, 1994, p. 140). Improved organisation results from a number of factors in ETUC's internal and external political environment. The first of these concerned the determination of Delors that the beneficiaries of European integration should include more than simply business elites. He is quoted as saying 'I want to make sure that the Trade Unions are written into Europe's social and economic decision-making' (Tongue, 1989, cited in Compston, 1992, p. 28).

In 1984, Delors announced that no new social policy initiatives would be undertaken unless they were sanctioned by a social dialogue between Europe's trade unions and employer organisations (Rhodes, 1995). The social dialogue was launched the following year, commencing with the 'Val Duchesse' discussions aimed at encouraging the social partners to develop fruitful dialogue at the EC level. Little progress was in fact made in the following years, largely because UNICE only participated on the basis that outputs should only be non-binding 'joint opinions', i.e. not even to the level of agreements. Nevertheless, the agenda had been set. Significantly, Delors chose the platform of an ETUC meeting in May 1988 to launch his crusade for the Community's social dimension (Story, 1996), and, with the Commission building coalition support among member states, the Social Charter was signed in 1989 by all member states with the exception of Britain. ETUC played an instrumental role in ensuring that the Commission revived the flagging social dialogue, and stood up to British objections in doing so (Story, 1996). In 1990, three joint opinions emerged by agreement between ETUC, UNICE and CEEP, on education and training, the functioning of the labour market and professional and geographic mobility, and the transition of young people into adult and working life (European Trade Union Confederation, 1991). Institutionalised labour market intervention was progressed further by the TEU, following agreement between the social partners, through delegating powers to private interests to initiate agreement through the social dialogue (Chapter 2). Although a limited degree of agreement has arisen to date, the creation of an institutionalised mechanism was a key step which shows all the signs of developing its own momentum, with both ETUC and UNICE acquiring limited collective bargaining rights from their members. The Commission has also progressed social integration, in part by pitting its wits against those of Britain in 'playing the Treaty game' by the selection of the appropriate legal basis for the introduction of measures reviewed earlier in this chapter, such as the Directives on Working Time, on Pregnant Women and on Information and Consultation (Rhodes, 1995). Towards the end of 1995 and throughout the first half of 1996, a number of initiatives arose which illustrate the increasing momentum of the social dialogue. In October 1995, the macroeconomic social partners agreed a joint declaration on national economic policies required to stimulate economic recovery, employment creation and improved competitiveness. In February 1996, the Commission began work on a communication designed to enhance the effectiveness of social dialogue. In March 1996, the Commission sought to drive the agenda forward by urging the social partners to negotiate an accord to protect the rights of workers with part-time and 'flexible' employment. In June 1996, the Commission adopted a voluntary code of practice on equal pay for equal work for those involved in collective bargaining, which was drafted in close co-operation with the macroeconomic social partners.

The Parliament has also been a strong supporter of progression of 'social Europe', although, ironically, it is partly excluded from the process because of the alternative course of action taken under the TEU. Both the Parliament and ETUC have made strong claims for the inclusion of the Parliament in the social process at the 1996 Intergovernmental Conference. If this is accepted, which now looks increasingly likely, the future for labour representation in Europe seems very bright indeed. The Parliament's present work includes a strong and effective trade union intergroup, with which ETUC meets monthly, and close connections between the majority Socialist party and European trade union leaders. ETUC has been able to table amendments in the Parliament through this route. Indeed, the relationship between these two actors is so strong that the UNICE secretary general Zygmunt Tyszkiewicz, has complained that 'ETUC has a privileged relationship with the European Parliament which shares its objectives and consistently passes resolutions by a large majority, advocating social policies that business finds unacceptable' (Stern, 1994, p. 141).

The development of 'social Europe' is a significant opportunity for labour interests, and has already exceeded the expectations of recent commentators (Visser and Ebbinghaus 1992; Streeck and Vitols, 1993; Roethig, 1995). Collective bargaining, albeit in a limited form, has now arrived at the European level, and, while integration has developed more by fits and starts than by a smooth incremental process driven by private interests, there is unquestionably a process of spillover type from the high politics of integration into functional labour market integration. Beyond the knock-on effects from the single market, Economic and Monetary Union (EMU) may lead to increased levels of harmonisation of working conditions and social partnership, because pressures upon member states to meet common convergence criteria may require labour collaboration in wage settlements in return for bargained conditions, and because a single currency would increase the transparency of comparisons in wage conditions (Coldrick, 1990; Compston, 1992).

The progressive advancement of social integration demanded adaptation from, and reform by, ETUC. It needed the ability to respond more quickly, and flexibly, to the new European agenda; and to take account of the increasing development of sectoral union organisation in Europe. A number of key reforms were therefore agreed at ETUC's seventh congress held in Luxembourg in 1991. These were based around: the dual membership pillars reviewed above; the allocation of voting rights according to size of membership; an enhancement of women's representation; the semi-incorporation of interests from central and eastern Europe; and the inter-regional trade union councils. Executive functions were split between a larger Executive, meeting less frequently (four times per year) and setting broad strategy parameters, and the insertion of a key operational tier, the 'presidium', relatively small in size with 19 members, meeting 8 times per year, with powers to take urgent decisions, and, significantly, to negotiate with employers organisations. This tier also undertakes, together with the secretariat, the work of lobbying with the institutions. Further reforms include: a strengthening of the role of the secretariat, whereby the general secretary and two deputies (of which one was an additional post created by the reforms), as well as the president, have a place and voting rights on the executive committee and the presidium; and an overall increase in staff numbers, to a total of forty-nine (Rath, 1994; Roethig, 1995). A similar total number of staff work for ETUC-related institutions, including ETUC's research and think-tank arm, the European Trade Union Institute (ETUI), formed in 1978, and the European Trade Union College, formed in 1990. As Roethig points out, this makes ETUC the European interest group with the largest staff (Roethig, 1995). Its operations are funded by contributions from the national confederations, and from the Commission. Stern estimates that the total Commission contribution to ETUC-related activities, including ETUI, the college, and cross-national meetings, amounts to around 4 million ECU each year (Stern, 1994). To be added to this figure are help with translation costs and support for pilot European works councils. Rhodes has identified the cost of this latter activity to the Commission in 1992–3 as 31 million ECU (Rhodes, 1995).

Undoubtedly, these reforms have contributed to increasing the effectiveness of ETUC, and have developed it somewhat beyond what one national union leader, characterising the pre-1991 period, described as 'a co-ordination body between national centres' (cited in Visser and Ebbinghaus, 1992, p. 223). However, the reforms have not completely overcome its problems, and they fall some way short of the creation of a supranational organisation. Much of the responsibility for policy-making still resides in the affiliates, rather than the secretariat. Its 8 standing committees and 6 working groups (covering areas such as women, youth, energy, education and training) meet too infrequently to be of sufficient value (only twice yearly), are too large and unwieldy, comprise officials of insufficient standing, and lack co-ordination. Departments are over-reliant upon the competency of their respective leadership, and there is a lack of co-ordination between them (Roethig, 1995). Labour organisation as a whole is over-reliant upon ETUC to directly engage the European level, which means that its resources are too thinly spread. Indeed, for the range of tasks it undertakes it is a relatively under-resourced organisation. Affiliates commit only a fraction of their resources to ETUC, typically well under 5 per cent. Above all, the reforms have done little to overcome ETUC's basic problem of diversity, and its federal structure makes it too unwieldy. Reflecting on ETUC's failure to get what it sought from the Pregnant Women Directive, Pedler comments that 'the Federal structure of ETUC was too unwieldy to transmit a clear and consistent message at the key moments and in the key places around the EU' (Pedler, 1994, p. 257).

This case is instructive of ETUC's problems, because although it had the ability to agenda set the issue with the Commission, it was unable to secure what it sought in later stages of the policy process, and the final result represented an advance from the position in only a very few countries. Because ETUC's membership is diverse, common positions, despite the reforms, are still too prone to compromise and relatively meaningless lowest-common-denominator positions. Thus, apart from the social dialogue, ETUC's recent work has tended to be focused on areas which are relatively uncontentious for its members. This includes policies to combat racial discrimination, promotion of the shorter working week, education and training initiatives, safety at work, and measures to assist the disabled and young unemployed to enter the labour market. Roethig argues that

> The outcome is often incoherent, reflecting the disparities within the trade union movement, but also being vague enough to allow everybody to agree and to interpret policies according to their own needs. As a result, the ETUC as a whole is able to project a common approach to the outside world while everyone, secretariat and affiliates, is left with the opportunity to work through its own channels and thus to maximise its individual impact on the EU policy-making process . . . in the end, everyone has to rely on their own strength. The ETUC is not a means to overcome an affiliate's domestic weakness (Roethig, 1995, p. 277).

Similarly, Visser and Ebbinghaus describe ETUC as 'united, yet fragmented, and with little internal cohesion' (1992, p. 222). It has a limited bargaining mandate from its members, and cannot influence the positions of national confederations, who are free to ignore the stances taken by ETUC. A great deal of reliance is placed upon national organisations to influence the positions taken by their domestic governments in the Council of Ministers. ETUC considers, for instance, that what success it did have in the passage of the Pregnant Women Directive arose in no small measure from the influence exerted by Italian member unions on their government (Pedler, 1994). On the whole, the governments of Germany and France have been most supportive of trade union concerns in the Council of Ministers. ETUC's work, however, is limited to addressing the European level. Only once has ETUC visited the national governments, prior to the Maastricht summit. Indeed, the role of

ETUC has historically been a contentious one among its members, with some affiliates preferring a simple co-ordination function which does not infringe upon their own activities, while others have sought a more supranational role. Thus, for the present, some national confederations are unwilling to see ETUC develop beyond its present role into a more powerful supranational actor, and will not, or cannot, commit the resources to enable it to so develop. For some national trade union confederations, there is more on offer at home than in Brussels. In most member states, for instance, there was little interest among labour-affiliated women's organisations in the Pregnant Women Directive, because they could not see how it would improve their national position (Pedler, 1994).

Although the European level represents few prospects for enhancement of labour conditions in the northern countries grouped round Germany (Chapter 5), the perspective among labour interests from these member states has been to progress 'social Europe' for fear of competitive losses through 'social dumping'. Indeed, it was a German presidency in the late 1980s which did much to progress the agenda for social Europe at a critical juncture in its development. The alliance between Chancellor Kohl and the German DGB provided crucial support in this promotion (Story, 1996), thereby illustrating the extent to which labour issues at the European level have very much been in the hands of national, rather than European-level, labour representatives. Despite the DGB being potentially the most important ETUC member, the participation of German trade union interests in ETUC has at best been patchy. It has been over reliant upon its *de facto* veto, and has paid little attention to alliance-building within ETUC. Rather, it is more of a singular actor, being outside the main alliance blocks (Roethig, 1994). One leading German trade union official never once attended an executive meeting on which he held a seat. The German DGB is strong, well resourced, and has a tendency to see Europe as an additional arena which can be adequately dealt with through the national environment (Roethig, 1994). The DGB, through its incorporation in decision-making in the social market economy in Germany, is able to secure its needs adequately at the domestic level. For British labour interests, however, the European level represents the only prospect of advancement because of their exclusion from domestic politics. Ron Todd the then general secretary of the Transport and General Workers' Union, told delegates at the organisation's 1988 conference 'The only card game in town at the moment is in a town called Brussels, and it is a game of poker where we have got to learn the rules and learn them fast' (Trades Union Congress, 1988, p. 572).

For British interests, the presence of ETUC, together with their own, more limited approaches to the European institutions, and their relationship with the European Parliamentary Labour Party, represent the only opportunities to exert influence in Europe. Indeed, in a number of countries the power of labour interests has been eroded at the national level, which, in turn, may help develop supranationality among labour interests at the European level. In some other countries, particularly those in the south of Europe where trade union incorporation into domestic politics has sometimes been weak, the European level represents significant new opportunities to develop their interests. For some national confederations, membership of ETUC also strengthens its role *vis-à-vis* its national members, because it provides the main route for them to address the European level.

The social dialogue may eventually develop ETUC into a truly supranational body, particularly as it is now part of the legal structures of the European Union. As it develops, the opportunities presented by the social dialogue may increasingly attract labour interests away from their national capitals. But, for the moment, some authors do not consider that ETUC yet merits application of the 'supranational' label (Roethig, 1995; Visser and Ebbinghaus, 1992). Roethig suggests that

> it is an instrument for assisting its national affiliates in influencing EU policy-making either through its own intervention, or through posing as a framework for co-operation between affiliates aimed at opening opportunities in other national subnetworks for particular national trade union interests (1994, p. 7).

The role of ETUC is thus one of taking centre stage in addressing the European level. Because the European level is its remit, ETUC has come to be a strong supporter of European integration, particularly over the last decade. Most of its members now share this perspective, although this is a relatively recent phenomenon for some. A strong value system therefore prevails among labour interests networking at the European level in favour of further integration, although sometimes for different reasons. For British and southern labour interests, the EU level therefore represents the chance to secure what they have not been able to obtain at home, whereas for German interests the EU level represents an opportunity to prevent hardship at home by ensuring labour market standards match their own. Belief systems to guide action are thus variable, and the fragility of the value system is likely to be tested by future demands exerted by the development of the social dialogue. However, together with the Commission, ETUC does share an interest in the development of European rules.

The promotion of positions within the European institutions on which ETUC's members can agree has proved somewhat more fruitful than the more difficult task of extending further platform-building among these members. ETUC has therefore sought to clearly define its role by seeking to address those issues which cannot be effectively pursued at the national level, and for which the European level is the most appropriate. This includes the special transnational issues for labour raised by the single market, such as the mobility of workers, the transfer of undertakings within public services, and industrial democracy issues raised by the transnational organisation of capital. It has also sought to develop a leadership role on more recent political concerns, such as environmental matters and the position of women in the workplace and in society (Leisink *et al.*, 1996). These authors therefore classify ETUC as

> principally . . . a lobbyist movement aimed at exerting some influence on the institutional decision-making process at Community level and at influencing the choices of its political actors such as the Commission, the European Parliament, and the Economic and Social Committee (1996, p. 258).

ETUC enjoys variable influence within the Commission. On the one hand, a number of Commission services are employer-orientated, although even the most important of these, DG III, does consult unions on a sectoral basis (Compston, 1992). On the other, it enjoys a range of formal and informal influences within the Commission. ETUC officials meet several times a year with the president of the Commission, with individual commissioners, and, periodically, the entire College of Commissioners. Individuals who are union allies are liberally sprinkled throughout the Commission (Turner, 1995). It therefore has access to early information about Commission proposals. It is well connected with the trade union unit within DG X (information, communication, culture, audio-visual), and in DG XVI (Regional Policies and Cohesion). But easily its best relations are with

DG V, where it enjoys insider status to the extent that one member of the Delors cabinet has described the Commission service as a 'union lobbying organisation, old style' (Ross, 1994, p. 507). This partnership was responsible for agenda setting the initiative on European Works Councils. Because UNICE is a reluctant partner, ETUC can often enjoy monopolistic access to public policies through this route. At times, however, as the Pregnant Women Directive showed, ETUC has been over-reliant upon its agenda-setting capabilities with the Commission, and finds itself unable to exert influence at later stages of the policy process. This over-reliance means also that it has not fully developed alliances with actors in a position to share interests. A case in point here concerned the Parental Leave Directive, the first accord to be negotiated under the Social Protocol, where some of the groups representing the professions acted alone in seeking to exert influence in favour of employee interests (Chapter 6).

ETUC is a fully institutionalised actor within the ESC, where Group II (workers) accounts for one-third of its members (Chapter 2). Although this represents an obvious channel of influence, possibilities are restricted in a number of ways. First, worker members are nominated by national governments and not by ETUC. Although there is considerable co-ordination by and with ETUC, labour interests are partly divided. Thus, the French Communist union CGT voted against other labour interests, and with the British government, in opposing the Delors social affairs package in 1989. Second, requirements for majority voting means that worker interests have to seek support from other groups. Third, the ESC is consulted relatively late in the decision-making process. Fourth, as was described in Chapter 2, the institution itself lacks weight, and what influence it may once have had has been steadily on the decline (Compston, 1992).

Conclusions

Although the development of social Europe is important for labour interests, it does not compensate for any loss of influence at the domestic level. Firstly, under the TEU, policies are to be implemented by national collective bargaining. As Rhodes has pointed out, this will prove the source of a great deal of unevenness and diversity across member states. For instance, Denmark requires ratification of collective agreements by vote of union members, while Belgium, France and Spain impose conditions on the representativeness of worker organisations. In the UK, the problem of the derecognition of trade unions, coupled with the lack of provision to extend agreements to non-unionised workers, will create difficulties in bringing agreements made at the European level to benefit workers at member state level (Rhodes, 1995).

The real problem for labour interests, however, remains the unfavourable conditions at the European level for the development of significant collective bargaining. Both ETUC and UNICE have rather limited mandates from their members to engage in collective bargaining, and UNICE remains opposed, in principle at least, to any significant form of binding collective agreement. There is no binding, European-level legal provision for the enforcement of collective agreements, and employer organisations continue in their determination not to replace agreements once made at the national level with full collective bargaining at the European level. Wage bargaining at the European level is not even on the distant horizon, and, even if it were, the ability of European trade unions to unite behind a common strategy is highly dubious. Most of ETUC's confederal members are not endowed by their own members with bargaining powers. As the social dialogue develops, so the ability of ETUC members to agree meaningfully will be seriously called into question, and the fragile harmony which at present prevails between ETUC members might collapse. Furthermore, there is no European law in the field of industrial action, and there are no signs of transnational union mass industrial action (Rath, 1994; Turner, 1995).

In 1992, Visser and Ebbinghaus concluded a review of labour interests at the European level by judging that this level did not, at that time, replace what had been lost at the national level. That judgement, by and large, continues to hold in 1996. Labour markets at the European level represent considerable high politics. The nature of high politics is such that it tends to involve competitive politics, and labour interests have struggled to find the capacities to match the players against which it is ranged. Labour interests can never expect to exert monopolistic influence in European public policies.

Yet the increased pace and depth of market integration at the European level has undoubtedly led to the creation of an agenda in the labour market field. As Armingeon argues from a review of national experiences, the development of the social dialogue may not ultimately depend upon the ability of trade union organisations to resolve their diversity problems (Armingeon, 1994). The agenda of today demands that the benefits of Europe extend beyond business interests, and in doing so provides a window of opportunity for labour interests. 'Social Europe' is no longer just about preventing unfair competition by uneven labour markets. DG V has recently (March 1996) released a controversial report rejecting the link between deregulation and employment creation which has informed much of European thinking in the 1980s and 1990s. Although the report was predictably rebutted by the UNICE secretary general, Zygmunt Tyszkiewicz, he did qualify his criticism by remarking that 'we must stress that we don't want to get rid of all regulation. What we need is re-regulation' (*European Voice*, 1996a, p. 2). Commissioner Flynn has continually emphasised in speeches throughout 1996 that Europe cannot progress without further social protection to oil the wheels of change and in another measure is now seeking to extend working consultation to firms with as few as 50 employees. Commission President Santer is presently seeking to balance monetary and financial issues at the present IGC with social aspects and a drive against unemployment, where the emphasis is as much upon public spending and investment in the labour market than in deregulating it. As experience with social Europe suggests, there really is no such thing as 'cheap talk' (Cram, 1993).

Labour interests now play an institutionalised role in the development of social Europe, and have demonstrated their ability to set issues on its agenda. The development of works councils illustrates the extent to which labour interests can achieve solutions to problems which could not be obtained by action elsewhere through acting at the European level; unions had been struggling unsuccessfully since the 1970s to influence multinational companies and address the globalisation of capital. Although there is nothing resembling a European mass labour movement, the development of works councils does provide tangible benefits at the grassroots level to worker interests. The internal market does create problems which cannot be dealt with at the national level, and trade unions have found something of added value at the European level.

Roethig remarks that the European division of the British Trade Union Congress is the only section of that organisation with a positive view of the future (Roethig, 1994). Trade unions across Europe have lost members, power and influence at the domestic level. While the European level does not replace this, it does partly compensate for it, and the increasing development of social Europe offers some bright prospects for labour interests. Leisink *et al.* remark that 'in 1995, the ETUC stands at a turning point in its history' (1996, p. 265), while Lecher suggests that its present structure does not preclude it from developing into a centre with powers as important as national confederations. Turner equally suggests that it is now developing into a supranational force. A combination of the development of the European political and economic environment, the development of the social dialogue, and the ability of ETUC to manage the diversity of its membership, may well result in such an outcome in the years ahead.

8

Public Interests

Taken as a whole, non-producer interests have become increasingly visible at the European level over the past decade, and undoubtedly play a greater role in European public affairs than was the case only a decade ago. Difficulty in ratifying the TEU in the member states was widely attributed to the remoteness of the European agenda from European citizens. 'Democratic deficit' (Chapter 1) has been a major concern throughout European politics in recent years, and a context for public interest politics to develop. It has been consistently used by the Parliament as a basis to claim further powers in European policy-making. The Commission and the Council have vied with one another to demonstrate their democratic credentials, and have sought to establish mechanisms for openness and transparency in decision-making (Chapter 2). In particular, the Commission, the most vulnerable of these institutions to the charge of remoteness, has engaged in a wide-ranging programme to explain the benefits of EU membership to citizens.

Interest groups have always been central to the Commission's attempts to overcome democratic deficit (Chapter 1) and to progress European integration (Chapter 10), and the Commission provides a range of incentives to groups to operate as representative structures (Chapter 3). Among public interests, it was mainly consumer groups which formed distinct European-level entities during the first decade of the European Economic Community. Today, the Commission provides significant funding for the development of a wide variety of European-level groups. Evidence from a sample of these (Chapter 1) suggests that some 59 per cent (45) of European-level public-interest groups receive European funding. The Commission also hands out places on its advisory groups to European-level groups first; only rarely are places allocated to national level groups. Most recently, public-interest groups have also been identified as

177

strategically important to the success of the 'Citizens First' campaign of 1996 (Chapter 6).

Public-interest European groups, concerned with public goods, can be roughly split into three categories, namely environmental, consumer, and the broadest of all, civil/social groups. These are considered in turn within this chapter. Despite variations in collective action and influence in public affairs, there are a number of similarities across the range of public-interest groups. While organising individuals is far more difficult than organising firms, many European-level public-interest groups are federations of organisations, and the ratio of federated to direct membership structures (two-thirds : one-third) for public-interest groups is very similar to that of business groups. Using the typology developed in Chapter 1, many public-interest groups cannot match the key power and associational resources of some producer interests with which to influence public policies. Many public-interest groups find their key concerns contested by producer (and, in particular, business) interests, although it is rarely as straightforward as analogies of 'opposing camps' might suggest; indeed, there are some key alliances between producer and non-producer interests in a range of public-affairs domains. Many public-interest groups find it difficult to remain involved throughout the policy cycle, from agenda-setting through to implementation, in the same way as some business interests are (Paterson, 1991).

For many public groups, the key issue is to ensure that potentially opposing interests do not have monopolistic access to the public-affairs domains which concern them. Some public-interest groups therefore seek to politicise issues, or to build upon their prior politicisation by public opinion, in order to make them accessible to input from a wide range of actors. Environmental issues, for instance, by and large, have mostly entered the arena of 'high politics', and public-interest groups both reflect, and are reinforced by, key public-opinion concerns. Indeed, public-interest groups are far from powerless in European public affairs. Some have demonstrated the ability to work together more cohesively than some producer interests, and many have become skilled at coalition-building. As is evidenced in this chapter, some have impressively resourced Brussels offices, in some cases with more staff than many business interest groups. Some public-interest groups have become institutionally involved in European public affairs, either as 'specialist' or 'peripheral' insider groups (Chapter 1). Most find the EP a receptive channel for their concerns. And today there is a culture within the Commission of deliberately seeking out the views of public-interest groups, and of attempting to create a level playing field for interest representation between public, and business, interests (Chapter 4).

As Table 3.1 suggests (Chapter 3), over one Euro group in five are public-interest groups, spanning consumer, environmental, citizen and social interests. Although these have a later period of formation than do business groups, the majority of a sample of public-interest groups had already formed by the single-market period (Table 8.1); however, as the same table shows, a majority of these interest groups only came to Brussels after conception of the single-market initiative.

Table 8.2 examines the size of the secretariat in a sample of public-interest groups, while Table 8.3 examines the turnover of these groups. These indicate a picture of a core of relatively well-resourced groups, and, at the upper end, it is interesting to note that higher proportions of public-interest groups have more than five staff, and a turnover in excess of 100 000 ECU, than do the more numerous business groups (Chapter 5).

Despite these surprisingly high levels of resourcing of public-interest groups, most find themselves having to use their resources across a wide range of fronts, and encounter some of the better-resourced sectoral business groups with specialist officials whose work is dedicated to some of the key concerns of public interest. This is most obvious in the case of environmental domains.

TABLE 8.1

**A sample of European-level public-interest groups:
periods of formation and Brussels establishment**

Period	Establishment		Location in Brussels	
	N	%	*N*	%
Pre-ECSC (pre-1950)	6	8	0	0
ECSC to pre-treaty of Rome (1950–5)	1	1	0	0
Treaty of Rome to de Gaulle crisis (1956–65)	8	10	4	7
'Eurosclerosis' (1966–83)	27	35	13	22
Single market (1984–92)	27	35	31	53
1992–1995	8	10	10	17
Total	77	100	58	100

Source: survey by author, February 1996.

TABLE 8.2

A sample of European-level public-interest groups: size of secretariat

Number of staff	N	%
0	7	9
1 to 1.5	5	6
2 to 2.5	16	20
3 to 3.5	7	8
4	4	5
5	6	7
6 to 10	16	20
Over 11	21	26
Total	82	100

Source: survey by author, February 1996.

TABLE 8.3

Turnover of a sample of European-level public-interest groups

Turnover (ecu)	N	%
0 to 20 000	6	10
20 001 to 50 000	8	14
50 001 to 100 000	7	12
Over 100 000	38	64
Total	59	100

Source: survey by author, February 1996.

Environmental interests

Environmental issues have assumed increasing importance in European public affairs. Axelrod, an American author, comments that the EU's environmental policies are the most advanced in the world, such that it has become a world leader in the domain (Axelrod, 1990). A number of factors explain the EU's activism. One is that environmental issues represent an opportunity for the Commission and Parliament to expand their fields of competence. A second is that environmental issues are now a central public interest concern throughout member states, and tend to be highly politicised. Thus, a Eurobarometer survey in 1989, the year the Green parties achieved unprecedented support in EP elections, making them the fourth largest party, indicated that 94 per cent of member state citizens thought environmental issues to be a key concern for them in public affairs, second only to unemployment (Axelrod, 1990). This concern manifests itself most obviously in Germany (where concern grew following reports of acidification damage to forests in the 1970s), Denmark and the Netherlands (with concerns about rising sea-level), where member state governments reflect domestic political pressures by seeking high environmental protection standards at the European level. Public concern on the international stage was also partly responsible for a 'landmark' summit held in Stockholm in 1972, a point from which European-level environmental policies developed with a series of 'environmental action programmes'. Because pollution does not respect national boundaries, international arenas have long been popular as the appropriate level to address the problem. The same Eurobarometer survey already referred to found that 64 per cent of member state citizens thought that environmental problems were best addressed at the EC level. Market behaviour by some citizens now displays significant green motives. Business has not been slow to acknowledge these concerns, and many firms have sought to advance their green credentials, both through product development and marketing, and by promoting a 'green corporate citizen' image. Some seek endorsement of their products from public-interest environmental representatives. Some firms have developed significant in-house environmental steering committees (Grant, 1993a).

A third factor explaining the growth of EU competencies in environmental issues concerns the development of the single market. Environmental issues were notably absent in the Cecchini assessment on the costs of 'non-Europe' (Cecchini, 1988). This deficit was filled by a 1989 high-level taskforce report, which argued that economic growth and environmental protection went hand in hand, and fitted with European product strategy in competing on the global stage by product quality. A broad consensus has emerged around this view, shared by many member state governments, Commission leaders, officials and parliamentarians, and representatives of business and public-interest environmental groups. The Environmental Fifth Action Programme (1992–7), by some way the most significant and far-reaching of the programmes to date, follows this thinking with its emphasis upon 'sustainability'. The number of environmental directives in the period from 1989–91 exceeded those of the preceding twenty years (Young, 1995), while DG XI (Environment, Nuclear Safety and Civil Protection) has grown in size from 55 staff in 1986 to

450 in 1992 (Weale and Williams, 1994). For some business interests and member states, however, the main economic linkage has been the possibility that differential environmental standards across the EU would constitute a barrier to trade. If Germany, Denmark and the Netherlands, for instance, imposed higher costs upon its producers in conforming to environmental regulation than exists elsewhere, firms primarily based in those countries would face competitive losses.

The Single European Market was therefore the first formal recognition of environmental policy in European policy-making. The TEU added to the environmental competencies of the EU. Environmental action can now proceed by reference to the single market, through Article 100a; or, following the TEU, by reference to Articles 129, 129a or d, or Articles 130r, s and t. Articles 100a, 129, 129a and d, and 130s(3), involve the Parliament fully in co-decision, whereas Article 130s(1) limits the Parliament's influence to co-operation procedure, or, in the case of 130s(2), to consultation only. Interests seeking higher standards therefore prefer the use of articles involving a higher degree of EP involvement (most notably those related to the single market, centred around Article 100a), and the choice of article therefore conditions the nature of interest representation. Those seeking lower standards advocate use of provisions under Article 130, or argue that subsidiarity concerns should prevail. Southern member states, in particular, led by Spain, have often argued that they are unable to meet the high costs of measures proposed by the Commission on northern member states (Cini *et al.*, 1994). Article 130 does not, however, prevent an individual member state from imposing higher standards, whereas regulation linked to the single market involving use of Article 100a imposes consistent standards to prevent barriers to trade being erected. Unsurprisingly, there have been a number of legal battles concerning the use of these instruments in the ECJ. The Commission took the Council to court over the latter's use of Article 130 provisions for a directive to limit pollution from the titanium dioxide sector, successfully arguing that the legal basis should have been Article 100a. In another move, DG III, spurred by multinational firm action, was the main influence behind the Commission's decision to refer to the ECJ the 'Danish bottles case' (Cini *et al.*, 1994), arguing that insistence on use of returnable bottles constituted a barrier to trade. Although the Court took the view that the system did constitute a minor trade barrier, it upheld the right of

Denmark to continue with the scheme on the grounds that the major purpose of the scheme concerned environmental protection. This important precedent emphasised the importance of environmental issues *per se* in European public policy, and established some degree of independence for environmental considerations from those of the single market. However, each case is taken on its merits, involving the extent to which a barrier to trade arises and the degree to which environmental protection is the main issue. The frequent use of Article 100a emphasises the extent to which environmental measures arise from the need to harmonise market conditions.

These factors mean that environmental policy has now come to be seen as fundamental to the sound development of the Community (Liefferink *et al.*, 1993). The multifarious nature of the influences behind the development of European environmental policy dictate that a wide range of actors seek to exert influence, and that the field as a whole has entered the high politics arena. Pluralistic patterns of interest intermediation can therefore be expected, with multiple arenas and multiple players. This is indeed the conclusion reached by Arp, in a study of car emissions standards regulation (Arp, 1991). However, of the main influences, economic motives seem to provide the most important authority behind the development of European environmental policy (Butt Philip, 1995; Cini *et al.*, 1994; Machmer, 1995; Porter, 1994; Weale and Williams, 1994).

Environmental issues are therefore far from being a simple contest between green citizen interests on the one hand and firms reluctant to meet the costs of compliance of environmental regulation on the other. Similarly, the strength of the linkages between economic and environmental issues predict that business interests are likely to be both active and influential in the field, and to use their superior resources to good effect. The international character of some industries has led them to seek international solutions (Paterson, 1991). These deductions, i.e. multifarious interest representation, but with economic interests predominating, is, indeed, what a number of authors have found. In a detailed study of the packaging and packaging waste directive, Porter found that in the three-year period 1990–3 some 279 lobbying entities contacted the Commission over the issue. Over 70 per cent (70.1 per cent) of these representations came from trade and industry sources; 15.8 per cent from government departments, politicians, and regional authorities; 8.2 per cent from research institutes; and 5.7 per cent from environmentalists consumers, and trade unions. Environmental interests were simply swamped by those from business (EEB, 1994). Consequently, the balance of this directive reflected more the interests of business than those of others, and business interests were able to exert key influence in amending drafts of the Directive (Porter, 1994). These balances of influences led Butt Philip to conclude that DG XI had been persuaded to work more towards an agenda that is acceptable to industry and commerce (Butt Philip, 1995). Indeed, although most business interests align themselves with the 'towards sustainability' slogan of the Fifth Action Programme, Butt Philip (1995) makes the point that the benefits to firms of enhancing their environmental credentials by adopting the rhetoric of EU environmental policies exceeds the relatively low costs for them of compliance and participation.

Significantly affected business sectors, such as the chemicals association CEFIC, with a secretariat of 80, and the ability to draw on the resources of 4000 personnel in expert committees (Chapter 3), can devote far more resources to environmental affairs than public-interest environmental groups can muster. It has intensive relationships throughout the Commission, including with DG XI (Paterson, 1991). The oil industry has a specialist Brussels trade association, the Oil Companies European Organisation for Environmental and Health Protection (CONCAWE), with thirteen staff, dedicated to environmental issues (Young, 1995). Other sectoral trade associations with significant interests in environmental affairs, such as those for automobiles, biotechnology, pharmaceuticals and agribusiness, sometimes have staff seconded to work permanently on environmental affairs, supplemented by the resources of multinational firms. Business interests have also demonstrated the ability to build effective issue coalitions when the need arises, including a number of business interest formal groups (of which some were formed in direct response to the packaging and waste packaging directive) and forums in packaging, waste management, and recycling. In comparison, public-interest environmental groups tend to be poorly resourced (Rucht, 1993). Rucht has dubbed the main civic interlocutor group, the EEB, an 'incoherent umbrella group' (Rucht, 1993, p. 88). The Brussels office Director of the World Wide Fund for Nature (WWF) recently reflected that 'in general the environmental organisations are unable to exercise power' (Long, 1995, p. 678). This view is worth evaluating more closely, starting with an examination of the public-interest environmental groups active in Brussels.

TABLE 8.4

The Brussels offices of environmental groups (April 1996)

Organisation; year of establishment of Brussels office	Staff	Core funding sources	Offices elsewhere?
European Environmental Bureau (EEB); 1974	11	Commission, national governments	No. Federated structure (136 organisations in 25 countries).
World Wide Fund for Nature (WWF); 1989	8	Commission, national and international WWF	Yes. Brussels office is policy office.
Transport and Environment (T&E); 1992	1.5	Commission, national members	No. Federated structure (27 organisations in 16 countries).
Birdlife International; 1993	2	Commission, partner organisations	Yes.
Greenpeace; 1988	4	International organisation	Yes. Brussels office is policy office.
Friends of the Earth (FoE); 1989	8	Commission, international organisation	Yes. Brussels office is policy office.
Climate Network Europe; 1989	2	Commission, network partner organisations, trusts	Yes. Brussels HQ and policy office.

Sources: European Environmental Bureau (1996a); Webster (1997).

Environmental public-interest groups

Table 8.4 details the Brussels offices of environmental groups, who collectively are known as the 'Group of Seven' (G7), although there is no formal membership organisation comprising them. Apart from some tensions surrounding the position of the EEB, described below, and despite significant differences in style, relationships between them are collaborative and well co-ordinated, with an unwritten agreement to divide their resources such that each specialises on particular environmental issues most central to their own remit. The range of issues they address can be classified under a number of headings constituting a variety of environmental 'threats' in the EU. These are matters concerned with air, water, soil, waste, the quality of life and high-risk activities such as nuclear power, the chemical industry, the transport of hazardous substances and genetic engineering (Axelrod, 1990). Co-ordination is particularly good between a core 'Gang of Four', comprising the EEB, FoE, WWF and Greenpeace, the best-resourced of the seven. These meet together every six to eight weeks for purposes of information swapping and co-ordination, and, on an annual basis, with the president of the Commission. Greenpeace takes the lead on issues of industrial and domestic waste, and marine life, FoE on matters concerning central and eastern Europe, the WWF on environmental concerns arising from the structural funds and the EEB on environmental standards issues, such as car emissions and water quality (Long, 1995). This division is not intended to be exclusive. Some of the other three actors in the G7 also make a significant contribution to a number of these areas. Birdlife International, for instance, works on a broad range of issues, including agricultural policy, coastal issues, marine life and the structural funds. A number of organisations join with Climate Action Network in working on CO_2 emissions, and renewable energies.

The EEB was formed in 1974, thereby predating the formation of most European environmental policies. As is discussed in Chapters 9 and 10, interests do not simply come to Brussels in response to Euro competencies. A significant influence concerns the behaviour of the European institutions, including their encouragement to interests to operate at the European level. In 1992, DG XI spent 6.5 million ECU on non-governmental organisations (NGOs) (Rucht, 1993), rising to 7 million by 1994 (European Environmental Bureau, 1994). The EEB receives around half of its total funding from the European institutions, of which the majority is accounted for by a core grant from DG XI, in 1995, of 409 477 ECU (European Environmental Bureau, 1996a). The EEB has been used by the Commission as its main interlocutor across the range of environmental interests, and has institutionalised its presence across a range of advisory committee structures. Apart from meetings with the Presidents of the Commission and the Council, the EEB was a member of the Commission delegation at the 1992 Earth Summit in Rio (European Environmental Bureau, 1996a), and in 1994, it was an observer at a Council of Environmental Ministers meeting (Bursens, 1996).

The EEB occupies a particularly problematic position among the G7. Until the late 1980s, the EEB was the sole representative of public-interest environmental concerns with a Brussels presence.

However, the growth of EU activism in the environmental domain, together with the difficulties faced by EEB in representing the broad constituency of environmental interests and in reaching meaningful agreement between the interests within it, and the ease of access to EU funding, meant that other actors began to set up camp in Brussels. With 136 member organisations (including 8 corresponding members) in 25 countries (EEB, 1996b), ranging from the Czech Academy of Sciences and the Romanian Rhododendron Club, through to Friends of the Earth (FoE) regional branches, and 'establishment' organisations such as the Town and Country Planning Association and the Council for the Protection of Rural England, the EEB has suffered from the classic incoherence inherent in federated, peak umbrella organisations. This partly accounts for a reactive, rather than proactive, approach (Grant, 1993b). Among the diversity of membership, Rucht draws attention to the contrast between the radicalism of German members and the moderation of those from Britain (Rucht, 1993). This diversity is clearly a weakness, but its breadth of constituency is also a strength, and provides it with recognition from the Commission as the most encompassing of all European-level environmental NGOs, and the status of institutionalised interlocutor. Indeed, it is networked with over 200 NGOs through the Centre for Our Common Future, in Geneva (Kamorotos, 1992), and has developed a wide-ranging set of institutional contacts (Bursens, 1996).

These strengths apart, the EEB also has some problems of style. Like some other organisations, it tends to exaggerate its membership; Rucht estimates that member organisations represent around 8.5 million individuals, rather than the 11 million presently claimed by EEB, and the 15 to 20 million claimed in 1992 (Rucht, 1993; European Environmental Bureau, 1996a). The Chairman of the EP Environment Committee, Ken Collins, has drawn attention to problems of presentation; 'instead of making it short and snappy they go in for awfully wearisome and hectoring briefings. Effective lobbying is about being selective with information' (*Financial Times*, 1994). EEB also does not make the best use of the expertise available to it, in that its expert groups meet little more than once a year. Many commentators take the view that the influence of the EEB, although never particularly strong, has been in steady decline since the establishment of a Brussels presence from other environmental NGOs. The EEB has not always welcomed the leadership the latter have sometimes given on particular environmental issues, largely because it seeks to be the lead actor in the domain, although it is often regarded as one of the less influential among the G7 (Rucht, 1993; *Financial Times*, 1994; Young, 1995). This is somewhat ironic, in that it is unique among the G7 in being established with the sole intention of influencing the European institutions (European Environmental Bureau, 1994). However, a programme of restructuring initiatives undertaken in 1995 may make it a more effective organisation. These include: the establishment of the European Environmental Foundation (EEF) as an association of individual members wishing to support EEB activities; an annual conference of NGOs; enlargement of the Executive; and the launch of a Technical Bureau responsible for standardisation issues (European Environmental Bureau, 1996a).

The WWF, and the Birdlife International network, have come in for particular praise from a number of institutional figures, including Ken Collins (mentioned above), and Ann Robinson, head of policy at the UK Institute of Directors (*Financial Times*, 1994). The WWF, the world's largest and best-established conservation organisation (founded in 1961, 28 national organisations, 1500 staff; Long, 1995) has something of an establishment image, with the Duke of Edinburgh as its president. Occasionally, its establishment links means that it is compromised; indeed, it was noticeably slow to join calls for bans on the ivory trade (*Financial Times*, 1994). While diplomatic in style and highly respected, it has resorted to the European Court of Justice where necessary, such as joining the National Trust of Ireland in seeking to prevent the Irish government from proceeding with controversial plans for a visitor centre in an environmentally sensitive area. Besides using established channels such as the national delegation offices in Brussels, it also makes use of classic 'outsider' tactics such as mass-membership letter-writing campaigns. Among the successes it claims are the incorporation of many of its demands in 1993 Commission proposals concerning the structural funds (Long, 1995) and ensuring compliance by contractors for the protection of habitat in the construction of a major bridge in Portugal (European Voice, 1996b). Birdlife International works in a very similar way to WWF, and has attracted a number of admirers in the European institutions; Gardner, for instance, documents its close involvement with an EC Directive on the Conservation of Wild Birds (Gardner, 1991).

Friends of the Earth and Greenpeace work in different ways to these two organisations. Whereas WWF and Birdlife are seen as 'light' green, FoE and Greenpeace are more 'medium to dark' green.

FoE, whose aims extend beyond the environmental domain into areas such as the achievement of social, economic and political justice, emphasises strong dialogue, but from the point of view of conviction. It has a reputation as a valuable contributor of information, and, despite its mass membership base (600 000 people in 26 European countries; Harvey, 1995), has concentrated rather more on the Commission and the Parliament. Like WWF and Birdlife, it has acquired a number of admirers in the Brussels and Strasbourg communities. At one point in the mid-1980s, using the name Co-ordination Européenne des Amis de la Terre (CEAT) to give its European operation some distinctiveness from its international structures, it sought to establish a rival cross-sectoral organisation to the EEB, seeking to attract direct-action-oriented groups. This name remains in use by FoE, although the idea of a rival organisation never came to fruition after EEB proposed greater co-ordination between the 'Gang of Four'. Greenpeace is perhaps the most aggressive (and most guarded in providing information about itself to outsiders) of the G7, geared to direct-action campaigns and boycotts, although it has also learnt how to interact with the European institutions. However, its Brussels office has been the subject of some internal turbulence, and has been scaled down in recent years, with responsibility for discrete policy areas often farmed out to national offices; thus, Greenpeace Austria and Greenpeace Switzerland, for instance, have responsibility for work on Trans European Networks. Indeed, the Brussels offices of Greenpeace and FoE are less well resourced than are some of their national offices. Greenpeace is alone among the G7 in refusing money from the European institutions so as not to compromise its independence. Indeed, Greenpeace is the most independent of the G7, and is the only one without membership of the EEB.

While there are considerable differences between these organisations, such differences tend to be complementary when used for collective purposes. The overall pattern of interest representation works well, with the style spectrum ranging from the respectable and 'establishment-friendly' WWF to the more assertive, direct-action-oriented Greenpeace, from the interpersonal contact style of Birdlife to the mass-membership power base of FoE and Greenpeace, and from the formal structure of EEB, with its institutional contacts, to the informal and loosely co-ordinated, but effective, Climate Action Network (Rucht, 1993). Some organisations have better institutional contacts, others have better direct-membership appeal. The relationships between the G7 are more harmonious than are many business coalitions, and the better-endowed organisations provide resources for the smaller groups to access. WWF and T&E have developed a particularly fruitful relationship (Young, 1995). Most of the Brussels offices of the G7 are not membership offices, and do not have to be overly concerned with platform-building, enabling them to respond quickly to issues. Transport and Environment was one of the first organisations to meet with incoming Transport Commissioner Kinnock (Young, 1995).

While collectively the G7 cannot compete with business interests on resource grounds, or match involvement throughout the policy cycle, they can contribute at a number of points. Most play an important whistle-blowing role; for instance, the WWF provided the European Investment Bank and the Court of Auditors with video evidence of environmental violations arising from use of the structural funds in Spain (Long, 1995), while FoE has provided important scientific evidence on the failure of some member states to meet water quality standards (Young, 1995). Something all organisations can contribute is considerable expertise. WWF, Greenpeace and FoE each have well in excess of 100 staff across the globe, while all have the resources of numerous sympathetic expert scientists to draw upon (indeed, these organisations are extremely large financial entities, with their own commercial structures; individually, they often have a world-wide turnover far exceeding the resources which some business associations can draw upon). These expert resources enable such organisations to engage European policy-making at a level of detail, as well as the provision of ideas.

It is perhaps at the level of ideas, and in politicising issues to bring them to the agenda, that these organisations work best in European policy processes (Grant, 1993b). With the exception of Greenpeace, all of these organisations have been commissioned by the European institutions for investigative work. They have the ability to turn science into politics, and therefore to influence the ways in which issues are perceived and defined. Most have excellent links with DG XI, sit on the General Advisory Forum on the Environment and Sustainable Development, and share in the work of the European Partners for the Environment forum, both established by the Environmental Fifth Action Programme, together with producer and governmental interests. The Car Free Cities Club is a further initiative established by DG XI in conjunction with 'Eurocities' (Chapter 9) in which G7 organisations play a role (Lenschow,

1996). They can share some of the credit for an increasingly warm culture which has been developed within DG III towards environmental affairs (Arp, 1993), and for developing voluntary schemes with business on eco-labelling of products and environmental audits, irrespective of the rather mixed success of these initiatives. G7 organisations have helped shape member state preferences towards environmental protection policies. Indeed, environmental NGOs have helped develop a culture where member states and firms see environmental concerns as congruent with their own interests. Some of the G7 have established meaningful alliances with producer interests over particular issues, such as those forged by Transport and Environment with road and rail lobbies (Young, 1995), and the EEB's 1990 Bergen negotiations with industrial representatives for a 'Joint Agenda for Action' (European Environmental Bureau, 1993). Andersen quotes CEFIC's president as reflecting that

> I think the demand . . . by the environmental organisations is less extreme. . . We have all gained from the experience. On the whole, therefore, it now looks as if the time is ripe for much more constructive dialogue . . . between the industry and the . . . realistic and responsible environmental groups (Andersen, 1992, p. 170).

All environmental NGOs have a natural ally in the shape of the EP, whose members are quick to take up concerns popular with their electorate. Indeed, membership of the EP Environment (and Public Health and Consumer Protection) Committee (where environmental issues dominate) is the most fiercely contested, and this Committee is easily the most powerful of all the specialist committees of the Parliament. Among its 'successes', the Committee lists Council Directives on baby seals (1982), disposal of batteries (1988), small cars (1989), the prompting of the Commission Green Paper on the Urban Environment, and initiatives on lead-free petrol and ozone-depleting substances (Arp, 1993; Machmer, 1995). The EP also has its own member interest group in the environment, GLOBE-EU, part of the world organisation of GLOBE International (European Environmental Bureau, 1994).

Perhaps the most noted 'success' of environmental interests with the EP concerns the Bio-patenting Directive of 1995, where intense lobbying activity led to the Parliament rejecting completely an industry-inspired Commission draft to permit the patenting of genetic modifications (Chapter 2). The case illustrates a number of broader issues concerning the role of public-interest representation. One is that it was precisely the sort of issue where the Parliament could demonstrate its democratic credential and assert itself. Conversely, however, the intensity of interest representation brought concern to the fore in the EP about the aggression of some public interests in seeking to pursue their causes, a factor which formed part of the parallel debate about the regulation of lobbying (Chapter 4). A third factor is that industrial interests did not exit from the issue once it had been lost, but continued to exert sustained influence over a redraft which has now been presented, and is likely to find its way to the statute-books in some form. Environmental interests need to be able to follow issues through to their conclusion, and they may lack the ability to exert continued decisive influence over an issue during the entire passage life of a directive, particularly where industrial inter-ests are determined, in their own interests, to see an issue through. Industrial interests have more influence in environmental affairs within the Commission, whereas public interests are stronger during the parliamentary phase. The parliamentary phase may bring spec-tacular 'victories', but it may in the end not be enough when set against the drafting powers of the Commission and its relationship with producer interests. But the issue does demonstrate the ability of environmental interests to make their presence felt.

Technical expertise held by scientists can determine access to a 'policy community', and drive perceptions of issues and the ways in which such issues are responded to, or not, on the policy agenda. As Peter Haas has indicated, such 'epistemic (knowledge) communities' have the ability to turn science into politics, or to seek to prevent science from entering the political arena. The role of expertise in acting as an entry barrier to such a community means that such affairs can often take the characteristics of low politics, with mono-polistic access to influence (Haas, 1992). Environmental issues can and do take the character of low politics, and yet the Parliament's activism in environmental arenas reflects the generalised status of such issues as high politics. In turn, this general high politics status means that environmental NGO interests have been able to exert influence in European public affairs, and they themselves have contributed to this degree of politicisation. Such patterns are rather less evident in the consumer and social-affairs arenas, though they are by no means absent.

Consumer interests

There are a number of similarities across the development of environmental and consumer policy domains at the European level. Both have grown in importance as quality-of-life issues have come to the fore, and European-level policies in both domains date largely from separate initiatives taken in 1972. Both have consistently been shown in Eurobarometer surveys as popular areas for the development of European wide standards and competencies. Indeed, both domains offer the prospect of democratic legitimacy as a means to demonstrate that 'project Europe' is more than just an opportunity club for business, and of relevance to the everyday citizen. Both domains have seen their status grow within the Commission, such that both now have directorate general status, although this was only achieved for consumer affairs (DG XXIV) as late as 1995. Both have been the subject of a series of 'action programmes', 5 for the environment and 7 for consumer affairs. Both areas acquired a firm legal basis for European-level actions as domains requiring action parallel to the single market, whereby a 'high level' of protection for environmental and consumer domains was provided for, and the use of QMV through Article 100a. Both areas acquired their own, specific legal base under the TEU, with Articles 130r, s and t (environment) and Article 129a (consumer protection). Consumer and environment groups have worked closely together on particular issues such as exhaust emissions from vehicles, and there are established structures of dialogue between them. Both express concerns about subsidiarity in each of their domains. Both have engaged in 'mass action' campaigns directed at the European level. In the consumer domain, the most notable example of this was an organised consumer boycott in 1980 of meat products subjected to hormone growth treatment, in which consumer organisations played a leading part, and which led to a ban on the use of such products by decision of the Council of Ministers.

There are, however, significant differences between European-level environmental and consumer affairs and the groups which represent public interest concerns. First, consumer policy is less driven than is the environmental domain by member state concerns with a level playing field in the single market. Firms from countries with a high level of consumer protection enjoy competitive advantages in selling their products in other countries through higher quality standards; Germany, for instance, has sought to protect its own high standards rather than to export them to the rest of Europe (Young, 1995). Second, consumer interests are far more diverse than are environmental interests. At the European level, consumer organisations are all federated, rather than direct membership, structures. The relationship between consumer organisations is far less cohesive than is the case between European-level environmental organisations, and, at times, has bordered on the hostile. Despite consumer groups in Europe setting up camp in Brussels much earlier than did environmental groups (largely in the early 1960s in the case of the former), it is much more difficult to identify their clear influences upon public policies. And third, consumer issues tend to be rather less politicised than do environmental issues, although they are also more prone to crises, such as those over concerns with the safety of eggs, and, more recently, beef products. Consumer issues which come to public attention tend, however, to be more prone to appear and disappear, than are environmental concerns which seem to be more durable concerns in public opinion.

In one sense, however, consumers are at the centre of the single market. In classical economic theory, the consumer is sovereign, with market mechanisms ensuring that producer activity is geared towards meeting consumer need. The single market, with its ability to deliver enhanced competition, should provide something approaching a consumers' heaven. There is no doubt that the consumer has benefited considerably from intensified competition in the single market. However, as consumer interest groups have not hesitated to point out, there is as yet no such heaven on earth for consumers in Europe, either with complete competition, or with necessary measures to protect the consumer from market distortions, and the extent to which market regulatory changes have been influenced by consumer groups is questionable. The political rhetoric of the single market, and of governments throughout Europe, however, continues to place the consumer at the theoretical centre of policy initiatives by emphasising market solutions. In some countries of Europe, for instance, governments have sought to enable the consumer to make self-interested choices in public life in much the same way as they would in the market, and reforms of public services have been driven by a customer orientation. On the whole, however, consumer-centred action tends to have arisen at the European level more as a by-product of European integration than as a focus in itself, although a number of directives and measures, particularly in recent years, have been driven in the first instance by a concern for consumer protection and safety.

There are six European-level organisations representing consumer interests, although one of these, the European Consumer Safety Association (ECOSA), based in Amsterdam, and dating from 1984, has a slightly different focus and operates somewhat apart from the other five. These are documented in Table 8.5.

All of these organisations are funded by the Commission, in some cases substantially, although the IEIC is the only one getting the majority of its core funding from the Commission. Taken as a whole, consumer organisations get around one-third of their funding from the Commission (Young, 1995). BEUC receives 750 000 ECU each year for the operation of ANEC, which in turn operates independently, and 300 000 ECU itself in core funding. Most of the organisations are therefore relatively well resourced, in European terms, although some have national organisations which are much better resourced. The London-based Consumers' Association, for instance, has some 500 staff, and BEUC has used this resource for particular needs (Young, 1995). Some of the national organisations are also in receipt of project funding from the European budget. The best-known example of this is the London-based Consumers in Europe Group (CEG), comprised of 32 UK consumer and professional organisations, which is geared towards the impact of European-level consumer policy upon the UK, and to the provision of research services. A number of national consumer organisations in southern Europe also receive financial support from the European budget.

The European budget for consumer affairs currently stands at 20.5 million ECU, including the funding provided to sustain consumer representation. The consumer budget experienced a substantial growth in the period from 1990 (6.5 million ECU) to 1992 (19 million ECU), although it thereafter suffered a decline (to 15 million ECU in 1994) (Maier, 1993). Indeed, there is now something of an annual ritual whereby the Commission proposes one level of funding in the budget, the Council seeks to substantially reduce it, and the Parliament ensures that the final level exceeds that initially proposed by the Commission (BEUC, 1995; Young, 1995). But consumer spending represents only 0.01 per cent of the EU budget, compared with 0.176 per cent on environmental policy, less than one-thirteenth of the amount spent by Germany on regional consumer advice centres (Maier, 1993). Put another way, the EU spends around £100 on every cow in the common market, but less than a penny per head on consumers (Dahl, 1993)! Grant sees the commitment of the Community to a consumer policy as largely symbolic, with little

TABLE 8.5

European Level Consumer Groups

Acronym	Name and Location	Date	Type	Staff	Members and Role
BEUC	European Office of Consumer Unions, Brussels	1962	Federation	13	25 national organisations across western Europe, although some recent loss of members. Only organisation dedicated solely to consumer interest representation, and seeks leader status among EU consumer organisations. Specialises on economic issues, noted for support for competition. Specialist organisational divisions. Co-ordinates consumer representation on technical standards committees with finance from Commission via the European Association for the Coordination of Consumer Representation in Standardisation (ANEC), located within BEUC. With COFACE, provides secretariat for EP Intergroup on Consumer Affairs.
COFACE	Confederation of Family Organisations in the EC (started in 1958 as European Committee of International Family Organisations)	1958/1979	Federation	8	73 member organisations in 14 EU countries; associate members in Eastern Europe. Interests in both family and consumer policy. Noted for support for consumer protection legislation (Young, 1995). Specialist Study and working groups. With BEUC, provides secretariat for EP Intergroup on Consumer Affairs.

Table 8.5 (*cont.*)

ETUC/ EURO-C	European Trade Union Confederation, Brussels-based EURO-C is a specialist consumer division	1972 (ETUC) 1994 (EURO-C)	Federation	49	See Chapter 7. A number of national consumer organisations in southern Europe arose from trade unions, and remain ETUC-affiliated. Has considered, and rejected, establishing own EU consumer organisation, preferring a specialist consumer division.
EUROCOOP	European Community of Consumer Co-operatives, Brussels-based	1962	Federation	5	19 national consumer co-operatives – thus distributive trades interests, specialising in food issues; operates own test laboratory. Represented on more than 12 EU advisory committes, including one on Commerce and Distribution.
IEIC	Consumer's Interregional European Institute, based in Lille, France	1989	Federation	5	Members are regional consumer organisations. Substantially funded by the Commission.

Source: BEUC (1994b); Roethig (1995) interviews by author, 1993-6; survey by author, February 1996.

incentive among the Commission and Council to pay attention to the view of consumer interests. Doubtless with their inability to influence agriculture and food policy significantly *vis-à-vis* the agricultural lobby (Nello, 1989) in mind – a view somewhat shared by BEUC – he characterises consumer groups as outsiders (Grant, 1993b). As will be evident later, this view is not one altogether shared by other authors. Undoubtedly, one difficulty common to all consumer interest groups concerns the diversity of consumers and the difficulties of overcoming free-riding problems, although these do not arise significantly at the European level because the organisations concerned are federations of national and regional organisations of consumers (Chapter 3).

A mechanism for institutionalised dialogue between consumer interests and the Commission dates from as early as 1961, with a continuous structure, subject to a number of reforms, to the present day. Today, the Consumers Committee (CC) provides a place for 20 consumer organisations, 15 from the member states (1 per country), and 1 each for the 5 European-level consumer organisations. Table 8.6 shows that the history of previous manifestations of the Consumers Committee has not therefore been a happy one. As in many large structures of the confederate type, decisions have been slow in forthcoming and highly prone to compromise, and members have been reluctant to defend them. The Commission is free to ignore the decisions of the CC, and rather little heed has been taken of them or of those of its predecessors throughout the Commission. Indeed, even the Consumer Protection Service (CPS) undertook only token consultation with the Consumers Consultative Council (CCC) about the content of the sixth action plan (1993–5) for consumer affairs, presenting it after it had been devised. The CPS has also been accused of citing CCC support for its action when in fact CCC had taken a somewhat different view (Goyens, 1993). The history of consumer consultative structures has been characterised by in-fighting between its members, in particular surrounding the demands of BEUC to be the leading representative of consumer interests, and the different perspectives of European-level consumer organisations. Most of its members have, however, welcomed its recent reconstitution, although it may be significant that its running costs are projected to be less than a quarter of its predecessor, a factor which may have contributed to the Commission seeking its reorganisation. 100 000 ECU each year is a relatively small price to pay for a

TABLE 8.6

The history of European-level institutionalised consumer representation (to April 1996)

Acronym	Dates	Name	Comments
CCC	1961–72	Consumers Contact Committee	Organised, operated, and fully financed by EUROCOOP. Dissolved because of member frictions about dominance of EUROCOOP.
CCC	1973–89	Consumers' Consultative Committee	No places for national representatives, and concerns in latter years that some newer EC countries had no consumer organisations. Committee decisions not actively defended by consumer organisations on committee, opinions not published by Commission (Maier, 1993). Commission declares its dissatisfaction with operation in late 1980s.
CCC	1990–4	Consumers' Consultative Council	National members incorporated, multiple seats for European-level organisations. 48 committee members. Frictions between European-level consumer organisations, mutual accusations of not being representative of consumer interest, and calls by BEUC for expulsion of ETUC and EUROCOOP on the grounds that they do not primarily represent consumer interests. ETUC and EUROCOOP retort that BEUC has commercial (testing) organisations within its membership as well as consumers. National organisations from southern countries oppose Council president nominations by BEUC (Petre, 1991). Walkouts and meeting boycotts, and moribund by 1993 (BEUC, 1992; 1993). Reforms in 1994 unsuccessful, such that in 1995 Commissioner Bonino declares history of mechanism unsatisfactory, with structure criticised as complex, unwieldy and slow (Commission of the European Communities, 1995).
CC	1995–	Consumers' Committee	20 members, one from each member state.

mechanism of consultation with a number of groups in an area of significant civil interest.

Of greater significance to CC type structures to date are the contacts which consumer organisations have developed throughout the European institutions. Most of these organisations command places on specialist and advisory committees, and most are represented in the ESC. BEUC and COFACE, in particular, have developed very good contacts throughout the institutions. BEUC meets each incoming Presidency, and enjoys regular meetings at Directorate General level, including a recent day-long meeting with the Directorate General of the prestigious DG IV. Indeed, BEUC has been able to develop a highly fruitful relationship with DG IV, resulting in a number of important initiatives taken against producer interests. COFACE, and in particular BEUC, have developed substantial reputations throughout the European institutions for their consumer work. Gardner, for instance, describes BEUC as a 'vigorous force in Brussels' (1991, p. 41), Andersen considers it a 'professional, well organised lobbying organisation with a good strategic approach' (Andersen, 1992, p. 203), while Stern describes it as a 'highly active monitoring and lobbying body, respected for its efficient organisation and effective lobbying' (Stern, 1994, p. 141). For its part, BEUC has engaged in issue alliances where necessary with producer interests, most notably in the fields of insurance, glass manufacture, pharmaceuticals, and automobile component making (Young, 1995). Impressively, some of these issue alliances have been formed against a background of hostility between the parties concerned over preceding issues. The Commission is also now brokering some of these issue alliances. Thus, most recently, the Commission has sought teams of business and consumer interests to work together in its 'Simpler Legislation for the Single Market' initiative, whereby these actors will examine a range of existing measures and, through the Commission, make recommendations to the Internal Market Council in November 1996.

The gradual elevation of consumer policy to the status of an independent directorate (DG XXIV) represents the ascendance of consumer affairs within the Commission. Initially part of DG XI, consumer policy attained independence as the Consumer Protection Service (CPS) in 1989, becoming a full DG in 1995. As a relatively young directorate, however, it has no more status and influence within the Commission yet than did the Consumer Protection Service, and, with 120 staff, is the smallest DG. The CPS had few friends among consumer organisations, and came under constant criticism from them (Young, 1995). There are instances where, despite producer and consumer groups agreeing on the need for consumer protection measures, the CPS did not take action. Nevertheless, there has undoubtedly been something of an increase in importance attached by the Commission to consumer affairs in recent years, and it is interesting to compare the views of BEUC in the early 1990s with those it espouses today. Writing in 1991, Gardner cites the comment of the former President of BEUC in opining that 'consumer issues are not on the Commission's agenda' (Gardner, 1991, p. 41). In 1992–3, with the CCC virtually moribund and the sixth action plan under heavy criticism from consumer organisations for its lack of substance, BEUC declared that there was 'no single market for consumers' (BEUC, 1992). It considered that the plan

> contained few concrete proposals to increase consumer protection. In fact, the Plan resembles more a balance sheet of past achievements and a statement of good intentions than a blueprint for future action. Regrettably, this was very much the standard tone on consumer policy emanating from the Commission throughout 1993. Hopefully the new year will see the beginning of a more courageous attitude (BEUC, 1994a, pp. 1–2).

BEUC recorded a number of complaints against the Commission during this period for failing to pursue producers' lack of compliance with European law, sometimes only inviting manufacturers to remedy digressions rather than taking enforcement action. It issued a 'balance sheet', which acknowledged historic achievements for consumers through directives and other actions in the following areas: food-related areas, cars, medicines, toys, foam-filled furniture, electrical appliances, agricultural commodities, banking, cross-border payments, telecommunications, utilities, air transport, VAT and excise, defective products, misleading advertising, doorstep selling, consumer credit, unfair contract terms, general product safety, and free movement of people; however it recorded more minus points than plus points in most of these fields (BEUC, 1992).

By 1996, with a different and somewhat enthusiastic Commissioner, an independent DG, a dedicated legal basis to consumer policy, a reformed Consumers' Committee, concerns to bring about a 'citizens' Europe' (Chapter 4), and a brand new action programme, the commitment of the Commission to consumer policy looks somewhat stronger. For its part, BEUC has welcomed the seventh action plan for consumer policy (1996–8), congratulating Commission Bonino on producing a 'comprehensive and forward thinking strategy to develop and protect consumer interests over the next three years' (Scotland Europa, 1995, p. 63). The plan contains proposals for a series of actions spanning consumer use of public utility services, financial services, credit cards, consumer indebtedness and food labelling. Most recently (April 1996), a directive on transparent pricing across member states, and initiatives to facilitate the settlement of consumer disputes with suppliers across borders, have been proposed, and measures taken to improve access to justice for consumers.

It is not clear to what extent consumer organisations can be credited with this improvement within the Commission. Indeed, drawing inferences between interest group desires and activity on the one hand, and policy outcomes on the other, is notoriously difficult. In its own literature and articles by its staff, BEUC claims campaign successes on issues such as the lead content of petrol (jointly with the EEB), bans on the use of growth hormones in animal husbandry, transparency of cross-border payments, the insertion of a cooling-off period into the doorstep selling directive (Goyens, 1993), and, somewhat daringly, the inclusion of Article 129a in the TEU (BEUC, 1994b, p. 2). Clearly, such self-credits cannot be taken at face value. However, Cram makes the point that interest groups need not directly influence hard policy outcomes to be effective, but rather can make a contribution by shaping preferences, enabling collaboration, and influencing the climate of debate (Cram, 1996). Some of the consumer organisations have made a contribution to European consumer affairs in these ways, although they have not been able to do so by acting in coalition. In a generalised sense, BEUC has been able to influence the climate of debate on issues such as food policy (Nello, 1989), in ensuring that there is no 'fortress Europe' in trade, and by its injection of specialist information into the policy process. More specifically, it has taken cases to the ECJ, and organised consumer representation on technical standards bodies, where consumer 'observers' have been able to ensure that producer interests, such as automobile manufacturers with safety standards, do not have things all their own way. Indeed, automobiles is the producer domain where BEUC has confronted business interests most, and here it has often come out on top, with notable successes in the ECJ against Ford concerning cross-border guarantees, in technical standards committees concerning safety issues, and through its campaigns in publicising differential car prices across member states (Andersen, 1992). Recently, its input to DG III's White Paper on industrial policy for the pharmaceutical industry indicates that its views are now taken account of across the Commission. Of interest also is that Ministers at the April 1996 Consumer Affairs Council stressed that consumer interests should be taken into account in all important political areas and in new Community legislation, and that implementation and enforcement of legislation should be strengthened, and further legislation introduced where necessary (BEUC, 1996). As was discussed in Chapters 3 and 5, the habit of collaboration between interests may be iterative.

Some recent work by Lund takes the climate of influence one step further, to show how industry in Europe has become more oriented towards quality in the manufacture of products, and how consumer affairs departments in large firms are now the norm, whereas once the issues in which they deal were the domain of consumer representatives (Lund, 1995). This climate has to some extent been institutionalised at the European level with the advent of the 1992 General Product Safety Directive, placing on manufacturers a duty to monitor marketed products for safety. Under the provisions of this directive, firms now have a duty to assess and investigate consumer complaints, to identify product batches and to sample-test marketed products. Her study suggests that while these techniques have only limited potential for the prevention of safety problems, they can also make an important contribution to lowering the incidence of releasing faulty products on the market.

The EP has been a kindred force for consumer interests throughout its existence. Its long-standing (since 1976) and high-status Committee on Environment, Public Health, and Consumer Protection has been a forceful promoter of consumer interests and a consistent critic of the Commission for its failings in the consumer policy field, while the Parliamentary intergroup on consumer affairs, jointly co-ordinated by BEUC and COFACE, is one of the more active ones. Both committees have been presided over by influential figures in the EP, and consumer organisations have been able to use these routes as a means of inserting amendments into Parliamentary business, or in encouraging the Parliament to use its powers of own initiative. BEUC's resources are heavily drawn upon by individual MEPs, such that it finds itself hard pressed to keep up with the steady demands upon it for information and commentary from this source (Gardner, 1991).

To a certain extent, the impact of the European institutions and consumer organisations upon each other has been mutually reinforcing. Consumer organisations have played a part in producing a general climate whereby consumer interests are taken into account at the European level, and European manufacturers have embraced consumer needs and desires through higher product standards. For influences in the other direction, the European institutions have played a part in improving consumer representation, at both national and European levels. Some of these types of outputs are also visible in the social field.

Social interests

Like environmental domains, 'social Europe' has principally developed alongside the single market. Indeed, in Euro speak, 'social Europe' is most frequently interpreted as matters concerning workers' rights, while the term 'social dialogue' refers to agreement between employers and labour interests (Chapter 7). Certainly, the soundest legal basis in the Treaties for social policy arises from measures to ensure a level playing field in production between the member states in the single market. Thus, the Treaty of Rome contained provisions concerning social security for migrant workers; for equal treatment of men and women; for protection of workers; and for health and safety of workers (Cram, 1993). In fields which can easily be related to employment, such as equal opportunities, training, exclusion from the labour market, disability, and protection and movement of workers, the Commission has had little trouble in developing and funding programmes and initiatives. Interest groups in these fields are relatively well established, often strong, and sometimes influential, with highly respected organisations operating in the fields of women's rights, young people, disabilities and refugees. This does not explain, however, why some groups (such as those concerned with young people) established themselves in Brussels in the early 1970s, whereas most of those concerned with women and with disability did not develop until much later.

Beyond employment-related fields, EU action in other social policy domains has been patchy, and, where it has arisen, has often encountered member state resistance. In 1994, for instance, Germany vetoed a fourth anti-poverty programme, demonstrating the fragility of social action initiatives. Despite the termination of this programme, however, the interest group network which the Commission sought to establish to run alongside its anti-poverty programme, the European Anti-Poverty Network, has remained, and has itself spawned a number of specialist networks. In areas such as housing, social services, public health, and education, Commission competencies are virtually non-existent, although the Commission has exploited opportunities to develop interest group structures oriented to the European level. Another well-respected group, FEANTSA, the European Federation of National Organisations Working with the Homeless, arose from a Commission-funded conference on homelessness and housing provision. Indeed, a range of funding programme areas spanning 'high-competence' and 'low-competence' fields have created European-level groups, from disability through to homelessness.

Implicit in the above analysis is the idea of the Commission seeking to expand its range of competencies. Cram describes the Commission as a 'purposeful opportunist' (1993, p. 142), working almost by stealth to enhance its competence and 'Euro build' by incrementally increasing its activities in fields which are unlikely to bring it into confrontation with the member states, and in the process stimulating demand for transnational activities by funding transnational interest groups. Using Lowi's typology of policies (Lowi, 1964) (Chapter 1), and building on earlier work by Majone (1993), Cram argues that regulatory policies are chosen by the Commission as a means of expansion because they disguise 'winners' and 'losers' (Cram, 1993). Despite occasional setbacks when the Commission clumsily pushes its luck too far (such as the German veto on extending the anti-poverty programmes into a fourth phase), it is able, through the legacy of stimulating the development of transnational groups, to ensure a stable system of influence upon member states, and, through the demands exerted by such groups through the Parliament, to influence the Council of Ministers. Certainly, the Commission has, in one way or another, been largely responsible for the development of transnational groups in the social policy field. There can be little denying that neither the Commission nor the Parliament is a disinterested disburser of funding to NGOs. Beyond the purposes of simplifying consultation structures, establishing a network of organisations capable of taking forward policy initiatives, providing expertise and meeting information deficits, and responding to citizen demands, the formation of such organisations undoubtedly creates forces in favour of further integration.

One problem with this otherwise convincing thesis, however, is its tendency to treat the Commission, in particular, as a singular, purposive actor moving in a uni-directional way, whereas its services have quite different perspectives (Chapter 2). DG XXIII, which has responsibility for liaison with voluntary and social organisations among a plethora of other responsibilities, is a relatively young service which has yet to fully establish itself within the Commission. DG V, also concerned with social issues, finds its concerns heavily contested by the more pro-industry services.

Another perspective sees the Commission as rather less purposeful, often moving forward without strategic oversight, partly in ignorance of demands from public interests, but nevertheless open to input from them. Commenting on a 1989 draft directive on animal testing for cosmetic products, Baker (1992), and Fisher (1994), both activists in the British animal welfare movement, record their considerable surprise when the Commission, having proposed a directive with rather less protection for animals than exists in many member states, welcomed input from animal welfare groups and removed offending clauses, despite input from the European Cosmetics, Toiletry and Perfume Association (COLIPA) and from US trade associations and individual firms. Throughout the issue, animal welfare groups found the Commission far more pragmatic than principled, again rather casting doubt on pictures of the Commission as a purposeful actor, although it does accord with Cram's description of it as an opportunist. The campaign experience led to the formation of the European Coalition to End Cosmetic Tests on Animals, comprised of more than thirty national organisations throughout Europe (Fisher, 1994). Today, the animal welfare lobbies are regarded as one of the most effective among social groups (Harvey, 1995), not least because of the ability of European-level groups (including the principal protagonist, the Eurogroup for Animal Welfare, half Commission-funded) to work together with active campaigning organisations in the member states, in addressing the European level (McKinney, 1994).

Another perspective again sees European (non-labour-market) social policy as so much window dressing, designed as a marketing device to persuade citizens that Europe is something more than an opportunity structure for business people. The anti-poverty programmes, for instance, had a budget of 55 million ECU over a five-year period, supporting small-scale 'pilot projects', research, and networking needs of interests groups, in the context of over 50 million EC citizens being trapped in poverty. Similarly, actions such as naming 1993 the 'European Year of Solidarity Between Generations', involving groups such as Eurolink Age, are relatively cheap forms of putting a 'human face on project Europe' (Baine *et al.*, 1992). Harvey refers to a 'grudging acknowledgement' of the role of voluntary organisations, and the need to work with them, in the TEU, which expanded competencies in the fields of health, culture and consumer protection (Harvey, 1995, p. 10). Here, however, Cram's point about rhetoric creating its own dynamic (Chapter 1) is relevant, not least because European-level interest groups have been created in the process which manufacture demands and seek an expansion of competencies. Certainly, Jacques Delors took a number of actions in the social policy field which seem rather more than simply 'cheap talk'. Among these was, first, a proposal for a 'Solemn Declaration on Exclusion', in 1993, providing for rights of citizens to culture, a minimum standard of living, education, training, and for freedom from discrimination. There were also measures to boost opportunities for tourism among excluded groups, and to protect particularly vulnerable consumers, plus a White Paper on Social Policy, in 1994, covering action in fields of anti-racism, equal opportunities and positive action for women, information collection, social security and protection, and illiteracy. In addition, the European Anti-Poverty Network was given consultation rights on measures concerned with economic and social exclusion, 'thus conferring on it a uniquely influential role in the voluntary sector' (Harvey, 1995, p. 137).

The Commission has undertaken a range of programmes in social fields, including those attached to the structural funds, research programmes, specialised programmes targeted at particular groups and problems, and monitoring initiatives including the establishment of 'observatories' to collect information on social problems. These programmes intrude into most areas of 'social' life; the most significant are those initiatives allied to employment, such as training and equal opportunities (for an excellent review of the range of these see Harvey, 1995). The last of these programmes has just commenced its fourth phase, reaching into the next millennium. It has itself spawned a further funding initiative, IRIS, concerned with occupational training for women, and provided the forum from which the Parental Leave Directive (Chapter 6) emerged. Of interest is that the Commission has chosen a research foundation, CREW (Centre for Research on European Women) to manage this programme, and an interest group, FEANTSA, as the home for one of its 'observa tories', while in another field the European Blind Union is institutionally involved in policy delivery in the Commission-funded disability programmes (Harvey, 1995). At the national level, a number of national councils for voluntary organisations manage social fund grants for training. Social NGOs have therefore become a mechanism of policy implementation for the Commission. Collectively, such measures indicate something more than simply 'cheap talk'.

There is no doubt that the Commission has been enormously influential in the construction and development of EU-level social groups. Table 8.7 indicates over 150 groups spanning over 20 sectors of activity. Many of these have arisen, quite deliberately, from Commission social funding programmes during the 1990s. Eurolink Age, FEANTSA, the European Disability Forum, the European Anti-Poverty Network, the Network for One-Parent Families, and the Trans European Rural Network (TERN), for instance, all started life in this way. Others resulted directly from the need of the European institutions to find representative fora with which to consult, such as a liaison committee bringing together voluntary organisations concerned with development, and a Migrants Forum, which resulted directly from Commission initiatives. Another type of example concerns the formation of the European Women's Lobby (EWL) from an initiative of a key group of women inside the Commission. Most other NGOs, even if they do not owe their existence to the Commission, are in receipt of Commission funding for core, and/or project, running costs. Many of these organisations receive up to 40 per cent of their funding in this way. Sometimes, little evaluation is evident of either the use to which these funds are put, or the value of them (Harvey, 1995). For many organisations, the availability of 'Euro gold' is a significant reason to set up in Brussels.

Table 8.7 identifies the number of organisations that can be found in each of the social fields. It shows that there are a plethora of European-level sectoral and cross-sectoral associations in virtually every social field, which, like the professions (Chapter 6), often draw in different types of organisations from different countries. Far from being under-represented in Brussels, it perhaps may legitimately be claimed that social interests are somewhat over-represented, particularly in some sectors where there are a number of organisations with very similar aims. Indeed, the map (figuratively speaking) of European-level associations, and associational membership, is extremely chaotic, although not necessarily disorganised, lacking in resources, incoherent or competitive. Diversity is germane to the voluntary

TABLE 8.7

Number of European-level associations in social fields

Type of network	Number
Anti-poverty	1
Child welfare	2
Church	15
Community development	4
Development	16
Family issues	4
Health	20
Housing and homeless	8
Human rights	11
Local-authority-based social networks	10
Older peoples	7
People with disabilities	10
Refugees, immigrants and migrants	7
Rural development	7
Social policy	6
Social services	7
Social economy and industrial development	5
Unemployment	2
Women's	10
Youth	9

Source: Euroconfidential (1996); Harvey (1995); Landmarks Publications (1995).

sector itself, and it would therefore be unreasonable to expect singular sectoral organisation at the European level. Diversity is sometimes managed by the creation of a further tier, with network organisations seeking to bring together the European-level groups in a particular field; thus, the Fondation pour le Progrès de l'Homme performs such a role for housing groups. However, competition between organisations does exist. Indeed, German organisations have often established their own Brussels offices, partly as a defensive posture to counter the possibility of voluntary organisations from other countries competing with them for domestic service contracts (Harvey, 1995). Some organisations, such as ECAS and the Centre for Non-Profit Organisations (CENPO) (Table 8.8) are in competition for the same market in seeking to provide consultancy services.

Some organisations, such as Amnesty International, have their own policy office in Brussels, and are not troubled by competing perspectives or in building common positions between members. Such an organisation, with 5 staff in a Brussels office, can also draw upon the resources of over 300 staff in its London international office. For a number of organisations in the social field, however, the reality may be more a cramped office sharing one or two staff and a fax machine. In the case of Amnesty, of interest is that its Brussels office was established in 1985, far ahead of the development of competencies in most of its interest fields by the European institutions (van der Klaauw, 1994). Indeed, Cram has argued that many organisations in the social field come to Brussels despite the fact that there are very few competencies in their interest arenas, sometimes because of the rhetoric of 'the importance of Europe', or with a mission to create Euro competencies, or because of actions by the European institutions designed to attract them (Cram, 1996).

A number of voluntary organisations operating at the European level arose from international associations. The involvement of these associations in European affairs has often historically centred around the Council of Europe, whose activities with non-governmental organisations somewhat predate those of the European Union. The Council of Europe has provided a number of NGOs with formal consultative status, provided they are transnational in nature, representative, and compatible with the aims of the Council. Entry costs are therefore low, while the benefits of working with the Council can be high. The Council of Europe, and its associated structures of the European Court of Human Rights and the Human Rights Commission, has asserted important rights for European citizens (such as rights of mental health patients, the abolition of birching, the decriminalisation of homosexuality), and is presently active in the fields of poverty, low pay, social security, homelessness and the protection of the rights of gypsies. Some of these fields are areas where the EU has developed few competencies, and Harvey considers that it is possible that the Council's work will fill the vacuum left by the termination of the anti-poverty programme (Harvey, 1995). Indeed, the work of the Council is an important reminder that the EU is one of a number of levels for NGOs to address. For public-health organisations, regimes such as the WHO are a more important player to address, and the European structures of bodies like Health Action International (HAI), campaigning on medicine safety, pricing and ethical-use issues, are part of a much wider international organisation. Indeed, some of the more established charities operating at the European level, such as the Red Cross, the Salvation Army and Oxfam, operate as branch offices of more significant international organisations. These activities partly explain why many voluntary organisations were already in place by the mid-1980s in Europe, although many have also come in recent years.

Sometimes, the kaleidoscope of membership of different organisations within the same sector defies neat explanation. Corresponding national organisations dealing with young people, for instance, may be members of quite different European-level youth associations simply because of interpersonal contacts. National organisations with cross-sectoral missions can be found located in European-level organisations with quite distinct sectoral missions. Some organisations have very similar aims, and overlapping membership, but nevertheless focus on quite different priority areas, and differ considerably in style; an example given by Harvey from the myriad of groups representing the interests of women concerns the roles performed by the European Network of Women (ENOW), and the EWL (Harvey, 1995), where there is membership affiliation between these organisations, shared members, and similar aims. The women's representation field also indicates some degree of specialisation, such as organisations geared to the training needs of professional women in employment. This indicates some degree of maturity in interest representation in the social field, although set against such a conclusion is the backdrop of a relatively high proportion of organisations only recently established. Similarly, there is considerable national diversity in social organisations, with many European-level sectoral organisations finding that there is no corresponding organisation in one or more member state. The voluntary sector tends to be relatively well developed in France, Germany and the UK, and rather less so in the southern countries, where church groups dominate the landscape of 'third-sector' provision.

Table 8.8 lists the organisations claiming to represent interests across the spectrum of social and community interests. Of these, the most high profile is perhaps ECAS. ECAS was formed by a number of leading individuals concerned with transnational NGO representation, including the former Director of BEUC, Tony Venables (and the present Director of ECAS), with the aim of increasing access for voluntary-sector associations to EU funding and the Community institutions. It at present employs seven staff. It provides a choice of level of membership service for affiliated organisations in return for different tiers of payment, ranging from corresponding to associate to full membership. One of the missions of ECAS is to build issue interest coalitions for the voluntary sector. Examples of these include VOICE (Voluntary Organisations in a Citizens' Europe), bringing together

TABLE 8.8

Cross-sectoral European-level associations in the social field

Acronym	Name	Role
—	Association pour le Voluntariat/Association of Volunteers	Brussels-based network of national volunteer bureau organisations
CEDAG	European Council of Voluntary Organisations	Established 1989. Paris-based federation. General voluntary organisation representative, focusing mainly on 'peak' national councils of voluntary organisations as members. 52 Members represent 50 000 associations and 9 million associates.
CEBSR	Combined European Bureau for Social Development	Hague-based. Seeks to promote community and social development throughout Europe. Lacks member organisations from all member states.
CENPO	Centre for Non-Profit Organisations	Established 1994. Resource and lobby centre for paying members. Seeks members from professions, local authorities and trade unions, as well as its main market of NGOs.
—	European Association for Social and Cultural Progress	Cross-sectoral, and sectoral, national association members.
ECAS	European Citizens Action Service	Established 1990. Direct-membership organisation, providing tiered services for 217 members drawn from spectrum of NGOs according to payment level, though dominated by UK members. Specialises in citizens' rights, health, social welfare and culture.
EFC	European Foundation Centre	Forum for grant-giving bodies.
	European Round Table of Charitable Social Welfare Organisations	Membership drawn from large, mainly (though not exclusively) cross-sectoral national voluntary organisations.

213

Table 8.8 (*cont.*)

ERAF	European Round Table of Associations and Federations	Established 1992. Association of 80 European-level NGOs, with focus on 'Citizens Europe' of democracy, openness and access to decision-making for citizens and NGOs. Present work focuses on regulation of lobbying (Chapter 4).
ESAN	European Social Action Network	Founded 1989 by UK and French national councils for voluntary organisations, now 100 members. Membership service organisation for NGOs in social welfare and development fields.
ICSW	International Council on Social Welfare	European regional office of world organisation founded in 1929, prioritising issues of poverty and social development.
IFS	International Federation of Settlements and Neighbourhood Centres European Network	Mainly community development, but welcomes any organisation with an interest in the social aspects of 1992. Birmingham-based.
	Volunteurope	Network of national volunteer bureaux, run from UK.

Source: Baine *et al.* (1992); CEDAG (1995); European Citizens Action Service (1996); Harvey (1995).

citizen views on the TEU; the European Public Health Alliance (EPHA); the European Forum for the Arts and Heritage (EFAH); and the European Third Sector Training Network (REEN) (ECAS, 1996). In many ways it is a pioneering organisation, performing roles which might otherwise be fulfilled by the European institutions. An example of this concerns its telephone hotline to advise European citizens. This service is better used than the 'Citizens Desk' service in DG X, and helps provide ECAS with grassroots information on the implementation of 'Citizens Europe'. It has used this information as the basis to request the Commission to pursue legal action against member states for non-implementation of EC law (Nentwich, 1995). The Commission sees the involvement of ECAS as crucial in its forthcoming 'Citizens First' campaign initiative.

A number of NGOs have good, established contacts throughout the European institutions, while a number of semi-formal institutionalised forms of contact exist between the Commission and NGOs. Apart from the European Anti-Poverty Network involvement in consultative structures, there are advisory, consultative or liaison committees between the Commission and citizen/social interests for issues concerning social security provision for migrant workers, elderly people, third-world development, human rights, and, most recently, for NGO umbrella European associations themselves. At present, the Consultative Committee of Co-ops, Mutual Societies, Associations and Foundations operates on provisional statutes, seeking to enhance the position of such organisations in representation and policy-making. This is also the subject of a soon to be issued White Paper, while for its part, the Council has recently agreed a multi-annual programme for NGOs (CEDAG, 1995). Most recently, in March 1996, a thousand participants, drawn mainly from social and voluntary NGOs but also including representatives from member states, the European institutions and producer associations, took part in the European Social Policy Forum in Brussels, aimed at widening contact between the Commission and those involved at grassroots level in economic and social action. A similar exercise was repeated in June 1996, aimed also at consolidating links between social NGOs (COFACE, 1996). There can be little doubt that the interests of social NGOs are now firmly on the European agenda, as much arising from the institutional actions of the Commission as from the demands of social groups themselves. These actions are exerting significant influences upon the development of social groups. Apart from the opportunities presented by institutionalised dialogue (such as advisory committees), the delegation of functions to social groups (such as observatories), the availability of core, project and conference funding (a recent example concerns funds provided by DG XXIII for a conference on lotteries and fundraising), there is evidence that social groups are restructuring themselves to improve their engagement with the European institutions. Thus, CEDAG has recently created its own committee structure which reflect the functional divisions of DG XXIII, in an effort to improve its dialogue with the Commission service (CEDAG, 1996).

Of all the European institutions, however, the Parliament is the most accessible for social interests, where popular pressure can most easily be brought to bear from citizens in the member states, and where an MEP's relationship with voters can best be exploited. Social issues are popular with MEPs because they are matters of concern in their own constituencies, and, as the Parliament has drifted to the left, social concerns naturally attract the interest of social-democratic politicians. Some European-level groups have arisen, or received significant boosts, from single-issue lobbying with the Parliament. Examples of such stimuli would include actions by animal welfare groups acting to prevent testing of cosmetic products on animals, or motorcyclists to prevent a Commission directive to ban powerful motorcycles. In August 1996, in a rare show of citizen protest, 25 000 motorcyclists from across Europe drove past the EU institution offices in Brussels to protest against measures designed to create a single market for motorcycles, impose restrictions on noise levels, and introduce safety measures such as the compulsory use of shear bolts, vehicle safety tests and stipulations on tyres. Drawing attention to the support it had received from the 93 per cent of MEPs to demand the measures, the Federation of European Motorcyclists (FEM) commented that 'we can see that the Parliament has at least listened to the arguments we have made. This campaign is for a Europe which is more responsible and responsive to its citizens, and more democratic' (European Voice, 1996, p. 3). Some of the funds to enable social groups to start up and network have their origins in budget lines voted by the Parliament (Baine *et al.*, 1992). One social group, Eurolink Age, is among the first of all groups to locate a Parliamentary liaison officer in Strasbourg, whose duties include providing the secretariat for an intergroup to operate. Other intergroups operate in the fields of the social economy, family policy (part staffed by COFACE), animal welfare (co-ordinated by the Eurogroup on Animal Welfare), public health (co-ordinated by the EPHA) and community development. Most of these are extremely active; the intergroup on age, for instance, has over a hundred MEP members. A number of amendments to parliamentary business have arisen from such intergroups. These groups have found that one of the best ways to lobby the Council and the Commission is through the Parliament, which is much more likely to take a stand on principle. Indeed, the EP has established structures for citizen and social protest, in the shape of procedures for receiving and referring petitions, and complaints of maladministration, directed through the Ombudsman, and continues to explore measures to create a level playing field with business interests (Chapter 4). As Harvey suggests, while there clearly never will be such a level playing field,

> at the same time, the voluntary and community sector may not be the victim of the forces of European integration that it sometimes imagines itself to be. The growth in European networks of voluntary organisations and associations suggests that the sector may have strengths and capabilities which will be to its advantage as key European decisions are taken over the next few years (Harvey, 1995, p. 100).

Conclusions

Public interest groups have increasingly participated in European public affairs, and often to good effect. The language of insider and outsider groups is no longer sufficient to capture the complexities involved. Indeed, even refinements of this model indicating core, specialist and peripheral groups (Chapter 1) seem insufficient to capture the ways in which public-interest groups interact with the European institutions. Specific degrees of influence over policy decisions and non-decisions by observers or by policy participants are largely incalculable, except in the case of events such as 'whistle-blowing' activities or delegated authority in implementation. Rather, the focus should be as much upon outputs as on outcomes (Chapter 1), such as the ways in which such interests contribute to, and are influenced by, the language of debate and the norms and understanding of those who participate in it. By any of these criteria, however, public interests have had an impact. Indeed, there have been some instances where public interests seem to have had a greater impact upon specific events than have producer groups. But it is rarely as straightforward as a contest between these interests; as well as competition there is collaboration. Public-interest environmental concerns have been processed alongside producer concerns in a climate where different interests can coincide. Interest representation landscapes respond to characteristics of the arena under consideration. The politicisation of some domains has itself contributed to a certain degree of shared perceptions, and such an extent of politicisation predicts multiple arenas with multiple players in which no one type of interest is likely to predominate. Naturally, public interests have contributed to, and are a reflection of, the climate of politicisation. In some instances, most notably in the environmental and social domains, coalition formation works well, with functional divisions of labour arising. Some of the Brussels offices of these groups are policy offices, and are not concerned with free rideable membership incentives which affect some producer groups. In these domains, interests have tangibly benefited from the experience of collaboration and the exchange of know-how. Equally, the development of public-interest groups at the European level has benefited considerably from deliberate actions by the European institutions, and in particular the Commission and the Parliament. This is consistent with expectations of neofunctionalist ideas of integration, a theme returned to in Chapter 10.

9

Territorial Interests

The focus of this chapter concerns subnational, regional and local interest representation at the European level, and in particular the perspectives of territorial public authorities. However, in practice distinctions between territorial public authorities and territorially based interests are difficult to make, because territorial public authorities work to attract, promote and protect key private interests within their domain. Indeed, the levels of complexity involved in territorial interest representation are perhaps greatest of all, because a territorial level can be a channel of influence for private interests, and a set of interests within itself, and because what constitutes a region means different things in different member states. The Committee of the Regions (CoR) is both a decision-making structure for regions and a source of interest representation in its own right. Collective action issues applicable to other actors do not arise in the same way for territorial public authorities, because they are a distinct level of governance, sometimes intertwined with national interests, sometimes separate, and with a whole range of competencies and interests. Indeed, the territories of the regions comprise the entire EU itself, and there is competition between them in the internal market, and, to an extent, for regional funding initiatives. However, there are also a number of reasons to collaborate, and territorial authorities do work both individually and collectively to pursue their interests in the EU. These collective structures span the formal and informal varieties.

A 'Europe of the Regions?'

A 'Europe of the Regions' is a phrase now most commonly reserved for romantics and nationalist separatists who seek the dissolution of states in favour of smaller regional identities. While some nationalist parties, such as those in the Basque country and in Scotland, seek independent membership of the EU, a scenario whereby member states would permit such a course of events would hardly be imaginable, either individually or collectively. Rather, to denote the increasing concern of public policy with spatial issues, the issue today is more one of a Europe 'with the regions' (Hooghe, 1995). Keating argues that regionalism was a response to the needs of national states for regional policies and plans, and to external pressures, not least from regions themselves and key interests within them (Keating, 1993). Some member states have decentralised into federal states (e.g. Belgium), while others have either provided greater autonomy to regions (e.g. Spain), and/or devolved increasing functional responsibilities from central government to the regional level (e.g. France). Some have created 'paper' regions to please the Commission for the purpose of conforming to structural-fund rules (e.g. Ireland and Portugal, while a similar process is underway in Finland and Sweden) (Hooghe and Marks, 1996). Britain is perhaps the exception to this process, in that Conservative administrations since 1979 have progressively centralised authorities, reversing earlier trends towards decentralisation. Federal states thus include Germany and Belgium; devolutionary centralised states include Spain, Italy, France, the Netherlands and Denmark, while unitary centralised states include Greece, Ireland, Portugal and the UK (Leonardi and Nanetti, 1990). Of the recent EU members, Austrian regions have strength on a par with those of Belgium and Germany, while Swedish regions are comparable with those of Denmark.

This differential degree of regional autonomy conditions the response of territorial interests to the European level. For instance, federal states do send Ministers from the regions to meetings of the Council of Ministers, whereas at the other extreme regions in centralised states largely lacking regional authorities can struggle to define, let alone represent, their interests. Where regions have considerable autonomy, so the European interface has tended to strengthen their powers; thus, in Belgium, central government has stepped aside and allowed the regions to deal directly with Brussels (Hooghe, in Keating, 1995). Where regions do not exist or are weak, central government has sometimes used the European level to strengthen its own powers *vis-à-vis* the regions. For instance, around 80 per cent of EU regional funding is disbursed from the national capitals (Kitt, 1995), and some governments have used this position to offset their own expenditure at the expense of the regions

(Greenwood *et al.*, 1995). In some member states, the EU has proved a force for centralisation, whereas in others it has meant considerably enhanced powers for the regions. Similarly, some issues reinforce member state power *vis-à-vis* the regions (such as acting as the gatekeeper of structural fund applications and the disburser of funds), while others favour the regions (such as Commission funding for trans-regional networks). However, as is evident later, different patterns also arise within countries themselves. The European level is not therefore a straightforward case of either reinforcing member states or dissolving them in favour of a 'Europe of the Regions'.

At the European level itself, regional policies have developed along three lines, namely the co-ordination of national regional policy measures to ensure conformity with the treaties, the development of EU funds for regional development, and the development of EU-level regional policies (Keating, 1995). Concerns with uneven regional development were referred to in the preamble to the Treaty of Rome, and were always a concern of the Coal and Steel Community. The European Investment Bank (EIB), providing low-cost loans for major projects in and across the European regions, was formed in 1958. Measures to support regions with particular difficulties were thus present from this period, although not in the context of an overall regional policy, because of the anticipation that the common market would automatically reduce regional disparities (McAleavy, 1994). In the absence of such a scenario, regional policy initiatives developed slowly, though controversially, in the 1960s. These included a major conference on regional disparities in 1961, the addition of the European Social Fund (ESF) in 1961 and the Agriculture Guidance and Guarantee Fund (EAGGF) in 1964, the Commission's first regional policy memorandum to the Council in 1965, and the formation in 1968 of a Directorate General for Regional Development (Deeken, 1993).

Regional policy took a quantum leap forward with the accession of Britain, which, as part of the accession negotiations, sought a 'pay-back' for its budget contributions in the shape of the availability of European-level regional funding programmes for its declining industrial regions. Italy, with its own marked regional disparities, had for some time also sought an active European-level regional policy. The result was the creation of the European Regional Development Fund in 1975, the major pillar of the structural funds, and a constituency of interests seeking receipts from this fund formed by membership accessions in the 1970s and 1980s. These accessions, of Ireland,

Greece, Spain and Portugal placed regional unevenness across the EEC in sharp relief. After a succession of reforms, particularly in 1988–9 and 1992–3, when these funds were doubled in absolute terms on both occasions, structural expenditure now commands approximately a third of the entire budget of the European Union. These latter reforms included the creation of a new Cohesion Fund, for countries with a GDP of 90 per cent or less of the European average (i.e. Greece, Ireland, Portugal and Spain, the 'cohesion four') (Armstrong, 1995). By the year 1999, such spending will amount to a peak of 30 billion ECU (in 1992 ECU) (Marks, 1993), the cumulative total value over the period 1994–9 having been 178 billion ECU (Hooghe, 1995). Although 60 per cent of the European territory is covered by these funds, 80 per cent of their value is spent on Objective 1 regions, concentrated in Greece, Portugal, Spain and Ireland. Further landmarks worthy of note in European regional policy include the establishment in 1988 of the Consultative Council of Regional and Local Authorities (CCRLA), annexed to DG XVI of the European Commission, comprising representatives of regional and local authorities, and its replacement in 1993 by the CoR, consisting of 222 representatives from (some) localities and regions in the member states. Looking ahead to the near future, EMU will have a significant impact upon regional economies, and, if regional policy initiatives spill over in much the same way as they have done from the single market, much more can be expected.

The recent growth of the structural funds is largely related to the single-market project. Although there is no agreement on the regional impact of the single-market project, one (rather simplistic) interpretation is that it will concentrate economic development in a 'golden triangle' between London, Paris and Milan (or a 'blue banana', stretching through Frankfurt), leaving a 'brown doughnut' of peripheral regions largely excluded from the benefits of the single market (Armstrong, 1995; Benington, 1994). Leaving aside the contentiousness of the metaphors (the prosperous cities of Aberdeen, Bordeaux, Copenhagen, Helsinki and Stockholm, for instance, lie well outside these configurations), the growth of the structural funds are therefore seen in such an interpretation as a form of side-payment to the poorer member states from wealthier countries in return for agreement for the single-market project, and as a means of smoothing out economic development. In 1989, national disparities ratios in the EC were at the extremes of 2.1 (Denmark): 1 (Portugal) of GNP per head (Andre *et al.*, cited in Keating, 1995). There is some evidence for aspects of the side-payment argument. Keating attributes Ireland's large positive vote for the Maastricht Treaty to the ability of that country to gain from the structural funds (Keating, 1995). A new Objective 6 for Arctic regions was created almost certainly with the intention of influencing the accession vote in the Nordic countries. However, the 'side payment' explanation is weakened because the regional impact of the single market remains disputed; indeed, it is possible that peripheral regions will attract inward investment in Europe from firms shopping around for the lowest production costs. Marks therefore argues that the growth of the structural funds arose more because of the vulnerability of potential losers in the event that the single market does concentrate wealth in the core of Europe at the expense of the periphery (Marks, 1992). However, there are other uneven effects of European policies, such as the CAP (Hooghe and Keating, 1994) and the research funds (Grote, cited in ibid.), which do tend to be concentrated in areas of economic development. Similarly, European policies have effectively dismantled or heavily slimmed down industries such as steel, textiles and fishing, and considerable assistance is needed for restructuring (Keating, 1993).

The liberal ethos of the single market provides much of the explanation for the growth in the European-level regional dimension. As was discussed in Chapter 1, however, deregulation has also brought with it re-regulation. Apart from the uneven development caused by market forces, the single-market project involved a whole host of new or revitalised initiatives and competencies deeply impacting upon territorial authorities. Competition policy has outlawed protectionism (indeed, DG IV remains a stubborn opponent of the growth of regional policy). Public-procurement legislation will disrupt favoured local-supplier relationships between producers and territorial authorities. As employers, landowners, and monitoring, enforcing and licensing bodies, local authorities are deeply affected by the range of competencies and activities of the EU. Martin, for instance, has estimated that some 85 per cent of trading standards legislation now comes from the EU (Martin, 1993). To this list could be added issues concerned with TENs and transportation, local economic development, encouragement to local interests to participate in Europe by way of information and advice, technology transfer and research framework programmes, the supply of public utilities, transfer of undertakings, and anti-poverty initiatives. The UK Audit Commission summarises these areas under three headings of where Europe impacts upon local authorities: regulation, integration, and funding (Audit Commission, 1991). All these competencies have attracted some territorial interests to set up camp in Brussels and to network extensively, albeit, as is evident below, in a rather uneven pattern from across the EU.

However, for territorial interests it is not simply a case of 'shooting where the ducks are'. Some regional alliances predate European competencies, whereas others have been stimulated as much by the encouragement of the European institutions themselves as by the presence of Euro competencies. The Commission and the Parliament, in particular, have encouraged alliances with regional interests, partly as a means of bypassing member states and reinforcing the authority of the central institutions. The 1988 reform of the structural funds established the notion of 'partnership' between territorial authorities and local interests, creating, enhancing and/or institutionalising local interest communities in the implementation of structural fund assistance. The Commission provides significant seedcorn funding for trans-regional networks to form and develop. Trans-regional interests and the Commission have teamed up to create new funding programmes for the regions, where the balance of power lies more with these parties than with member states. Thus, the RECHAR funding initiative for the adaptation of coalmining regions was proposed by the Coalfield Communities Campaign, a grouping linking coalfield communities in the UK, Germany, Belgium, France, and Spain, for one of the Commission's 'own-initiative' regional funding schemes. This was seized upon by the then Regional Commissioner Millan as the opportunity both to develop the Commission's own competencies, and as a mechanism to trap the UK government and expose it for failing to pass on money to target regions. The scheme did act as a catalyst to resolve this dispute over 'additionality', whereby member states have to ensure that European funds are additional to their own regional spending programmes (John, 1994; McAleavy, 1994). Member states themselves signed up to these rules in 1988, and yet, in certainly the cases of the UK, Italy and Spain, and undoubtedly others, governments have found themselves later constrained by, or even opposed to, the working of these regulations, such that, in some cases, they have had to resort to tactics little better than fraud (Keating, 1993) to reconcile their interests. This is some way from intergovernmentalist caricatures of member states as calculating and rational actors, in full command of the consequences of their decisions to pool sovereignty. Such additionality problems have led directly to further efforts from the Commission to encourage input directly from the regions and localities, with some limited opportunities for bypassing member states as they do so.

Some good relationships are developing between the Commission and the regions at grassroots level. Commission officials now regularly visit the regions, particularly on structural fund business; in 1992, they were involved in 240 such committee meetings (Marks, 1993). Officials were sent out to visit cities to consult over a Green Paper on the Urban Environment (John, 1995). A further example of Commission attempts to team up with the regions concerns the April 1996 initiative from the information services of the Commission in producing a series of public-information booklets on and for each of the European regions, cultivating regional identity and a sense of linkage with Europe. The standard preamble to this asserts in bold face type that

> In this radically reshaped (European) Union, the sense of regional identity will be a healthy counter balance to the decision-making by Ministers which member states Governments will undertake at the level of the Union itself (European Commission Representation in Scotland, 1996, p. 3).

In the Scottish edition, the foreword is somewhat different from the common entry for each of the English regions. It plays somewhat to Scottish nationalist sentiment and to the cultivation of Scottish–Europe links by reflecting that

> Historically, Scotland has always been a European nation with strong economic, cultural, legal, educational and ecclesiastical links with the Continental mainland. As European integration both widens and deepens, Scotland is strengthening these links. The realisation is strong among Scots that . . . Europe is where our future lies and the more vigorously and positively we participate the greater will be the rewards . . . the Scots, as public opinion polls so clearly demonstrate are enthusiastic participants in the European Union . . . (Scottish interests) demonstrate daily that being at the physical extremity of Europe does not prevent a people being politically at its heart (ibid., p. 1).

The rest of the document includes reminders of English invasions and Scottish resistance heroes, and the security and cultural benefits brought by historic alliances with other European countries. It is, perhaps, one of the more explicit examples of rhetoric in recent years from one of the Commission offices aimed at building 'Euro bridges' directly with interests in the regions.

The organisation of territorial public interests at the European level

Subnational territorial public authorities engage the European level directly in a number of ways. There are multiple access points. The first 'channel' to consider are the institutional sources. Some regions play a role in national representation through the Council of Ministers, particularly in federal states, although even in centralised unitary states such as the UK, Scottish Office Ministers will attend Council discussions where a Scottish interest predominates in national affairs, such as fishing. Another forum for ministerial contact, albeit outside the framework of the EU, is through the Council of Europe, which has a secretariat and forum for the regions, the Standing Conference of Local and Regional Authorities, established in 1957. This forum: discusses matters concerned with local and regional authorities throughout Europe and submits opinions to the Council's Committee of Ministers; organises public hearings on local and regional matters of interest; is active in town twinning; maintains close relations with conferences of European Ministers responsible for questions of local administration; and maintains direct contact with the EU within the framework of the relations established between the Council of Europe and the EU. In 1986 it opened a joint office with the International Union of Local Authorities (IULA), as a means of engaging the EC (Keating, 1995).

In the Commission, the foremost regional structure is DG XVI, which has developed strong links with regional and local-authority interests. As major employers, a number of territorial interests have also developed good links with DG V, while the peak public-sector employers' organisation, the CEEP, is a 'first-level', or 'macroeconomic' social partner. The Parliament also contains a natural constituency of interests in regional affairs, and it was this institution which proposed the establishment of the CCLRA, the predecessor to the CoR. The Parliament has a Committee on Regional Policy, Regional Planning, and Relations with Regional and Local Authorities, and an established Intergroup of Local and Regional Representatives (Chapter 2). Although the latter has not been an active structure, local authorities have provided speakers on key issues at meetings (Kitt, 1995), while a variety of other, specialist, regional intergroups exist, such as those concerned with mountainous regions, and regions with large airports (Gardner, 1991). Finally, regions and local authorities provide members for the CoR, although at present, representatives to the CoR are mostly appointed by member state governments. To date, this forum has been riddled by wrangling and conflicts, mainly between regions (accounting for most representatives in federal countries) and local authorities (accounting for most representatives in unitary member states). Its limited advisory powers mean that it has yet to be taken seriously in European decision-making, although it is somewhat more promising that its predecessor, the CCRLA, which was widely regarded as little more than a creature of the Commission for one-way communication (Grayson and Hobson, 1992). It is, however, the weakest of the present institutionalised channels available to territorial interests (Hooghe, 1995). Of these institutionalised channels to EU decision-making, not surprisingly, regions with the greatest degree of devolved autonomy have done most to exploit the available opportunities.

Some regions have sought to create an overt sense of identity for communities of officials working in, and interfacing with, the European institutions, such as directory books of citizens from a particular region working in Brussels (Chapter 2), or have sought to capitalise upon the regional identity of commissioners, such as Strathclyde's links with former Regional Policy Commissioner Bruce Millan. Most, if not all, regional and local authorities of any size have appointed European officers to manage the EU interface. A number of territorial public authorities have set up their own Brussels offices, and/or participated in formal and informal trans-regional networks in Europe. These latter two strategies are considered in detail below.

Vastly differing numbers have been cited in a count of the regional offices based in Brussels, ranging from 54 at the lower end (Marks *et al.*, 1995) to 80 (Baird, 1994). Others have hedged their bets; the Parliament Research Services, for instance, puts the figure at 'more than 50' (European Parliament, 1993). This may reflect some differences in perception as to what constitutes a European regional 'office', which in turn partly reflects differences in resource levels, and patterns of sharing offices, missions, and staff. Table 9.1 provides the most up-to-date information on regions and localities with direct representation in and around Brussels, and, in listing these, provides transparent criteria for the count. Thus including individual anomalies, such as

TABLE 9.1

Regions and localities with direct representation in Brussels (April 1996)

Austria

Landes Burgenland Information Office for the European Union; Representation of the Länder; Land Kärnten Verbindungsbüro; Land Niederösterreich; Oberösterreich Information Office; Land Salzburg Information Office; Steiermark Office; Office of Europaregion Tirol; Vienna Business Promotion Fund; City of Vienna; Association of Austrian Cities

Belgium

Permanent Representation of the Brussels Capital; Permanent Representation of the Flemish Region Community; Permanent Representation of the French Community; Permanent Representation of the Government of the German Community; Permanent Representation of the Walloon Community; Brussels–Europe Liaison Office; Brussels Region; French Community; Ministry of the Brussels Region; Social and Economic Council for Flanders; Ministry of the Flemish Community; Flemish Government; Association of Belgian Cities and Towns

Germany

Observer of the Länder; German Local Government European Office; Information Office Baden-Württemberg; Representation of the Free States of Bavaria to the European Union; European Office of the Bavarian Communities; Senate and Administration for Federal and European Affairs Berlin; Information Office Brandenburg; Information Office for the Free City of Bremen; Hanse Office; Information Office Hessen; Information Office Mecklenburg Vorpommern; Information Office Niedersachsen; Information Office Nordrhein Westfalen; Information Office Rheinland-Pfalz; Information Office Saarland; Information Office Sachsen; Information Office Sachsen-Anhalt; Information Office Thüringen

Denmark

Aalborg EU Office; Aalborg Development Agency; Aarhus Development Agency; Association of Danish County Councils; Copenhagen City; Eura; National Association of Local Authorities in Denmark; Odense Denmark EU Office; South Denmark

Finland

Helsinki Office in Brussels; The Association of Finnish Local Authorities; Vaasa municipality

France

Alsace Office; Association for Co-operation Between Brittany and the Loire Region; Atlantic Centre; Armor Coast; Apcci-Eurodom Office; Corsica Office; Datar; Association of French Regions Brussels Grand Est Branch; Lot-and-Garonne, Gers, Tarn-and-Garonne; Lorraine Office; Martinique General Council; Espace Moselle; Nord-pas-de Calais Region; Lower Normandy Association; Upper Normandy Region; Paris Ile de France Delegation; Picardie Regional Council; French Polynesian Office; Rhône-Alpes Regional Council; Grand Sud Association; Departement de Vaucluse

Italy
ASTER/Region Emilio-Romagna; Desk Basilicata; Latium Branch Brussels; Lazio Region; Lombardy Association; Mezzogiorno Office; CIAPI-Sicily Region; Trentino European Region; Tirol European Region; Tuscany Office

Ireland
Dublin European Representative Office; West Ireland

Netherlands
City of Amsterdam; East Netherlands Provinces; VNG – Association of Netherlands Municipalities; Region Randstad Holland and Utrecht

Portugal
Industrial Association of the Minho

Spain
Andalucian Institute of Marketing; Government of Aragon Office; Office of European Affairs in the Asturias Region; Sofesa Office of the Canary Islands; Council of Castilla and Leon; Catalan Pro-European Association; Galician European Foundation; Imade; Institute of Marketing of the Region of Murcia; Government Delegation of the Navarra Region; Basque Country Delegation; Community Office of Valencia

Sweden
Federation of Swedish County Councils; Swedish Association of Local Authorities; Mid-Sweden; South Sweden European Office; Stockholm Meeting Point; West Sweden

United Kingdom
Bedford European Office; Birmingham and West Midlands European Office; Cheshire; Convention of Scottish Local Authorities; European Liaison Office for the Counties of Cornwall and Devon; East of Scotland European Consortium; Essex County Council; Gloucestershire Brussels Office; Hampshire–Dorset Brussels Office; Highlands and Islands European Office; Kent European Office; Lancashire Enterprises; Local Government International Bureau; Association of London Government; Luton Borough Council; Manchester; Brussels Merseyside Office; East Midlands; Northern Ireland Centre in Europe; North of England Office; Nottingham Brussels Office; Oxfordshire County Council; Scotland Europa Ltd; Scottish Enterprise; South of Scotland Liaison Office; Strathclyde Region; Surrey County Council; East Sussex; West Sussex County Council; Wales European Centre; West of Scotland European Consortium; Yorkshire and Humberside European Office.

Source: Scotland Europa (1996).

some national associations of regional and local authorities with Brussels offices, the number of regions and localities from member states with direct representation in Brussels is 135. A number of observations can be made. The first is that one of the most centralised countries in Europe, the UK, has the most regional and local offices in Brussels. Paradoxically, however, and as might be expected (without considering receipt of structural funds), regions from other countries with centralised states (Greece, Portugal, Ireland) are the worst represented in Brussels. Ironically, however, it is these three countries, together with Spain, which are the greatest recipients of the structural funds. Greek localities are not represented, reflecting the almost complete absence of regional structures in that country until 1995; Portugal has only one representative (and, in the absence of real regions in Portugal, that office is a delegation of industry in the northern, and, relative to the rest of Portugal, semi-prosperous, region); and Ireland has two regional offices. Indeed, Norway, ineligible for many of the structural funds as a non-member, has as many offices in Brussels as do Greece and Portugal combined. Similarly, Italy, with marked regional problems in the south, has the same number of offices as Denmark, where regional development is much less uneven.

Marks *et al.* have done a more systematic study of the factors influencing the establishment of regional offices in Brussels. They found that there is no relationship between money and the presence of regional offices; that is, neither the 'pull' of the structural funds, nor the capacity of a region to fund representation, were statistically significant factors in determining the establishment of a regional office. Rather, the independent variables were more political factors, and, less strongly, factors related to the strength of regional associational traditions. Regions with a distinctive political and cultural identity are almost all represented in Brussels. Political autonomy of regions was also a strong predictor of a Brussels presence (Marks *et al.*, 1995). One qualification to these arguments, however, is that all of Portugal, Greece and Ireland have designated Objective 1 status, so there is no need for individual regional representation for funding purposes. In Spain, the fourth country (and somewhat the leader) of the 'cohesion four', where some regions are not designated for assistance, there are thirteen regional offices in Brussels. Spain, however, has devolved a great deal more autonomy to the regions that have the other three countries, an independent variable predicating establishment in the study by Marks *et al.*

The resources, functions and roles of the 135 offices vary considerably. Most have been recently (within the 1990s) established (the first, Strathclyde, dates from 1982), and are still developing and feeling their way. Among them can be found individual cities, local and regional authorities, grouping of authorities, country offices within unitary states, national local authority organisations, and local quangos. Some territorial representations share the services of one executive-cum-consultant, who in turn may share support services of a regional office with others. Regional groupings of authorities sharing offices are now increasingly common. One untypical example concerns a cross-regional office, Essex and Picardie. In some cases, however, there are cleavages, with localities not participating in a regional office, or setting up their own alternative representation (John, 1994). Some representations, such as Bavaria, have as many as twenty employees who are envoys of federal ministries. Most of the better-resourced offices tend to act not just for territorial authorities, but for the interests contained within those regions. Scotland Europa, for instance, as well as being an umbrella structure for the representation offices of public territorial offices in Scotland, has a paying membership spanning large and small private enterprises, trade unions, voluntary organisations and universities. Reflecting on the benefits for a firm in joining this structure rather than relying on a sectoral trade association, its former chief executive has argued that 'it is better to have your own poodle than a part share in someone else's Rottweiler' (Baird, 1994, p. 5). Scotland Europa is also available as an enquiry point for any Scottish organisation which cares to use it, irrespective of membership. However, experience to date is that not all Scottish interests use this outlet, and some firms in particular remain wedded to their own channels of interest representation.

All offices are hungry information-gatherers for their paymasters. Just as with business interests, the relative uncertainty of the European environment makes a Brussels office seem essential to many. But some representations are restricted to this function, either on resource grounds, or because it is politically too sensitive to extend the role further. Some regional offices represent a number of individual local authorities which have competing interests or perspectives on matters concerning regulation, integration and funding. Most have to be extremely careful not to create tensions with national permanent delegations to Brussels; this applies particularly in the case of the UK, where funding for Scottish and Welsh representations is partly provided by central government offices or agencies. As one UK office put it, much of the work of UK regional offices is technical liaison rather than subnational diplomacy. However, Marks *et al.* found that where conflicts exist with central government, so a region was more likely to set up an office in Brussels, not least because of the need to rely upon themselves to represent their interests (Marks *et al.*, 1995).

It should be noted, however, that with the exception of Article 10 of the European Regional Development Fund (ERDF) and Article 6 of the European Social Fund (ESF), regions cannot engage directly with the Commission as a means to secure funding from the ERDF, ESF and European Agricultural Guidance and Guarantee Fund (EAGGF), because the rules require that the member states are the gatekeepers for these applications. In many cases, the Commission is powerless to respond to specific demands from the regions and localities. Some delegations from localities which have sought to obby Brussels directly over structural fund decisions have been turned back and referred to their member states offices, even in cases where a member state has refused to include a particular location within an application. In most cases, however, the Commission is pleased to listen to what territorial interests have to say, without being able to involve them at the decision-making level for these funds, and in any case it feels obliged to listen to representations from an MEP on behalf of a particular locality. Nevertheless, partnership arrangements under the structural funds have created or consolidated hundreds of local-interest communities of territorial authorities, producers and social interests, which have some degree of autonomy in the management of structural fund programmes (Balme, 1991). As Marks comments, the Commission has created 'social partnership' at the local level (Marks, 1993), particularly in centralised member states where these might otherwise have been absent.

In Brussels itself, some coherent identities of geographical collections of regions have been created through the presence of representative offices in Brussels (John, 1994), with particularly dense networks between offices within the same country (Hooghe and Marks, 1996). However, as has been evident from other chapters, formal collective structures with wide constituencies often suffer from coherence and lowest-common-denominator problems. Both national and European-wide collective structures of territorial interests suffer severely from this problem, not least because, at the European level, the structure, funding, competencies and democratic legitimacy of the territorial authorities across western Europe differ significantly, and because of economic and funding competition. Because of the diverse range of governmental type competencies possessed by territorial authorities (within themselves and in comparison), it would indeed be unreasonable to expect such actors to work well collectively.

Collective actors for the regions and localities are multifarious. Examples of neighbouring regions who act in collective structures for European purposes and who divide and share membership of wider European-level associations of territories between themselves (Chapter 3) include the East of Scotland European Consortium linking four Scottish regions, and regions in Denmark, England (in each of the North West, South Yorkshire, and the South West regions), Portugal, and Spain (Jeffery and O'Sullivan, 1994). As is evident from Table 9.1, some regions have developed trans-regional Brussels offices, spanning national boundaries. The English county of Kent and the Nord-Pas-de-Calais region of France have together created the strongest trans-regional links, such that their combined area is now dubbed the 'Trans-manche' region, and have persuaded the Commission (without too much difficulty, not least because of the Commission's interest in the development of trans-regional networks) to recognise this for the purpose of distribution of structural funds under the INTERREG programme. This organisation has been extended, as much for economic identity as for political purposes, to include Wallonia, Flanders and Brussels, under the adopted name of 'EUROREGION'. Indeed, there are a range of political, social and economic networks of regions, or regions clustered around European programmes dedicated to bringing regions together for particular purposes. Examples of these are listed in Table 9.2; some of them predate many EU funding initiatives. Indeed, municipalities are involved in thousands of twinning networks across national boundaries. But there are signs that some trans-regional networks are developing into far more significant structures than perfunctory meetings between civic dignitaries. Even twinning arrangements are now creating access to trans-regional networks for some towns. Dunfermline, in Scotland, for instance, was able to join a funding application directly as a result of its twinning with Wilhelmshaven in Germany and by sharing the German town's network contacts. Apart from twinning, trans-regional networks such as Quartiers en Crise, in particular, are highly regarded, and considered 'to be at the cutting edge of European thinking on urban regeneration and social exclusion' (Harvey, 1995, p. 60). Some networks are funded under the Commission RECITE (Regions and Cities of Europe) scheme, launched in 1991 with the explicit purpose of trans-regional network formation. In 1989, the European Parliament launched the Exchange of Experience programme, which was then adopted and part financed by the Commission, to transfer know-how between regions (Hooghe, 1995). Trans-regional collaboration, whether across or within national borders, has thus been facilitated by the European

TABLE 9.2

Transregional networks in the European Union (April 1996)

Acronym	Name	Constituency (where unclear from name)	Comments/function (additional to interest representation)
AEBR	Association of European Border Regions		Partly interfaces with Commission's INTERREG programme, linking border regions.
AIRLINE	Aerospace Industry Regional and Local Authority Network	12 local authorities (Benington, 1994)	Networking.
—	Arc Atlantique	30 members bordering the Atlantic in 5 countries. Hosted by Galician representation	Some interface with Commission Atlantis funding programme.
—	Baltic Gateways	North Tyneside (UK), Esbjerg (DK), Gdynia (P), Rostock (D) (Benington, 1994)	Shipyard networking, influenced funding decision under RENEVER programme.
C6	—	6 French and Spanish Mediterranean cities (Hooghe and Marks, 1996)	
CCC	Coalfield Communities Campaign	97 UK authorities, and like regions in Germany, France, Belgium and Spain	Seeking assistance for restructuring of former coalmining regions. Interests in RECHAR programme.
CERCLE	European Local Authorities Research and Study Centre	85 European municipalities, 45 firms (Goldsmith, 1991)	Expertise and think-tank capacity; sharing expertise and interaction.
COAST	Co-ordinated Action for Seaside Towns		

Table 9.2 (*cont.*)

CPMR	Conference of Peripheral Maritime Regions	Formed in 1973 in response to creation of ERDF. 120 member regions. Four specialist 'commissions' (subregional membership units): Atlantic Arc, North Sea, Intermediterranean and Islands	Includes specialist 'Commissions', e.g. 28 North Sea regions. Consultative Status with the Council of Europe (Harvey, 1995).
DEMILITARISED	—	Regions with defence interests	Restructuring of defence industry regions; interface with programmes such as KONVER.
DIONYSOS	—	10 French, Italian, Spanish, Portuguese wine-growing regions (Hooghe, 1995)	Part Commission funded project to pool resources and for technology transfer.
EARLIE	European Aerospace Regional and Local Authority Information Exchange		
EFCT	European Federation of Conference Towns		
EIC	European Middle-Sized Cities Network	Includes large towns such as Brighton, Chartres, Charleroi (Benington, 1994)	
EURADA	European Association of Development Agencies		Regional development agencies.
EUROCERAM	—	Regions with ceramics interests	
EUROCITIES	EUROCITIES	60 metropolitan cities (12 from UK) with populations of at least 250 000.	Share knowledge and experience, help non-EU European cities; subnetwork of 'Telecities', promoting telematic applications in urban life (Harvey, 1995).

Table 9.2 (*cont.*)

Acronym	Name	Constituency (where unclear from name)	Comments/function (additional to interest representation)
—	EUROREGION	5 regions: Kent, Nord Pas de Calais, Wallonia, Flanders, Brussels	European regional identity for economic and funding purposes.
EUROSYNET	—		For cross-national co-operation on public procurement, and the promotion of SMEs.
—	EXCHANGE	Local Authorities	Creation of transnational teams to assist with EXCHANGE programme to combat poverty
—	FOUR MOTORS	Baden Würtemburg, Catalonia, Lombardia, Rhone Alps. Wales part association agreement	'Economic motor' and motor economy regions.
—	GREEN LINKS TO EUROPE		To develop strategic transport corridor from Ireland to Eastern Europe.
—	HORIZON (localities)	Local authorities	Local government network clustered around Commission programme to improve opportunities for disabled.
LEDA	Local Economic Development Action (localities)	Local authorities	Cluster around Commission funding programme.
MILAN	Motor Industry Local Authority Network	Mainly UK-based, run from University of Warwick, UK	Developing links with other European motor industry areas, manufacturers and trade unions.

Table 9.2 (cont.)

Quartiers en Crise/Districts in Crisis	31 cities	Seeks assistance for declining cities; urban development and social exclusion network, know-how exchange, research and seminars, new project and ideas development (Harvey, 1995).
RENAVAL (localities)	Regions with interests in civil shipbuilding restructuring	Interests in RENAVAL programme.
RETEX (localities)	Regions with interests in textile industry restructuring	Interests in RETEX funding programme.
RETI Regions of Industrial Technology (formerly Assn of Traditional Industry Regions of Europe)	Majority of objective 2 regions	Protection and improvement of EU funding for Objective 2 regions.
Roc Nord	Danish–Crete network (Hooghe, 1995)	Knowledge transfer in economic and environmental planning.
Union of Capital Cities		
Working Community of the Jura	CPMR provided significant impetus for creation	
Working Community of the Pyrénées	CPMR provided significant impetus for creation	

institutions in a significant way. Indeed, this form of 'grassroots' collaboration has brought far more tangible results for the regions and localities than has the Committee of the Regions, whether through knowledge transfer, learning and mutual socialisation, or in directly shaping and/or influencing funding programme decisions.

Examples of influence over EU funding initiatives involving the RECHAR, RENAVAL and INTERREG schemes have been provided earlier in this chapter. The Commission's Atlantis programme is another where a regional network, the Arc Atlantique, claims a 'lobbying success', while the Conference of Peripheral Maritime Regions (CPMR) and Coalfield Communities Campaign (CCC) are also regarded as influential organisations. CPMR includes among its successes the adoption by the Council of Ministers of a European Coastal Charter in 1986, protecting coastal zones, controlling tourism and preventing pollution (Harvey, 1995). Elsewhere, the influence of RETI has been frequently cited as a factor in the increase in funds applied to Objective 2 regions in the 1994–9 funding programme (Hooghe, 1995; John, 1994; McAleavy, 1994; McAleavy and Mitchell, 1994), and the influence of the UK Association of County Councils in enhancing the PEFRIFRA programme (John, 1996). Hooghe (1995) also cites the border regions network as being particularly effective. For the future, trans-European networks will create and/or strengthen linked communities of regional interests across national borders. The range of Commission 'own-initiative' funding programmes, in particular, has created relatively good links between it and territorial interests, and it is in these that there is most scope for a 'member state bypass'. The course of European integration will unquestionably develop, and be developed by, this process. Indeed, some of these networks have become more influential within their own interest domains than are the peak associations of territorial interests at the European level. For instance, the author has seen a recent (June 1994) document from the former Central Regional Council, in Scotland, recommending that affiliation to peak bodies be discontinued on the grounds that its interests can be better secured through sectoral networks such as the Coalfields Communities Campaign.

Of course, there have also been some lobbying failures of regional coalitions. John provides some examples of poorly executed campaigns, and others of instances where local-authority and European political-party interests diverge (such as over-issues of environmental compliance costs versus green ideology), even where the same political party is involved (John, 1996). Greenwood *et al.* (1995) show

how some authorities have pursued completely the wrong targets, not least in concentrating lobbying resources at the Brussels level for structural funds and in paying insufficient attention to member state level. These mistakes were not untypical when territorial authorities first became interested in 'Euro grantsmanship', although subsequent attempts to secure funding became more sophisticated as learning curves were mastered.

The contribution of trans-regional networks to integration has been nothing like a smooth or unidirectional process. Some networks are little more than shells, while others such as RETI have a history of collective action problems, with authorities joining and leaving. Once again, however, the Commission has been instrumental in trying to resolve problems. DG XVI, for instance, sought a gathering of Objective 2 regions for reasons of promoting dialogue and identity. When RETI seemed unwilling or incapable of organising one, the Commission service prompted a meeting of all sixty regions in 1991. This was far more than RETI's total membership; the end-result, after considerable shifting of coalition sands, was that RETI sought to become a far more inclusive organisation seeking to represent the interests of all Objective 2 members (McAleavy and Mitchell, 1994).

Beyond the specialist trans-regional networks, the peak associations of territorial interests at the European level are the Assembly of European Regions (AER), and the Conference of European Municipalities and Regions (CEMR). The AER started life as the Council of European Regions in 1985, changing its name in 1987. Comprising 289 member regions from 23 countries, it covers 85 per cent of the European population, and is based in Strasbourg with a secretariat of 20. Because representatives come mainly from elected regional assemblies, there are significant membership gaps in many of the centralised states, and in particular Greece, Ireland and England, as well as Denmark. Its objectives include the promotion of co-operation between the regions of Europe, and to promote regionalism and federalism in Europe. It has created its own policy-specific networks of regions, such as the Interregional Cultural Network (ICON) for exchange of information and implementation of joint projects (Hooghe and Marks, 1996). In 1992, it was significantly reorganised, with a structure including an annual General Assembly, a steering committee ('Bureau') of 40 members, meeting at least 4 times each year, and 6 specialist committees. It performed a semi-institutionalised role with the European Commission prior to the formation of the

Committee of the Regions, doing much of the preparation work (Hooghe, 1995).

The CEMR has much earlier roots. It is the European section of the Hague-based IULA, formed in 1913. This section has its roots from 1951 as the Council of Municipalities, and has twice had a Brussels office. The first of these closed in 1976 due to lack of use and finance (Keating and Waters, 1985), while the second has been open since 1990. Its Paris headquarters now has a secretariat of 30. Its objectives are to: defend and strengthen regional autonomy; represent the interests of local and regional authorities before the EU institutions; promote co-operation between the municipalities and regions of Europe; and develop local democracy in eastern and western European countries. IULA and CEMR have also developed programme responsibilities, such as the Support Programme for Employment Creation (SPEC), a co-financing project with the Commission for pilot employment creation schemes (Harvey, 1995). This illustrates the extent to which interest structures have, in places, becomes mechanisms of European-level public policy delivery.

While the AER is more geared towards regional interests, the CEMR primarily represents local and municipal interests. Both have members drawn from across western and eastern Europe. As peak associations representing large constituencies, they suffer from typical coherence and lowest-common-denominator problems. Like the Committee of the Regions and its predecessor the CCRLA, they have been beset by conflict, both within and, mainly, between these organisations, which are largely divided along the lines of the regions (AER) and the municipalities and local authorities (CEMR) (European Parliament, 1993). A more distinct form of such conflict arises between urban and regional needs. Both organisations perform similar roles; typically, this leads to a limited degree of collaboration as well as competition, not least because the actors have had to work together on a range of issues, including shared institutional involvement (including the nomination of members) in the CCRLA. The AER, in particular, has gained influence in the last decade, and is now treated by the Commission on an even footing with the CEMR (Kitt, 1995). Indeed, DG XVI has tried extremely hard to be even-handed in its dealings with these actors, including allocating equal numbers of seats to them in the CCRLA (Hooghe and Keating, 1994). They are the most representative outlets of territorial authority for the Commission to engage with.

Conclusions

Measures for regulation, integration and funding certainly provide much of the explanation for subnational mobilisation in Europe. The logic of the single market has led to the development of a number of compensatory initiatives in regional policy, and more may arise from further attempts at monetary union. Some Euro competencies have offended territorial interests, but many have delighted local and regional actors throughout member states, and these have formed demand structures for the development of regional policy initiatives. The Commission has not been an impartial actor in this process, deliberately cultivating bridges directly between the territorial and supranational levels where it is able to, assisted by the Parliament. Subregional mobilisation cannot therefore be accounted for by the growth of Euro competencies alone, although the single market has undoubtedly altered the structure of both political opportunities, and the nature of regional policies, in Europe. Rather, institutionalist explanations focusing on the actions of the supranational institutions, together with issues concerning regional identity, and the relationship between subnational actors and member states, are also important factors in explaining subnational mobilisation in Europe.

In centralised states, some territorial interests have sought a presence in Brussels because they seek to stiffen the resolve of central government actors in the interests of regional players. The European level has contributed to the development of regional bureaucracies in some of these countries, and to the mobilisation of interest coalitions around them. In federal states, the European level has involved a partial strengthening of regional interests *vis à vis* member states. But the overall analysis is nothing like as simple as this. Responsibility for regional policy has not been removed from member states. Member states remain the decision-makers in key areas of European integration, and in matters concerning regions and localities, such as structural fund global financing and applications, and the development of the CoR. Yet some member states have clearly been caught out by rules which they themselves signed up to, such as additionality. There is no clear-cut 'national bypass', and nor is there a clear pattern of the European level strengthening, or weakening, of the position of member states *vis-à-vis* the regions and localities. The subnational level is neither superseded nor made subordinate, and nor is there a nascent 'Europe of the Regions' emerging, as a result of the European level. Nor are regional interests straightforwardly enhanced by the EU. Notable trans-regional networks have arisen and developed, and a significant quantity and quality of partnerships of regional, local, national and European-level interests have been created. As John remarks, there is a complex interplay of interests involving a triad of local authorities, national governments and EU institutions; sometimes all of these can be winners, and sometimes different actors can be (John, 1995). To this complexity might be added the cleavages between regional and local interests. Collective action is also complicated by patterns of inter-regional competition and collaboration.

It is these complexities which have led a clutch of authors to search beyond state-centric accounts of European integration (Chapter 10) to adequately conceive of a 'Europe with the Regions' (Hooghe, 1994; Hooghe and Marks, 1996). The question is not so much what the territorial level does to the position of member states in the EU, but what dynamics arise from the subnational level itself, and throughout interactions with the European level. Marks (1993), and Hooghe (1994; 1995), in particular, therefore propose the label of 'multi-level governance' as

> a system of continuous negotiation among nested governments at several territorial tiers – supranational, national, regional, and local – as the result of a broad process of institutional creation and decisional reallocation that has pulled some previously centralised functions of the state up to the supranational level and some down to the local/regional level (Marks, 1993, p. 392).

These ideas have some currency beyond the issue of territorial interest representation. While they are, for the moment, awaiting some flesh on the bones, they do at least present some promise for fully conceiving of the territorial level in its own right, and the 'mobilization and empowerment of subnational governments' (Marks, 1993, p. 407) in the analysis of European integration.

10

Conclusions: Interests and European Integration

Despite key differences in emphasis, actions by private interests are more or less present in most accounts of European integration. Rather than the artificially polarised debate of previous years between neofunctionalist and international relations perspectives on the integration process, considered below, more recent offerings have created some degree of awareness that a range of ideas are partial to explain the realities, dynamics and complexities of European integration (O'Neill, 1996). There is also now some agreement among authors associated with one or other of the classical traditions that an emphasis upon the role of states (international relations), and supranational 'institutionalist' dynamics (neofunctionalism), in the integration process need not be mutually exclusive (Keohane and Hoffman, 1990; Sandholtz, 1993). Most modern accounts of the integration process draw from both traditions rather than exclusively from one.

In part, the search for 'mid-range' ideas arose because both neofunctionalism, apparently moribund by the turn of the 1980s, and (then) dominant international relations accounts, were taken somewhat by surprise by the arrival and significance of the single market and the relaunching of 'project Europe'. Member states were themselves unclear about where the single market would lead them, and did not adequately foresee the ways in which the loss of their national veto, and the agreements they entered into at summits, would lead to supranationalist outcomes. These realities cast doubt upon characterisations drawn from international relations of member states as rational utility-maximisers in interstate bargaining, jealously guarding their sovereignty and calculating the limits to which sovereignty needed to be pooled for their own advantage. Such events demanded fresh perspectives on integration.

Despite acknowledgement throughout different theories of integration of the role of private interests in shaping forces in the integration process, there are substantial differences in emphasis upon the roles which private interests play. The sharpest distinction remains between accounts of integration derived from international relations, and those drawn from other traditions. While Realist and neorealist ideas stress the extent to which interests contribute to domestic preference formation among member states, they continue to under-emphasise the role of transnational-level aggregations of interests. The clarity of such a distinction remains today in modern usage of neorealist variants of international relations theory, where Moravcsik, in particular, continues to emphasise the interests of states (and the global and domestic arenas in which these are defined) as the primary source of integration (Moravcsik, 1991; 1993). Of all the other ideas in integration, the greatest emphasis upon groups is provided by neofunctionalist accounts and derivatives thereof. Because of this emphasis, a brief review is warranted here.

Interests and neofunctionalist accounts of integration

The roots of functionalist theory can be traced to David Mitrany's *Working Peace Systems* (1943), and, as applied to the EEC, to the work of Ernst Haas (1958; 1964). In a nutshell, Mitrany, writing in a time of war, saw the solution to nationalism, and the prospects for peace, in the progressive transfer of specific functional responsibilities away from national governments to supranational agencies. In the first instance, this would involve the gradual transfer of relatively uncontentious, technical, low politics functions to which states would be unlikely to object, until finally states were locked in a web of interdependence in which war would be impossible. It was this vision which inspired the founding fathers of the EEC, Monnet and Schuman, to embark on 'project Europe', first with the coal and steel community, then with atomic energy, to be followed by the development of a single market envisaged by the Treaty of Rome.

In an adaptation of Mitrany's work, Haas identified spillover as the central dynamic to regional integration in Europe, of which two types, functional and political, could be identified. Functional spillover involved the necessity of seeking integration in functionally related areas to resolve the problems of limited integration in one sector, with the gradual buildup of a virtually unstoppable momentum of integration. Thus, the single market brings problems which cannot be adequately dealt with at the national level. For instance, it brings the prospect of uneven development across the regions of Europe, and arguments for significant expansion in regional development programmes. Similarly, market-building in deregulating national rules has brought the need to build new rules of market exchange, such as competition policy (Chapter 5), preventing national barriers to the free movement of workers by providing for European-level rules, and preventing market distortions through differential labour market and environmental production costs by measures for harmonisation (Chapters 7 and 8). Support for these measures can be provided by member states keen to 'export' production conditions to provide a level playing field, and through their public-interest impact. Thus, in the case of environmental policy, there is considerable public support for the development of European level policies to tackle problems such as pollution because it does not respect national boundaries, and the Commission has used this support to seek enhanced competencies. In the 'cohesion four' countries, the benefits to be derived from the structural funds have helped popularise the EU (Chapter 9). Public support, however, remains context-specific and an uncertain factor in the integration process. Thus, more controversially, the Commission at present sees monetary union as a necessary next 'functional-spillover' step in integration following the single-market programme.

The second type of spillover, namely political, involved the demands of interests for further integration to arise at the supranational level, and the associated transfer of loyalties of political actors from the national to the supranational level. Private and public interests therefore play a central role in this account of integration. In the first instance, business interest groups, in particular, would come to see the value of European integration, perhaps from tangible benefits achieved in other sectors, and exert demands upon member states for integration at the supranational (European) level. As integration initiatives arose, so pressure would build up in favour of further integrative measures, and transnational groups would form to exert demands at the transnational level in tandem with those made at the national level, and to form a barrier against the possibility of any retreat in integration. A key role in this transfer of loyalties is posited for the Commission, which, interested in the development of a European 'superstate', or at least further powers for itself, manipulates the formation of transnational-level interest groups as demand and protection structures at national and transnational levels for further integration. The integration process is posited as developing with its own momentum, carried forward by the role of rhetoric, ideas, and the creation of institutionalised structures in which the actors become enmeshed, which in turn restructures their preferences. Something of this nature seems to be emerging in the field of 'social Europe' (Chapter 7). The end result of these processes would be the creation of a European 'superstate', and the erosion of the nation state as an entity. Thus, Haas defined integration as

the process whereby political actors in several distinct national settings are persuaded to shift their loyalties, expectations and political activities toward a new centre, whose institutions possess or demand jurisdiction over the pre-existing national states (Haas, 1958, p. 16).

This account of integration seemed to fit at least some of the realities in the first years of the EEC. In the first instance, initiatives to achieve European integration arose from political leaders in the context of some disinterest from the European business community. Once the benefits of integration became clear, however, there was something of a role reversal, with business in the forefront of demands for integration that were made to more reluctant politicians. Transnational-level business groups did grow apace in the years between the Treaty of Rome and the 'empty chair' crisis of 1965, with the Commission playing an active role in their development. As was evident from the review in Chapter 5, some of these groups did come to play a significant role in securing European integration within the sectors in which they operated, although in many instances not until the advent of the single-market project. The contribution of transnational-level groups was uneven, however, and some of those which formed in the early years of the EEC were shell structures unable to contribute anything very significant. Spillover, while recognisable in some sectors, was often not unidirectional towards further integration, such that terms like 'spill around' and 'spill back' were created in revisionist accounts of neofunctionalism. As Haas and other proponents of neofunctionalism came to recognise by the mid-1960s in a highly self-critical way, nothing like an incremental and self-sustaining momentum towards further integration could be claimed, but rather 'fits and starts'. And the extent to which 'spillover' integration extended from low politics into high politics fields, a claim made in some versions of neofunctionalism, was at best dubious.

This latter point provided one of the main foci of attack on neofunctionalist theory by scholars in the field of international relations, who, while acknowledging that states might not be too concerned with the transfer of powers from the national to the supranational level in technical, low politics fields where it suited them to pool their respective sovereignties, insisted that governments would never permit spillover into high politics fields such as defence, national security and monetary union (Hoffman, 1965; and Tsoukalis, 1977; both cited in George, 1991). Notions of low and high politics are thus central to accounts of integration, but as was discussed in Chapter 1, there is a blurring of the boundary between low and high, with some issues, such as competition policy, actually straddling it; similarly, different actors would be prone to classify different issues in different ways, depending on their importance. However, for the purposes of this discussion some sort of low–high politics continuum is useful to distinguish between technical and more politicised issue arenas, and the ways in which perceptions of issues condition the responses of interests.

Indeed, many and significant criticisms and revisions have been made of neofunctionalist theory, some by its proponents, and some by its opponents (for a review of these see, for instance, the collections by Nelsen and Stubb, 1994, and O'Neill, 1996). Consequently, Haas finally abandoned the theory by 1976, the mid-point of the so called 'dark' years of 'Eurosclerosis', because of the absence of incremental spillover in the direction of further integration, and the extent to which events since the 'empty chair' crisis of 1965 had seemed to confirm the supremacy of member states in the integration process (Haas, 1976). International relations accounts, focusing on the supremacy of member states as actors in the integration process, therefore came to dominate explanations of integration in the period from the de Gaulle crisis until at least the advent of the single-market project.

International relations ideas and the challenge of large firms as political actors

The consequences of the single-market project in leading to a variety of integrative measures which states had clearly not foreseen when they signed up to it, and the role of the supranational institutions and non-state actors in the accelerated integration process since, have considerably brought into question the determined focus upon states as the principal source of integration in some versions of international-relations theory. There is, however, undoubtedly a considerable richness in depth of international relations accounts of integration. The less Realist accounts, for instance, posit how 'preference convergence' among states arises from their interdependence, and their participation and mutual socialisation as network actors in a global context. Yet most international relations accounts continue to see integration as little more than the outcome of rational strategies pursued by states, seeking limited integration in as far as it met their calculated needs to so do.

Some recent work in the related field of international political economy does focus upon the way in which markets are part of an integrated pattern of political authority and governance, examining the interrelationships between the interests of states and those of socioeconomic coalitions underpinning the operation of the global market economy. Here, politics and markets are seen as indivisible. Firms are seen as integral to the politics of relations among states, rather than a disaggregation between relations among states on the one hand and market forces on the other (Strange, cited in Underhill, 1997). This is a quite specific way of recognising the way in which global forces have shaped governmental preferences. Away from offshoots of international relations, these themes have also been present in a more familiar way in Marxist analyses (Baran and Sweezy, 1966; Holland, 1976), and in work on meso and micro corporatism (Cawson, 1985). However, as Lindblom has remarked, no particular theoretical sophistication is required in order to recognise the privileged position of business in governance (Lindblom, 1977).

Multinational firms, in particular, play a central role in politics. The role of these actors in the creation of the single European market has been well documented by Cowles (1995a), particularly when it has been expressed in the form of organised business through the

AMCHAM-EU and the ERT, and their institutionalised relationships with national governments and with the European Commission. Large firms moved away from 'national champion' strategies towards the end of the 1970s because of their multinational character, and because their interests could not and were not being particularly well served by any one particular government. They sought instead a transnational solution to the future of wealth creation in Europe and to Europe's competitiveness *vis-à-vis* global trade. The strategy they chose was the completion of the single market first envisaged by the Treaty of Rome. In preparation, the run-up to the single market saw a hectic process of concentration such that transnational European networks of capital were in place (Jacquemin and Wright, 1994; Chapter 1). Most legislation directed at industry in Europe now has a 'made in Brussels' stamp on it (Cowles, 1995a; Chapter 5). Trade between member states has grown exponentially, such that the European market is today the largest home market in the world. Eurobarometer evidence suggests that the single-market process drove on a wave of 'Euro enthusiasm' among business interests and public opinion, in a manner quite anticipated by Euro architects such as Davignon, Cockfield and Delors (Sandholtz, 1993), but not perhaps by member states. In turn, the role of transnational level groups in supranational structures questioned international relations perspectives on integration, and reawakened interest in explanations of an institutionalist type.

Although business groups did mobilise in response to the Treaty of Rome by forming transnational level groups (Chapter 5), large firms were not in themselves active players much before 1980 (Cowles, 1995b). But the investment by multinational firms in, and partial shift of loyalties to, the European level in the early 1980s (Chapter 5) is not too far removed from what Haas (1958; 1964) had envisaged in his theory of neofunctionalism. The largest firms in Europe, through their CEOs in the European Round Table of Industrialists, played a driving role in conceiving the solution in the form of project 1992, in élite socialisation, and, where governments looked like faltering, in binding their commitment, if necessary by threatening the removal of investments, sometimes directly through their ability to use a prime-ministerial hotline (Cowles, 1995a; Chapter 5). Some of these ERT members were directly recruited by Commissioner Davignon with this purpose in mind (Sandholtz, 1993). Delors has paid tribute to the role of the ERT, and, where necessary, used the support of the ERT with the member states to seek further integration, sometimes by directly quoting their enthusiasm in summitry, sometimes by appearing on joint platforms with the ERT, and sometimes by asking ERT and/or AMCHAM-EU to establish strategic think-tank groups. Thus, the Commission has used this support to make the functional spillover claim about the necessity of following up the single-market programme with monetary integration.

There is also some, albeit more limited, evidence of political spillover with business groups mobilising at the transnational level in favour of monetary union, and exerting influence on both the European institutions and member states (Sandholtz, 1993). More certainly, the ERT exerted significant influence upon the development of competition policy, a relatively high politics field. From such evidence, the Commission certainly appears as a manipulator and shared leader of integration, and business and transnational authority seem almost indivisible in pursuing integration. The sources of change came as much from within Europe as from the member states. Certainly, changes in member state politics, and in particular the change in emphasis in France and Spain upon market solutions in the 1980s, led to some kind of preference convergence to accept market-driven visions provided by business and the Commission. Clearly, the global environment, in the words of Sandholtz, created 'the context of choice and cast up problems to be resolved' (Sandholtz, 1993, p. 127). And, true, governments negotiated the details of the SEA and ratified it. But the 'decisions and strategies' (ibid.) came mainly from within the European level itself, not least from the capacity of business to shape the response, and integration seems to have developed, at least in part, its own dynamic. Similarly, the ERT has been credited with either the ideas, or decisive support for, later high politics initiatives, such as initiatives on growth, competitiveness and employment, and TENs (Cowles, 1995a). Some ERT strategic thinking and actions have provided decisive leadership in times when national political leaders have been in disarray. The ERT told Cowles:

Governments are pleased to regard themselves as sovereign decision-makers . . . (I)n fact they are very much at the mercy of conflicting pressures and severe constraints. Indeed, the powerlessness of governments is one of the important themes of our time. What the ERT does is to help and encourage governments to move in certain directions. We do this by providing analysis and advice, by posing questions and influencing the general climate of opinion and by warning of the consequences of mistaken policies. In other words, we add to the pressures (1995b, p. 21).

Realist theories, which seemed good explanations of the European Community in the 1960s, were no longer adequate in the 1980s. As Cowles (1995a) comments, the experience of the 1980s was that big business can interject their agendas, ideas and ideological views in matters that were traditionally reserved for member states or other formal EU bodies twenty years ago. As Keohane and Hoffman (1990) suggest, the process (if not the context) of EU policy-making is now undoubtedly supranational. Supranational institutions do have autonomy, and, often in tandem with transnational groups, they do seek to advance the course of integration. Indeed, the realities of European integration in the 1980s and 1990s have led to a search for a revised version of neofunctionalism, and in challenging the lack of emphasis placed on transnational groups by mainstream international relations theories.

A revised neofunctionalism?

Political spillover remains a central problem in assessing the contribution of private and public interests to the integration process, because the process of transfer of loyalties and competencies has been neither incremental nor unidirectional, and nor (as Haas originally acknowledged) has it been automatic. The formation and maintenance of interest groups, and the roles and perspectives of actors from interest communities has been nothing like as predictable as the process of political spillover suggested. For instance, some groups representing the professions have remained in the national capitals and have sought to retain their advantages at the national level (Chapter 6). Equally, while there is evidence of political spillover in low politics fields arising from the activities of interest groups and other types of interest aggregations, the extent to which such interests contribute to high politics fields, where multiple actors (including member states and supranational institutions) engage in multiple arenas, is somewhat debatable. This debate is a crucial one in evaluating the role of interest groups in integration, and one which is examined further at a later point in this chapter. However, it has never been refuted that political spillover does occur. EFPIA, for instance, one of the best resourced, authoritative and effective Euro groups, has been able to achieve far more by acting at the European level than was possible at the national level, and the European pharmaceutical industry has successfully persuaded governments to shift competencies for medicine authorisation, patents, some pricing issues, and information regulation to the transnational level. EFPIA has become institutionally involved in these changes itself, to the degree of delegation of authority from the Commission for self-regulatory arrangements. It has even persuaded the Commission to take the governments of Italy and Belgium to the ECJ over arrangements that the industries in those countries were until recently a party to (Chapter 5).

Evidence of spillover mechanisms in action has led to efforts among researchers to adapt neofunctionalist ideas from where Haas left them in 1976. Part of the answer in seeking a revised form of neofunctionalism has been to turn to different kinds of institutionalist – 'new institutionalist' – explanations, taken from comparative politics, the 'institutional features' which 'organise the behaviour of the actors and structure the conflict' (Hix, quoted in Cowles, 1995a). Partly reviewing some of these, Caporaso and Keeler comment that 'increasingly, scholars assume that some institutional structure is in place and examine what goes on inside those structures. Politics and policy making within institutions have assumed an analytic place alongside the politics of institutional change' (quoted in Cram, 1995, p. 3).

International relations scholars have focused upon the way in which EU institutions provide a framework in which intergovernmental bargaining occurs, and see these in a rather passive way with capacities of limited autonomy which enhances prospects for state-level bargaining. Other writers provide for a more active role for these institutions, beyond that permitted by member governments, both as independent actors with a significant degree of autonomy (and in particular the Commission and the ECJ), and in socialising the actors who participate within them (Fuchs, 1993; Sandholtz, 1993; Cram, 1995a; Marks *et al.*, 1996). In the latter context, Cram retains the idea from earlier neofunctionalist theory of the Commission as manipulator, in seeking to depoliticise, select and define issues to ensure that member states do not see issues in terms of 'winners' and 'losers' (Cram, 1995a; Chapter 8). Also central to this strategy is the ability of the Commission to draw private interests, both domestic and transnational, into the European policy process, in acting on both national governments and transnational structures.

Although a reservation must be expressed about the way in which such accounts tend to treat the Commission as a singular actor acting in a cohesive and unidirectional way (Chapter 8), the emphasis upon the ways in which supranational institutions possess autonomy to develop the integration process does mean that the trap is avoided of seeing national governments as fully rational, independent actors, in command of information resources and in full view of the consequences of decision-making. This position is close to that of Sandholtz (reviewed earlier), who holds that member state preferences and positions are shaped by their historic and present participation in the EU, which move them to work in ways in which they would not otherwise have done had they not been in membership. Crudely speaking, years of collaboration within the structures of the EU has had an impact on the ways in which member states see issues, respond to them, and relate to one another and to supranational structures. Actors come to share assumptions and belief systems as a product of the institutions and interests in which they participate and interact, and socialise one another in so doing.

A further dimension is given by the ways in which the natures of the issues themselves shape the integration process, such as how competition from developing economies, or competing technologies in product standards, may shape perceptions of issues, the interaction of political actors and the solutions developed to problems (Chapter 5). Cawson, for instance, has shown how high-definition television policy changed from an industrial policy issue of protecting a 'Euro champion' firm in consumer electronics manufacture, Philips, to concerns about the ways in which such a firm could prevent competition in digital broadcasting by restricting market entry of new firms (Chapter 5). Such a change in perception was caused by the entry of new forces into the policy arena, involving different units of the Commission and different business interests. 'Everyday politics' therefore matter (Cram, 1995a; Peterson, 1995b). Similarly, private interests also contribute to, and are socialised by, the value systems to which they participate, and are deeply influenced by the institutional structures, positions taken, and architecture within the EU. This type of work significantly advances institutionalist explanations of integration, through acknowledging the role of member states, the supranational institutions themselves, and that of transnational private interest groups in the integration process. As is evident from some of the arguments reviewed later, institutions and everyday politics considerably shape interest intermediation in the EU.

'New' institutionalist explanations feature strongly in the work of some of the more recent ideas on European integration, in particular that of multi-level governance. Associated most closely with the work of Marks (1993), Bulmer (1994), Peterson (1995b), and Marks *et al.* (1996), the literature suggests

> that institutions shape preferences and outcomes; that the complexity and contested character of policy making on multiple levels makes for dispersed and disjointed decisions, and for incomplete implementation; and that national governments have struggled both to use the EC level to serve their own national objectives and to maintain control over inputs and outcomes, with varying success in different areas (Wallace, 1996, p. 445).

While this work acknowledges the primary role of states in high politics arenas and their control of the integration process through treaties, it places considerable emphasis upon the autonomous role of supranational institutions, and on the dense networks they form with a variety of political actors, in exploiting and developing the vacuum left by the outline nature of member state agreement. Integration therefore proceeds beyond the complete control of state actors, in ways not always envisaged by them. In particular, the complexity of European-level decision-making takes integration away from state control. In these respects, multi-level governance has more in common with neofunctionalism than with intergovernmental explanations, because of the failure of latter accounts to adequately conceive of the autonomy of supranational institutions and the importance of their relationships with non-state actors for the development of integration. Multi-level governance accounts are particularly critical of statecentric approaches, stressing: the importance of disaggregating state actors; that state actors have other goals in addition to preserving state sovereignty; that state executives are just one type of a variety of influential actors in the EU, with supranational institutions exerting important influences; and that state-centric accounts fail to take into account both supranational and sub national arenas (Marks *et al.*, 1996). These critiques of state-centric approaches place the ideas of multi-level governance far closer to neofunctionalist accounts.

Yet both neofunctionalist and international relations perspectives are seen in accounts written from the multi-level governance viewpoint as failing to recognise fully the multi-dimensional character of European integration, and the dynamic character of EU decision-making in shifting between arenas and actors. Hooghe and Marks, in particular, had in mind the arrival of sub-national government as a tier of authority and governance, and its interaction with other tiers. This variant of multi-level governance is seen as a result of processes whereby European integration and regionalism 'converge in pulling decision-making away from national states' (Hooghe and Marks, 1996, p. 23). 'Multi-level governance' is therefore characterised by 'co-decision-making across several nested tiers of government, ill-defined and shifting spheres of competence' (Marks, 1993, p. 407). In this, there are however still resonances of a process with its own momentum which is central to neofunctionalist theory.

Ideas and socialisation (Chapters 1, 2, 5, 7 and 8), a range of interacting interests at a variety of levels with differential influences in different arenas (Chapter 2), the institutional pull and push upon the behaviour of individual and collective political actors (Chapters 3, 5, 7, 8), everyday politics (Chapters 4–9), and the ways in which particular types of policies and issues can structure underlying politics (Chapters 3, 5, 7, 8 and 9), are the ingredients for a modern-day neofunctionalism. In such accounts, actions by private and public interests, and a shift in the horizons of actors to the transnational level, are central to explanations of integration.

Interests and the integration process

The study of 'business and European integration' is by now almost a historic endeavour. The single market is all but established as an arena, at least for market exchange, and we know from the numerous sectoral case studies reviewed in Chapter 5 that business interests have not been insignificant in the achievement of integration within their domains. We know, most notably from the work of Cowles, that a variety of forces, global and domestic, drove large firms in Europe to see a single home market as the solution to the future of their wealth creation capacities (Chapters 1 and 5). In the shape of the ERT, they helped provide the blueprint and much of the impetus for the single market, and, where member states faltered or showed signs of a loss of nerve, business was there encouraging, prodding, or, if necessary, threatening removal of investment. Europe's future wealth creation depended upon the ability of business, in partnership with key elites in the supranational institutions, to socialise themselves and a variety of political actors with a definition of the problems and the solutions, and to create the momentum for the solutions to become a reality.

Much of market integration in low politics fields has been achieved, or is well under way. In 1996, consistent with President Santer's theme of 'managing what we do better', the Commission announced only nineteen new initiatives in its work programme. The agenda in economic fields has largely shifted back again to the realms of high politics, to which of course business interests do not have monopolistic access. Some business groups, like the ERT and the AMUE, with powerful large-firm members, can and do contribute to high politics arenas at the level of ideas (Chapter 5), but these are multiple arenas with multiple players. Indeed, the present IGC reminds us that the focus of integration is back upon member state bargaining.

Even in low politics fields, it is methodologically almost impossible to definitively prove the specific 'influence' of interests over policy outcomes. It would be somewhat naïve to draw simple connections between the aspirations of private interests on the one hand, and public policy decisions and non-decisions on the other, or to take at face value the claims of interests or the ways in which the recollections of public officials are constructed and presented. In any event, few researchers ever get near enough to the centres of decision-making, and those who do can be too closely involved to examine the complexities of power and norms which structure decisions and non-decisions. A simple reading of the physical resources of Euro groups such as personnel and turnover does not on its own imply effectiveness, although the lack of these, together with a history of collective action problems, does indicate a reduced ability to wield influence. Network analysis, focusing on constructs such as resource exchange, policy communities and the ways in which belief systems arise and are shared, among elite participants (Chapter 1), and the interrelationship between values and facts in knowledge communities (Chapter 8), can help to identify influences over policy outcomes. Similarly, wider social values structure debate and governance; an example which comes to mind concerns the ways in which the aftermath of the TEU referendum debates has favourably influenced the climate for the development of citizen and consumer interests at the European level (Chapters 4 and 8). Subsequent measures have developed their own logic, such that rhetoric to construct a 'Citizens' Europe' is no longer 'cheap talk'. Indeed, citizen and social interests in Europe now have the organisational capacity to ensure that rhetoric does not stay empty, and have flourished in the climate of 'Citizens First' (Chapter 8). This suggests that a simple reading of wider resource exchange capacities does not on its own predict influence. In the environmental domain, for instance, while environmental protection is driven more by concerns among business interests than those of public interests, there has been something of a 'preference convergence' between the two. Business now talks the language of 'sustainable development', and has come to see a high level of environmental protection as consistent with the market positioning of its products on the global market, where products compete through recognition of quality standards. Something similar has arisen in some aspects of consumer affairs, where business has equated consumer protection with quality issues, now partly enshrined in policy implementation mechanisms for the General Product Safety Directive (Chapter 8).

The success of public interests in the EP vote over the draft Bio-patenting Directive (Chapter 8) illustrates the ability of public interests under certain conditions to compete with the most powerful business interests by politicising issues, and the ways in which the Parliament offers public interests the opportunity to exert influence. Any increases in power for the Parliament is likely to strengthen the role of public interests. Many public-interest groups, however, have been genuinely surprised to find how easy it is to gain access to public-policy arenas in Brussels (Chapter 8). What is perhaps of greatest significance from the review in Chapter 8 is the remarkable degree of mobilisation of public-interest groups, and the relative strengths of these. Some 20 per cent of Euro groups are public-interest groups, and, surprisingly, a higher proportion of these have more than 5 staff, and a turnover in excess of 100 000 ECU, than do the more numerous business groups. In some fields, most notably environmental public interests, coalition-building between Euro groups has worked well (Chapter 8). Some Brussels-based public-interest groups are Brussels policy offices of wider movements, such as Amnesty International and the World Wide Fund for Nature, and do not suffer from the collective action problems present in some federated structures of business. Nevertheless, business interests are often able to call upon a more diverse range and strength of resources across sectors, and through the firms represented through groups. The multinational oil industry, for instance, has a specialist association dedicated to representing the environmental interests of oil firms, as well as a variety of other powerful associations with interests in the field (Chapter 8). While the discussion on preference convergence indicates patterns of collaboration between producer and public interests, there are also entrenched arenas of competition.

Clearly, interests with significant bargaining chips, in the form of economic power to exchange in governance structures are more likely to be influential than those without (Chapter 1). An illustration of this is provided by Porter's comprehensive study of interest input in the Packaging and Packaging Waste Directive (Chapter 8). The 'privileged position of business' posited by Lindblom (1977), and the superior resources of these actors, does mean that the voice of business tends to be heard above those of others over specific measures for which there is a range of interest input. Such actors have the capacities to exert influence throughout the policy cycle, whereas public interests may be more restricted to involvement at the level of ideas (Chapter 8), or, using the example of the bio-patenting issue, at dramatic points in the decision cycle to which the resources of these interests have been intensely directed in politicising issues. The ability of public interests to sustain such a level of politicisation is also questionable. Indeed, the bio-patenting directive will soon be re-presented in a revised format after a period of quiet discussion between the Commission and the business interests to whom the directive is so essential (Chapter 8). As so often happens, issues seem to lose some of their controversy when they are presented second time round because actors have become accustomed to the arguments, see re-presentation as a sign of inevitability that the measure will eventually be passed in some way, or find it difficult to sustain the same level of novelty and enthusiasm among interests likely to object. The ability of some business interests to be ever present in decisional arenas, and to see issues through the length of their policy life span, suggests a more sustained capacity among such interests to exert influence (Chapter 5). Even in relatively politicised domains, the power of business to structure debate does mean that it is able to exert important influences in the all-important issue definition stage. Thus, in a recent contribution, Sbragia has shown how business interests have focused the policy debate on TENs away from public-interest environmental concerns and towards the needs of business (Sbragia, 1996).

In low politics domains, the influence of interests, while methodologically problematic, is somewhat more discernible than it is in high politics arenas. The nature of low politics predicts that interests with exclusive and indispensable resources, such as expertise, will be able to obtain monopolistic access to the policy process through closed and integrated elite policy communities (Chapter 1). Business interests are more likely to be in possession of such resources, and the ability to exploit them, than will other types of interests. Such interests will therefore try to ensure that issues remain within the low politics fields where they are able to exert significant influence over both the character and detail of governance. Public interests are rarely able to enjoy such monopolistic access. But, as was argued in Chapter 8, the effectiveness of any interest might best be gauged by assessing impact on policy outputs, such as by structuring debate and in the injection of ideas. This is particularly applicable throughout high politics arenas because of the characteristic multiplicity of players and arenas.

Groups with significant think-tank capacities, such as the ERT, or the AMUE (with somewhat overlapping large-firm memberships), have the ability to structure debate within high politics arenas. But even in the grey areas of politicised arenas in between high and low politics, such as environmental protection, a range of interests can contribute at the level of outputs. Thus, the contribution of interests to integration may go somewhat beyond the boundaries of low politics arenas acknowledged by international relations accounts. Ideas matter, particularly where there is a vacuum. Member states do not operate in arenas that correspond precisely to those of the supranational institutions and interests, which latter therefore have the opportunity to develop integration within such a vacuum. In the absence of ideas, firm directions and detailed involvement in the integration process by member states, networks of groups and supranational actors can drive integration by defining issues, identifying and choosing options, and delivering policy in implementation structures. Where member states do operate in European integration, they do not always have the coherence to provide leadership, or the monopoly over issues to exclude ideas generated by non-state actors in structuring debate. Indeed, interests contribute to shaping the preferences of member state actors, and therefore to the consequent positions they take in the integration process. Interests can also enter the vacuum left by the management deficit of the Commission by providing key resources and fulfilling functions in the integration process (Chapter 1). Indeed, the very complexity of European policy processes tends to disperse control of integration and provide vacuums for other actors to fill.

Particularly under conditions of uncertainty, therefore, where member state involvement in the integration process in nature only an outline one and is lacking in detail, unclear and/or divided, networks of interests and supranational institutions possess considerable opportunities to progress integration. The development of the social dialogue (Chapters 5 and 7) is one illustration of this general phenomenon. Considerable leadership was provided for the construction of a 'social Europe' by Delors, and taken forward in a rather determined way by DG V, in which the European Trade Union Confederation is institutionally involved as a network actor. Member state perspectives sharply contrast on a spectrum ranging from, at one end, those countries keen to export higher production conditions to, at the other, those seeking competitive advantage by insisting on the ability to retain locally determined production conditions. The Social Protocol ended the ability of some member states to get away with 'cheap talk' in the enhancement of labour market conditions, creating a configuration of one member state (the UK) versus the rest (Chapter 5). The macroeconomic 'social partners', UNICE, ETUC and CEEP, wrote the draft social agreement, which was appended to the Maastricht Treaty almost unrevised under conditions of intense and hurried intergovernmental summitry within the confines of a crowded agenda (Chapter 2). Just as the single market has developed the pace of integration in ways not wholly anticipated by member states, so the framework of social dialogue has developed at a level of detail by the partners within it and has delivered consequences which may not have been foreseen. These partners were invested by the TEU with legal responsibility to initiate and develop social Europe through the parameters of the social dialogue. Such responsibilities have considerably strengthened the otherwise threatened positions of UNICE, CEEP and ETUC *vis-à-vis* their members and in European public affairs as a whole. The influence of UNICE, in particular, had been eroded by the advent of the ERT and AMCHAM-EU. UNICE, CEEP and ETUC now have limited collective-bargaining mandates from their members (Chapters 5 and 7). True, business has historically been a reluctant partner, although in turn this particular *type* of vacuum has enabled ETUC to exploit divisions and to progress integration (Chapter 7). What is significant, however, is that UNICE has become increasingly less reluctant as the social dialogue has developed, and that meaningful public-policy initiatives, no matter how awkwardly, are arising (Chapter 5). To some extent, both

UNICE and ETUC have 'gone native' by participating in the European public-policy arena.

The Social Protocol has now moved some way beyond relatively uncontentious agreement on education and training, into more meaningful fields such as works councils, the Parental Leave accord, and the protection of the rights of part-time workers. True, the Commission has had to play an interventionist role in bringing debate to legislation (Chapters 5 and 7). But 'social Europe' is no longer 'cheap talk'. UNICE has become enmeshed within a structure with its own momentum from which it cannot escape, and, through participation in it, its own preferences have been restructured. The clock cannot be turned back to the days when labour market issues were effectively excluded from the agenda of the EU as a result of the alliances between employers and the British government. Integration has proceeded within the 'mushiness' of the boundaries established by member state summitry to such a degree that the interest networks which are exploiting the vacuum (in this instance ETUC and parts of the Commission) may themselves be able in the future to expand the boundaries of integration which member states set, having partially restructured the preferences of UNICE *en route*.

The recently accelerated pace of development of European integration in labour market fields provides an opportunity to watch forces in the integration process unfolding in current affairs. The development of integration in labour market fields may not be dependent upon the role of ETUC. Certainly, ETUC has found a role by locating issues which are most appropriately dealt with at the European level. But periods of high unemployment do not favour trade union actors, and the preference for market solutions means that the European level does not yet compensate for loss of influence at home. For some national union interests, Brussels is indeed 'the only card game in town' (Chapter 7). Yet at the other extreme, it is difficult to identify how workers can gain added value from the European level to conditions enjoyed in their own states. The parameters of labour market integration seem to be driven less by ETUC than by member state concerns for a level playing field in production conditions, although, as was argued above, parameters can leave plenty of room for network actors to exploit 'drift'. As with competition policy, market deregulation has led to some degree of re-regulation, and re-regulation has in turn developed its own momentum. But in addition, the agenda of today demands that the benefits of Europe extend beyond business interests, and in doing so provides a window of opportunity for labour interests. 'Social Europe' is no longer just about preventing unfair competition by uneven labour market conditions, where the recent emphasis in Commission rhetoric is as much upon public spending and investment in the labour market than in deregulating it (Chapter 7). Instead of the erratic 'fits and starts' of integration historically characterising labour market integration, rather more incremental progression seems now to be in evidence.

Interests, integration and the role of the European institutions

The expansion of European integration in labour market fields can also be illustrated by recalling from Chapter 7 the debate on the drawn-out workers' consultation arena. Long stalled by a veto exercised by member states and business in the 1980s, the issue has now returned in the guise of the Directive on Information and Consultation. Far less offence has been caused by the common use of this name than by the title of Works Councils Directive. The initiative illustrates the ways in which determined network building by the supranational institutions (and in particular, actions by the Commission with the support of the Parliament, both interested in the achievement of further European integration and a consequent enhancement of their role) can develop European integration. In 1992–3 alone, the Commission spent 31 million ECU on the development of forerunner European Works Councils, and 4 million ECU on ETUC-related activities. European works councils have created transnational networks of workers at grassroots level, and strengthened the role of sectoral industry union federations at the European level as independent structures and within ETUC. They have also brought tangible benefits for their members in the firms where they have been established (Chapter 7). In performing these roles, they have created forces for the transfer of loyalties of political actors to the European level.

In establishing transnational networks, the Commission undoubtedly also creates demand structures for integration at the European level, and for the expansion of competencies. Commission activity in this endeavour is evident throughout the interest arenas reviewed in Chapters 5–9. It makes crystal-clear its preferences for engaging with transnational actors, and provides incentives to these to form and develop, ranging from encouragement and criticism at the 'soft' end, to advisory committee places and funding at the 'hard' end of the spectrum. So strong are these incentives that a least one 'Euro champion' multinational firm has created an associational structure largely for the purpose of 'playing the game' and pleasing the Commission, while other business interests have disbanded groups following criticism by the Commission of the extent to which they are representative and coherent (Chapter 5). In a survey of the constituency of Euro groups, the majority (160, or 53 per cent) rated their allocation of EU advisory committee places from the Commission as an important membership incentive. But most visible of all are the initiatives of the Commission and the Parliament in providing funding or activities dedicated to the establishment of new groups.

In business domains, the Commission has brought together key interests for the purpose of forming groups where these were absent, and, if necessary, provided funding for these. Its programmes, from research collaboration schemes through to TENs, create new network structures of interests. In territorial domains the Commission has established a programme dedicated to the funding of trans-regional networks (Chapter 9). Some of these networks have been directly responsible for helping the Commission establish own-initiative funding programmes deliberately aimed at bypassing member states or challenging member states interpretation of funding rules, as was the case with the Coalfield Communities Campaign and the RECHAR initiative (Chapter 9). Indeed, the latter case is instructive because member states signed up to 'additionality' rules which they later found it difficult to live with. In turn, this illustrates once again the lack of control of member states in the integration process in that they sign up to framework agreements without fully appreciating the consequences of them, and which develop in ways unanticipated by them, shaped by other forces in the integration process.

The Commission now creates or sustains local-interest networks around implementation of the structural funds, and is increasingly present itself at the local level in consultation and implementation (Chapter 9). In some member states without significant devolved territorial authorities, some of these networks might otherwise have been absent. Where transnational territorial groups have lacked breadth of membership, the Commission has itself brought together interests through activities such as convening meetings of regions interested in a particular structural fund, and through such initiatives have provided the basis for groups to improve the range of interests they represent (see, for instance, the case of RETI in Chapter 9). In social and citizen domains, both the Commission and the Parliament have been busily and explicitly prompting, establishing and funding transnational networks in recent years, such that there are now over 150 groups spanning 20 sectors of activity, mostly funded by the EU. Groups such as Eurolink Age, FEANTSA (homelessness), the European Disability Forum, the European Anti-Poverty Network, the Network for One-Parent Families, and the Trans-European Rural Network, all started life from Commission funding programmes or Commission conferences designed to kick-start European-level interest aggregations. Some of these have themselves spawned further specialist networks – six in the case of the European Anti-Poverty Network. As an example of how groups move into the 'vacuum' left by 'management deficit', some have become part of policy implementation structures, operating Commission training and 'observatory' programmes, while ECAS operates a citizens' telephone hotline that is in greater use than one provided by DG X for this purpose, and which provides the Commission with policy-relevant information on issues such as the free movement of workers across borders (Chapter 8). Beyond these arrangements, so ingrained is the relationship between public authority and some private interests that arrangements of neocorporatist, 'private-interest government' type arise at the meso level (Chapter 5).

Unsurprisingly, the effect of establishing new groups is to create pressures for further integration, and the expansion of Euro competencies. In housing, for instance, there are virtually no Euro competencies, but the Commission deliberately inaugurated a conference on homelessness from which FEANTSA emerged, with Commission support and funding. Only rarely is the Commission clumsy enough to mobilise member state resistance; the German veto of the Fourth Anti-Poverty Programme in 1994 provides an exception. But in the main, the Commission uses networks of European level interests to promote integration by stealth, establishing pressure structures, most notably through the Parliament where social concerns are strong and reflect the interests of constituents, for the expansion of Euro competencies (Chapter 8).

The Commission's relationship with private interests is, however, far from uni-directional. Difficult integration problems remain in fields such as competition policy, where the interests of private firms can compete with those of states, such as disputes over airline subsidies. As further exemplar material, it is worth recalling events from Chapter 6, where sectoral directives aimed at facilitating the ability of professional workers to work in other countries took up to seventeen years to complete, or were wholly abandoned. Rather than facilitating the process of integration, a number of groups were either unable to deliver agreement, or, in the case of certain measures aimed at liberalisation, resisted integration. In the end, the Commission found it easier not to consult with interests and to abandon the difficult sectoral integration approach in favour of a general directive aimed at mutual recognition of qualifications. Groups representing the professions remain far stronger at the national level, where entrenched powers offer far more prospects than the more uncertain, and in some instances, threatening, Brussels environment. Some sectoral interests have sought to prevent peak groups from acting as anything more than listening posts, and despite the three peak groups representing the professions working on very similar issues, there is not so much as an issue network between them. Nothing like a political spillover mechanism can be detected. Conversely, however, interests in this field have made an impact in that their failure to contribute significantly has hampered the integration process.

The professions apart, few would deny that interests do tend to respond to the development of Euro competencies, and indeed many groups have set up in Brussels since the start of the single-market project. But it is possible that this factor has been overemphasised in some accounts in recent years. Some interests, such as Amnesty International, arrived in Brussels some time before the development of significant Euro competencies within their interest areas (Chapter 8). The same is true of some transnational regional alliances (Chapter 9). Some, like the EEB, were established to help develop Euro competencies within their field (Chapter 8). Some came in search of 'Euro gold', although, as the discussion on territorial interests suggested in Chapter 9, those regions benefiting most from the structural funds are, ironically, often least present in Brussels. Indeed, an issue ever present throughout Chapters 5–9 concerns the considerable differences between northern and southern traditions of organising interests. Throughout many of the interest arenas, interest organisation is less developed in the south of Europe, although, as is evident from a recent study of biotechnology (Greenwood and Ronit, 1995a), the presence of the European level is itself developing interest organisation in these countries in fields where it has been weak or absent.

What is remarkable about present-day European integration, from the preceding analysis, are the ways in which the Commission and the Parliament, in a manner very much foreseen by neofunctionalist accounts of integration, are acting as development agencies for the construction and consolidation of interest networks at the European level. Besides providing the impetus and incentives to create and sustain groups, the architecture of the European institutions fundamentally influences the landscape of groups. Grote, for instance, attributes much of the fragmentation in European level SME representation to the fragmentation of competencies within the European institutions (Grote, 1995; Chapter 5), while historic cleavages in the organisation of biotechnology interests can be attributed to sharp divisions and competition between the services of the Commission (Chapter 3). In both of these fields, however, the Commission has sought to respond to the problem by seeking and/or funding the development of co-ordination structures between groups, and has played a role in encouraging mergers between different group structures.

The presence of encompassing transnational-level groups provides the Commission with a whole range of advantages, including loyalty transfer, pressures for further integration, a simplified consultation and participation structure, channels of communication, and resources such as information exchange, co-operation, and implementation mechanisms (Chapter 1). Such groups can participate through the range of formal and informal channels for network dialogue. Cram, in particular, has drawn attention to the ways in which actors become socialised in the structures in which they participate, and norms and value systems arise as forces in favour of integration (Cram, 1995a; Chapters 1 and 5). Similarly, by participating in structures such as standardisation committees, forms of collaboration can arise between interests which would not otherwise have done so (Greenwood and Cram, 1996; Chapter 3). This indicates how institutional dynamics impact upon the rationality of collective action, an issue which has been a durable debate within the literature in recent years.

Capacities and collective action in European level interest representation

A variety of private-interest structures have been identified throughout this volume, ranging from single entities such as firms, through to informal and formal collective structures, at subsectoral, sectoral, peak, sub national, national, transregional and transnational levels of organisation. The most common transnational interest structure remains that of the formal European-level groups. A great deal of the literature focusing on the contribution of interests to the integration process has centred around the capacities of these actors. There are a number of aspects to this focus. One concerns the physical resources of the groups themselves. A second issue concerns the ability of groups to work as meaningful collective actors themselves, and issues of the relationship between groups. A third concerns the format of the group, whether federated or direct-membership, at peak or sectoral levels of organisation, and the extent to which such a format shapes the effectiveness of the collective actor to effectively represent the interest concerned. These three debates were reviewed extensively in Chapter 3, and arise periodically throughout Chapters 5–9. The fourth issue, centred on claims of European-level pluralism, was introduced in Chapter 1.

These issues have somewhat over-dominated perspectives on European-level interest representation, and a number of unhelpful, and sometimes rather unfounded, orthodoxies have arisen from them (Chapter 3). These problems may have weakened the theoretical contribution which the study of interests might otherwise have made to the study of the integration process, because the assumption implicit from claims of 'weak Euro groups' or assertions of 'Euro pluralism', informed by ideas of group fragmentation and competition, is that groups do not have the capacities to contribute significantly to the integration process. Although such claims have been periodically repeated from the 1960s until the present day, it is remarkable how thin the evidence actually is for such caricatures. Nowhere in the preceding literature is there a constituency-wide survey of the resources of Euro groups, or comprehensive studies of collective action capacities across groups. Some recent restatements of the 'weak Euro groups' thesis have cited evidence little more substantial or up to date than Sidjanski's study of the agricultural group, COPA, during the 1960s, or, at best, have cited highly selective case studies with little claim to substantive generalisability, or else have focused on groups which have long been reorganised into more effective structures (Chapter 3). In point of fact, the weight of case study evidence, at least in the field of business, accounting for two-thirds of all Euro groups, leaves the impression of well-resourced, coherent and effective Euro groups (Chapter 5). Outside business fields, some case studies identifying abiding weaknesses among pub-lic-interest groups fail to take account of recent developments, which indicate that such caricatures are by no means typical (Chapter 8).

Most frequently, claims about the weakness or fragmentation of groups cite a somewhat speculative article by Streeck and Schmitter (1991). As was argued in Chapter 1, this article has frequently been taken out of context, and rather more importance has been attached to it than the authors may have intended. One reason for this may be because these two writers have been closely associated with the corporatist tradition, and seemed to be discounting its development at the European level. The article foresaw Washington-like fragmen-tation and competition in the European interest group architecture, and drew attention to the likely failure of 'Euro corporatism' to develop. The article did not claim to be based upon comprehensive evidence drawn from the resources or capacities of groups; rather, it was more deductive and intended to be speculative in character. It is hard to disagree with their point about the absence of 'Euro corporatism', because the European level possesses nothing of the state-like properties needed for such a scenario. More particularly, what they had in mind was the absence of macrolevel corporatism, and indeed nothing like macro corporatism is discernible at the European level. Despite some interpretations that Streeck and Schmitter had ruled out the possibility of corporatist arrangements at the EU, and that therefore 'pluralism' was a more appropriate label for interest intermediation at the European level (Chapter 3), their contribution had almost nothing to say at all about meso-level corporatism. Schmitter's later recognition of the development of meso-level corporatism at the European level, citing some of the evidence concerning the pharmaceutical domain reviewed in this text, acknowledges the presence of interests in the economic division of labour with sufficiently strong associational capacities (Traxler and Schmitter, 1994; Chapter 1).

The popularity of claims of 'weak Euro groups' and 'EU pluralism' seem to arise more from the frequency with which they are repeated than from substantive evidence. Most Euro groups were formed prior to the single-market period, and half were in Brussels before this time. Most have a turnover in excess of 100 000 ECU. Over a third have 5 or more staff. Some, like CEFIC, have as many as 80, while secretariats of 20 are not uncommon. Groups such as the ERT, AMCHAM-EU, EFPIA, ACEA, EUROFER, CONCAWE, CEGA, CEA and CAOBISCO are also well endowed (Chapters 5 and 8).

Many business groups now have specialist divisions, and are able to draw upon considerable additional resources made available by their members. Over a quarter of a sample of public-interest groups have more than 10 staff. Many of these are in receipt of considerable EU funding. Specialisation is now evident, with considerable new group formation in territorial, labour and social–citizen fields, and the growth of less formal business collective fora. Indeed, the problem today is not so much the absence of transnational level groups but one of overcrowding, leading to attempts from the institutions to seek to manage the EU level interest group environment (Chapter 4).

Apart from the physical resources of groups, many of the 'weak Euro groups' claims relate to inherent collective action problems. In particular, peak, federated structures are often compromise-prone, find platform-building difficult, and spend considerable time mediating between conflicting member interests. Such a problem is evident among groups in the fields of business (UNICE), the professions (SEPLIS), labour (ETUC), the environment (EEB) and territorial structures (AER; CEMR). But such problems do not necessarily mean that these groups are necessarily fatally flawed, and nor does it mean that a caricature of weakness can be applied to the universe of groups. As was evident in Chapter 5, federated sectoral structures can work well under certain conditions, while direct-firm-membership structures have often proved highly effective in representing the interests of large firms. Fragmentation does not necessarily imply competition and pluralism. Where different types of groups exist alongside one another within the same sector, such as information technology, they can perform mutually complementary roles. Federated structures possess breadth of membership, and direct firm structures offer ease of platform-building and the strength of representing large-firm interests (Chapter 3). Undoubtedly, there are examples of 'weak' Euro groups, and a number of cases have been reviewed throughout this book. But it is important not to over-generalise the rather specific problems of a few groups to all, as some accounts seem to have done (Chapter 3).

Associability of interests at the European level may not be that complicated (Chapter 3). The provision of hard, selective material incentives by groups is virtually non-existent in an environment where Euro groups are favoured by public authorities. Membership costs are relatively low, whereas the costs of non-membership, including the loss of market and political information in an uncertain environment, and loss of influence over group strategies, seem relatively high (Chapter 3). Two-thirds of Euro groups are federated structures, where mechanisms of associability are virtually automatic because they centre more on membership by collective national association actors, where particular dynamics operate in favour of associability, than by individual actors such as firms. Even in direct-membership structures, where the rational calculus of membership might be more applicable, the logic is still towards membership among large firms well rehearsed in the habits of collaboration. Indeed, working through the rationality of collective action for large enterprises, a firm might have to think harder about its reasons not to join than to associate (Chapter 3). At least for most business groups, potential collective action problems have either been solved or do not arise by the time groups are formed. The European level imposes distinctive dynamics upon collective action, such that for most interests associability is a matter of going with the flow.

For large firms, formal groups provide just one of a range of strategies in meeting their needs at the European level (Chapter 5). Most need some capacity for independent action, or exclusive collaboration between them. These resourceful actors exert significant dynamics upon the outcomes and output of European public policies (Chapter 5), to member state input, and to collective action structures (Chapters 3 and 5). A range of informal collective configuration of interests, primarily based around large firms, provides flexible structures as: think-tanks; ideas, issue and leadership forums; information and socialisation networks; and quick-response mechanisms. They can provide added-value commodities to the political and economic strategies, and operations, of large firms as single and collaborative actors, and to those of groups in the integration process. The experience of collaboration in them may be iterative (Chapter 5).

The future role of interests in integration theory

Much of the recent discussion of the integration process has proceeded without full consideration of the roles which groups and other aggregations of interests perform. This is some loss, not least because many of the recent approaches to integration offer synthesised, theoretical insights of some explanatory promise. No modern account of integration is foolish enough to claim discovery of a single dynamic of integration, nor the ability to be able to predict the pace and direction of future integration. Yet without consideration of the role of interests in the integration process, accounts will always be incomplete. In part, the uncertainty arises from the contribution of European-level interest representation analysis to date, where a focus upon a posited weakness of Euro groups has implied a lack of ability of these actors to contribute to integration dynamics. Equally hampering has been a lack of comprehensive evidence spanning the range of interest domains, and detailed insights into the ways in which groups operate as network actors with public authority in the integration process. These exercises would help develop further insights into: the role of the supranational institutions in network-building, as agents with autonomous capacities; the transfer of loyalties to the European level, and the consequent creation of demand structures for integration, which exert forces on the boundaries of integration; the ways in which member states conclude agreements for which they cannot foresee the consequences, and the subsequent vacuum and conditions of uncertainty in which network actors of interests and supranational institutions operate, expand, provide ideas for and exploit; the vacuum left for interests to develop by the management deficit of the Commission; the contribution of interests to outputs in high politics arenas, and to certain specific outcomes in low politics fields; the ways in which integration proceeds by stealth from such networks; the associated power of rhetoric, leadership, socialisation, and ideas, as forces in European integration; and the ways in which iterated co-operation among interests and actors in the integration process leads to preference convergence between them.

Bibliography

Agence Europe (1994) 'EU Commission to Define Aims and Means of its Transparency Policy' (Brussels: Agence Europe).

Altenstetter, C. (1994) 'European Trade Associations; Mobilizing for the Regulation of Devices in the European Community', in V. Eichener and H. V. Voellzkow (eds), *Europäische Integration und verbandliche Interessenvermittlung* (Marburg: Metropolis Verlag) pp. 349–83.

Andersen, C. (1992) *Influencing the European Community* (London: Kogan Page).

Armingeon, K. (1994) 'The Regulation of Trade Unions and Collective Labour Relations in the European Union', paper prepared for presentation to the Joint Sessions of the European Consortium for Political Research, Madrid, 17–22 April.

Armstrong, H. (1995) 'The Role and Evolution of European Community Regional Policy', in B. Jones and M. Keating (eds), *The European Union and the Regions* (Oxford: Clarendon Press) pp. 23–64.

Arp, H. (1991) 'Interest Groups in EC Legislation: The Case of Car Emission Standards', paper prepared for presentation to the Joint Sessions of the European Consortium for Political Research, University of Essex, 22–28 March.

Arp, H. (1993) 'Technical Regulation and Politics: The Interplay Between Economic Interests and Environmental Policy Goals in EC Car Emission Legislation, in J. D. Liefferink, P. D. Lowe and A. P. J. Mol (eds), *European Integration and Environmental Policy* (London: Belhaven Press), pp. 150–72.

Aspinwall, M. (1995) 'International Integration or Domestic Politics? Anatomy of a Single Market Measure', *Journal of Common Market Studies*, vol. 33, no. 4, December, pp. 475–500.

Aspinwall, M. and Greenwood, J. (eds) (1997) *Collective Action in the European Union: Interests and the New Politics of Associability* (London: Routledge) forthcoming.

Aspinwall, M. and Greenwood, J. (1997) 'Introduction', in M. Aspinwall and J. Greenwood (eds), *Collective Action in the European Union: Interests and the New Politics of Associability* (London: Routledge) forthcoming.

Audit Commission (1991) *A Rough Guide to Europe: Local Authorities and the EC* (London: Her Majesty's Stationary Office).

Averyt, W. (1977) *Agro Politics in the European Community: Interest Groups and the Common Agricultural Policy* (New York: Praeger).

Axelrod, R. S. (1990) 'Environmental Policy and Management in the European Community', in N. Vig and M. E. Kraft (eds), *Environmental Policy in the 1990s: Towards a New Agenda* (Washington DC: Quarterly Press) pp. 253–73.

Baine, S., Benington, J. and Russell, J. (1992) *Changing Europe: Challenges Facing the Voluntary and Community Sectors in the 1990s* (London: NCVO Publications).

Baird, G. (1994) 'Representing Scottish Interests in Europe: Scotland Europa after One Year', lecture to the Europa Institute, University of Edinburgh, 21 January.

Baker, M. (1992) 'Voluntary Group Lobbying in the EC – A Case Study in Animal Testing of Cosmetics', *European Access*, vol. 4, August, pp. 8–9.

Balme, R. (1991) 'EEC Regional Policies and Policy Networks in the Member States', paper prepared for presentation to the Joint Sessions of the European Consortium for Political Research, University of Essex, 22–28 March.

Baran, P. and Sweezy, P. (1966) *Monopoly Capitalism* (New York: Monthly Review Press).

Benington, J. (1994) 'Local Democracy and the European Union: The Impact of Europeanisation on Local Government' (London: Commission for Local Democracy).

BEUC (Bureau Européen des Unions de Consommateurs) (1992) *No Single Market for Europe's Consumers on 1 January 1993* (Brussels: BEUC) 17 December, 92.22.

BEUC (Bureau Européen des Unions de Consommateurs) (1993) *Annual Report 1992* (Brussels: BEUC).

BEUC (Bureau Européen des Unions de Consommateurs) (1994a) *Draft Annual Report 1993* (Brussels: BEUC).

BEUC (Bureau Européen des Unions de Consommateurs) (1994b) *BEUC: The Consumers Voice in the European Community* (Brussels: BEUC).

BEUC (Bureau Européen des Unions de Consommateurs) (1995) *BEUC In Brief*, no. 15 (October) ((Brussels: BEUC).

BEUC (Bureau Européen des Unions de Consommateurs) (1996) *BEUC In Brief*, no. 17 (April) (Brussels: BEUC).

Bulmer, S. (1994) 'The Governance of the European Union: A New Institutionalist Approach', *Journal of Public Policy*, vol. 13, no. 4, pp. 351–80.

Buitendijk, G. J. and van Schendelen, M. P. C. M. (1995) 'Brussels Advisory Committees: A Channel for Influence?', *European Law Review*, vol. 20, no. 1, February, pp. 37–57.

Bursens, P. (1996) 'European Integration and Environmental Interest Representation in Belgium and the EU', paper prepared for presentation to the Joint Sessions of the European Consortium for Political Research, Oslo, 29 March–3 April.

Butt Philip, A. (1985) *Pressure Groups in the European Community*, Working Paper no. 2 (London: University Association for Contemporary European Studies).

Butt Philip, A. (1995) 'David Versus Goliath? The Challenge for Environmentalists in the Making and Implementation of EU Environmental Policy', paper prepared for presentation to the Fourth Biennial International Conference of the European Community Studies Association, Charleston, South Carolina, 11–14 May.

Button, K. and Fleming, M. (1992) The Changing Regulatory Regime Confronting the Professions in Europe, *The Antitrust Bulletin*, vol. 37, summer, pp. 429–452.

Calamaro, R. (1992) 'European Law: A Code for EC Lobbying', *Financial Times*, 20 July, p. 32.

Camerra-Rowe, P. (1996) 'Firms and Collective Representation in the European Union, paper prepared for presentation to the annual meeting of the American Political Science Association, San Francisco, August 29–September 1.

Caporaso, J. (1974) *The Structure and Function of European Integration* (Pacific Palisades: Goodyear).

Cawson, A. (ed.) (1985) *Organised Interests and the State* (London: Sage).

Cawson, A. (1992) 'Interests, Groups and Public Policy Making: the Case of the European Consumer Electronics Industry', in J. Greenwood, J. Grote and K. Ronit (eds), *Organized Interests and the European Community* (London: Sage), pp. 99–118.

Cawson, A. (1995) 'Public Policies and Private Interests: The Role of Business Interests in Determining Europe's Future Television System', in J. Greenwood (ed.), *European Casebook on Business Alliances* (Hemel Hempstead: Prentice-Hall) pp. 49–61.

Cecchini, P., Catinat, M. and Jacquemin, A. (1988) *The European Challenge: 1992: The Benefits of a Single Market* (Aldershot: Wildwood House).

CEDAG (European Council for Voluntary Organisations) (1995) *CEDAG – Euro Letter*, no. 10 (September) (Paris: CEDAG).

CEDAG (European Council for Voluntary Organisations) (1996) *Annual Report* (Paris: CEDAG).

Cigler, A. J. and Loomis, B. A. (4th edn) (1995) (eds), *Interest Group Politics* (Washington, DC: CQ Press).

Cini, M., Porter, M. and Pridham, G. (1994) 'Environmental Standard Setting and the Single European Market: Southern Europe as a Special Case', paper prepared for presentation to the Economic and Social Research Council Conference on The Evolution of Rules for a Single European Market, University of Exeter, 8–10 September.

Clark, P. B. and Wilson, J. (1960) 'Incentive Systems: A Theory of Organization', *Administrative Sciences Quarterly*, vol. 6, pp. 129–66.

Claveloux, D. (1993) *Talking to the EC: Consultation, Lobbying and Openness: A Background Briefing for the June 15 Conference at the Palais des Congrès in Brussels* (Brussels: Forum Europe).

Coen, D. (1995) 'The Firms Political Action in the European Union', paper prepared for presentation to the Fourth Biennial International Conference of the European Community Studies Association, Charleston, South Carolina, 11–14 May.

COFACE (Confederation of Family Organisations, in the EC) (1996) 'The European NGO's Platform for the Social Sector, COFACE-CONTACT, July-August, p. 7.

Coldrick, P. (1990) 'Collective Bargaining in The New Europe', *Personnel Management*, October, pp. 59–61.

Colebatch, H. (1991) 'Getting Our Act Together: A Case Study in Regulation and Explanation', paper prepared for presentation to the XVth World

Congress of the International Political Science Association, Buenos Aires, 21–5 July.

Collins, M. (1993) *A Complete Guide to European Research, Technology and Consultancy Funds*, 2nd edn (London: Kogan Page).

Commission Office London (1996) 'Recognition of Diplomas Facilitates Free Movement', *The Week in Europe* (London: European Commission Office) 22 January, WE/7/96.

Commission of the European Communities (1990) *Appendix to the 1990 Budget, Part III, Commission – Part A* (Brussels) SEC (90) 2025; 19 October.

Commission of the European Communities (1992a) *An Open and Structured Dialogue Between the Commission and Special Interest Groups* (Brussels) CEC: SEC (92) 2272 final.

Commission of the European Communities (1992b), *Directory of EC Trade and Professional Associations 1992* (Brussels/Luxembourg: Editions Delta).

Commission of the European Communities (1993) *Communication Concerning the Application of the Agreement on Social Policy Presented by the Commission to the Council and to the European Parliament* (Brussels) COM (93) 600 final, 14 December 1993 (Brussels: CEC).

Compston, H. (1992) 'Trade Union Participation in EC Economic Policy Making', Strathclyde Papers on Government and Politics no. 90 (Glasgow: University of Strathclyde).

Confédération Européenne des Cadres (CEC) (1995) *Presentation of the CEC* (Brussels: CEC).

Cowles, M. G. (1994) *The Politics of Big Business in the European Community: Setting the Agenda for a New Europe*, PhD thesis, American University, Washington DC.

Cowles, M. G. (1995a) 'Big Business and Two Level Games: Conceptualizing the Role of Large Firms in EU Affairs', paper prepared for presentation to the Fourth Biennial International Conference of the European Community Studies Association, Charleston, South Carolina, 11–14 May.

Cowles, M. G. (1995b) 'The European Round Table of Industrialists: The Strategic Player in European Affairs', in J. Greenwood (ed.), *European Casebook on Business Alliances* (Hemel Hempstead: Prentice-Hall) pp. 225–36.

Cram, L. (1993) 'Calling the Tune Without Paying the Piper? Social Policy Regulation: The role of the Commission in European Social Policy', *Policy and Politics*, vol. 21, no. 2, pp. 135–46.

Cram, L. (1994) 'Rationalising EU Intervention: Rhetoric and Soft Law in European Policy Making', paper prepared for presentation to the IXth International Conference of Europeanists, Council for European Studies Chicago, 31 March–2 April.

Cram, L. (1995a) 'Policy Making and the Integration Process – Implications for Integration Theory', paper prepared for presentation to the Fourth Biennial International Conference of the European Community Studies Association, Charleston, South Carolina, 11–14 May.

Cram, L. (1995b) 'Business Alliances in the Information Technology Sector', in J. Greenwood (ed.), *European Casebook on Business Alliances* (Hemel Hempstead: Prentice-Hall) pp. 23–37.

Cram, L. (1996) 'Providing the Catalyst for Collective Action: The EU Institutions and Euro Interests in EU Social Policy', in D. Fink-Hafner and T. Cox (eds), *Into Europe: Perspectives from the UK and Slovenia: European Social Policy* (Ljubljana: Academic Press), pp. 339–62.

Dahl, B. (1993) 'Consumer Protection within the European Union', *Journal of Consumer Policy*, vol. 16, pp. 345–53.

Deeken, J. (1993) 'Regional Policy and the European Commission: Policy Entrepreneur or Brussels Bureaucracy', paper prepared for presentation to the Third Biennial International Conference of the European Community Studies Association, Washington, DC, 27–29 May.

Ebbinghaus, B. and Visser, J. (1994) 'Barriers and Pathways to "Borderless" Solidarity: Organized Labour and European Integration', paper prepared for presentation to the Economic and Social Research Council conference on The Evolution of Rules for a Single European Market, University of Exeter, 8–10 September.

Ebbinghaus, B. and Visser, J. (1996) 'European Labour and Transnational Solidarity: Challenges, Pathways & Barriers', MZES University of Mannheim Working Paper AB2, no. 11, Mannheim, MZES.

EBIS (European Biotechnology Information Service) (1993) 'Editorial: Openness – The Case of Biotechnology', *EBIS*, (Brussels: Commission of the European Communities) vol. 3, no. 4, pp. 1–2.

Eckstein, H. (1979) 'Case Study and Theory in Political Science' in F. Greenstein and N. W. Polsby (eds), *Strategies of Inquiry* (Reading, Massachusetts: Addison-Wesley) pp. 79–137.

Egan, M. (1997) 'International Standardization, Corporate Strategy and Regional Markets', in J. Greenwood and H. Jacek (eds), *Organised Business and the New Global Order* (London: Macmillan) forthcoming.

EFPIA (European Federations of Pharmaceutical Industry Associations) (1994) *INFOBRIEF*, 24 May 1994, (Brussels: EFPIA).

EUROCADRES (1994) *Report on Activities: February 1993 to July 1994* (Brussels· EUROCADRES) 504/94/E/b.

EUROCHAMBRES (1996) 'The Active Partner for European Enterprise' (Brussels: Eurochambres).

Euroconfidential (1996) *Directory of Information Sources in the EU 1995–6*, (Geneva: Euroconfidential).

European Citizens Action Service (ECAS) (1996) *What is ECAS?* (Brussels: ECAS).

European Commission (1995) 'The Commission Approves the Creation of a Consumer Committee', (Brussels: European Commission News Services) 13 June, IP/95/609.

European Commission Representation in Scotland (1996) *Scotland in the European Union* (Edinburgh: European Commission Representation in Scotland).

European Environmental Bureau (EEB) (1993) *The European Environmental Bureau: European Federation of Environmental NGOs* (Brussels: EEB).

European Environmental Bureau (EEB) (1994) *EEB Twentieth Anniversary* (Brussels: EEB).

European Environmental Bureau (EEB) (1996a) *Activity Report 1995/Programme of Activities 1996* (Brussels: EEB).

European Environmental Bureau (EEB) (1996b) *Members List* (Brussels: EEB).

European Parliament (1992) Committee on the Rules of Procedure, the Verification of Credentials and Immunities, PE 200.405 fin.

European Parliament (1993) *The Powers of Regional and Local Authorities and their Role in the European Union*, European Parliament Directorate-General for Research, DOC-EN\DV\246\246137.

European Parliament (1995a) Committee on the Rules of Procedure, the Verification of Credentials and Immunities, *Study by the Directorate General for research on 'Rules Governing lobbying in the National Parliaments of the Member States'*, DOC-EN/CM/268/268842.

European Parliament (1995b) Committee on the Rules of Procedure, the Verification of Credentials and Immunities, *Preliminary Draft Report*, 12 April, DOC-EN/PR/268/268845.

European Roundtable of Associations and Federations (ERAF) (1994) 'European Union: Participatory Democracy, Openness and Transparency', *ERAF Conference Report, European Parliament* (Brussels: ERAF).

European Round Table of Industrialists (ERT) (1996) *The European Round Table of Industrialists*, June 1996 (Brussels: ERT).

European Voice (1996a) 'Report Reignites Labour Row' Brussels, *European Voice*, 28 March–2 April, vol. 2, no. 13, p. 2.

European Voice (1996b) 'Bridge given go-ahead despite criticism from environmental lobbies', *European Voice*, 25–31 July, vol. 2, no. 30, p. 5.

European Voice (1996c) 'Curbs on Bikers Spark Noisy Protest', *European Voice*, 1–7 August, vol. 2, no. 31, p. 3.

European Trade Union Confederation (ETUC) (1991) *VIIth Statutory Congress: Report on Activities 88/90* (Brussels: ETUC).

Evetts, J. (1995) 'International Professional Associations: the New Context for Professional Projects', *Work, Employment and Society*, vol. 9, no. 4, pp. 763–72.

Falkner, G. (1995) 'Social Europe in the 1990s: After All an Era of Corporatism?' paper prepared for presentation to the Fourth Biennial International Conference of the European Community Studies Association, Charleston, South Carolina, 11–14 May.

Falkner, G. (1996) 'The Transformation of Governance in the EU: Dilemmas of Corporatism', paper prepared for presentation to the joint sessions of the European Consortium for Political Research, 29 March–3 April.

Financial Times (1994) 'Business and the Environment: Same Journey, Different Routes', *Financial Times*, 13 July, p. 20.

Financial Times (1996a) 'Turkey's "gifts to MEPs" Under Fire', *Financial Times*, 19 January, p. 11.

Financial Times (1996b) Unions to Press 800 EU companies to set up works councils, *Financial Times*, 23 September, p. 3.

Fisher, C. (1994) 'The Lobby to Stop Testing Cosmetics on Animals', in R. H. Pedler and M. P. C. M. van Schendelen (eds), *Lobbying the European Union: Companies, Trade Associations and Issue Groups* (Aldershot: Dartmouth) pp. 227–40.

Friedson, E. (1986) *Professional Powers* (Chicago: University of Chicago Press).

Fuchs, G. (1993) *The Telecommunications Highway for Europe After 1992, or Paving a Dead End Street? The Politics of Pan-European Telecommunications Network Development* (Cologne: Max Planck Institute).

Gardner J. (1991) *Effective Lobbying in the European Community* (Dordrecht: Kluwer).

George, S. (1991) *Politics and Policy in the European Community*, 2nd edn (Oxford: Clarendon Press).

Goldsmith, M. (1991) 'Beyond the Blue Banana: The Single European Market and Local Government in the 1990's: A British View', paper prepared for presentation to the Joint Sessions of the European Consortium for Political Research, 22–28 March.

Gorges, M. (1993) 'Interest Intermediation in the EC After Maastricht', in A. Cafruny and G. Rosenthal (eds), *The State of the European Community*, vol. 2 (Harlow: Longman).

Gorges, M. (1996) *Euro-Corporatism? Interest Intermediation in the European Community* (Lanham, MD.: University Press of America).

Goyens, M. (1993) 'Where There's a Will There's a Way!', *Journal of Consumer Policy*, vol. 16, pp. 375–86.

Grant, W. (1978) *Insider Groups, Outsider Groups and Interest Group Strategies in Britain*, Working Paper no. 19 (Coventry: University of Warwick Department of Politics).

Grant, W. (ed.) (1985) *The Political Economy of Corporatism* (London: Macmillan).

Grant, W. (1990) 'Organised Interests and the European Community', paper prepared for presentation to the 6th International Colloquium of the Feltrinelli Foundation, Corton, 29–31 May.

Grant, W. (1993a) 'Transnational Companies and Environmental Policy Making: the Trend of Globalisation', in J. D. Liefferink, P. D. Lowe and A. P. J. Mol (eds), *European Integration and Environmental Policy* (London: Belhaven Press) pp. 59–74.

Grant, W. (1993b) 'Pressure Groups and the European Community: An Overview', in S. Mazey and J. Richardson (eds), *Lobbying in the European Community* (Oxford: Oxford University Press) pp. 27–46.

Grant, W. (1995) *Pressure Groups, Politics and Democracy in Britain* (Hemel Hempstead: Harvester Wheatsheaf).

Grayson, L. and Hobson, M. (1992) *Inlogov Informs on Europe* (Birmingham: Institute of Local Government Studies).

Greenwood, E. (1965) 'Attributes of a Profession', in M. Zald (ed.), *Social Welfare Institutions* (London: John Wiley), pp. 509–23.

Greenwood, J. (1995a) *European Casebook on Business Alliances* (Hemel Hempstead: Prentice-Hall).

Greenwood, J. (1995b) 'The Pharmaceutical Industry: A European Business Alliance That Works', in J. Greenwood (ed.), *European Casebook on Business Alliances* (Hemel Hempstead: Prentice-Hall) pp. 38–48.

Greenwood, J. (1995c) 'Tourism: How Well Served, and Organised, Is the "World's Largest Industry" in Europe', in J. Greenwood (ed.), *European Casebook on Business Alliances* (Hemel Hempstead: Prentice-Hall) pp. 128–42.

Greenwood, J. and Cram, L. (1996) 'European Level Business Collective Action: The Study Agenda Ahead', *Journal of Common Market Studies*, vol. 34, no. 3, September, pp. 449–63.

Greenwood, J., Grote, J. and Ronit, K. (1992) 'Introduction' in J. Greenwood, J. Grote and K. Ronit (eds), *Organised Interests and the European Community* (London: Sage) pp. 1–41.

Greenwood, J. and Jordan, A. G. (1993) 'The UK: A Changing Kaleidoscope' in M. P. C. M. van Schendelen, (ed.), *National Public and Private Lobbying in Brussels* (Aldershot: Dartmouth) pp. 65–90.

Greenwood, J., Levy, R. and Stewart, R. (1995) 'The European Union Structural Fund Allocations: "Lobbying to Win" or Recycling the Budget?', *European Urban and Regional Studies*, vol. 2, no. 4, pp. 317–38.

Greenwood, J. and Ronit, K. (1991) 'Pharmaceutical Regulation in Denmark and the UK: Reformulating Interest Representation to the Transnational Level', *European Journal of Political Research*, vol. 19, pp. 327–59.

Greenwood, J. and Ronit, K. (1994) 'Interest Groups in the European Community: Newly Emerging Dynamics and Forms', *West European Politics*, vol. 17, no. 1, January, pp. 31–52.

Greenwood, J. and Ronit, K. (1995a) *The Organisation of Biotechnology Interests in the European Union*, Report to the Commission from Study Contract BIO2-CT93-0603, June.

Greenwood, J. and Ronit, K. (1995b) 'European Bioindustry', in J. Greenwood (ed.), *European Casebook on Business Alliances* (Hemel Hempstead: Prentice-Hall) pp. 128–42.

Grote, J. (1989) 'Guidance and Control in Transnational Committee Networks: the Associational Basis of Policy cycles at the EC Level', typescript, Florence, European University Institute.

Grote, J. (1995) 'Size and Territory in the Organization of Business Interests', in J. Greenwood (ed.), *European Casebook on Business Alliances* (Hemel Hempstead: Prentice-Hall) pp. 237–58.

Guardian The (1996) 'MEPs Tackle Influence of Lobbyists', *The Guardian*, 18 July 1996, p. 14.

Haas, E. (1958) *The Uniting of Europe: Political, Economic and Social Forces, 1950–1957* (Stanford, California: Stanford University Press).

Haas, E. (1964) *Beyond the Nation State: Functionalism and International Organization* (Stanford, California: Stanford University Press).

Haas, E. (1976) *The Obsolescence of Regional Integration Theory* (Berkeley, California: Institute of International Studies).

Haas, P. (1992) 'Introduction: Epistemic Communities and International Policy Coordination', *International Organisation*, vol. 46, no. 1, pp. 1–35.

Harris, R. and Lavan, A. (1992) 'Professional Mobility in the New Europe: The Case of Social Work', *Journal of European Social Policy*, vol. 2, no. 1, pp. 1–15.

Harvey, B. (1995) *Networking in Europe: A Guide to European Voluntary Organisations* (London: NCVO Publications).

Hayward, J. (1995) 'Organized Interests and Public Policies', in J. Hayward and E. Page (eds), *Governing the New Europe* (Cambridge: Polity Press) pp. 224–56.

Heclo, H. (1978) 'Issue Networks and the Executive Establishment', in A. King (ed.), *The New American Political System* (Washington: AEI).

Hix S. (1994) 'The Study of the European Community: The Challenge to Comparative Politics', *West European Politics*, vol. 17, no. 1, January 1994, pp. 1–30.

Hoffman, S. (1966) 'Obstinate or Obsolete? The Fate of the Nation State and the Case of Western Europe', *Daedelus*, vol. 95, pp. 862–915.

Holland, S. (1976) 'Meso Economics, Multinational Capital and Regional Inequality', in R. Lee and P. E. Ogden (eds), *Economy and Society in the EEC: Spatial Perspectives* (Farnborough: Saxon House) pp. 38–62.

Hooghe, L. (1994) 'Political-Administrative Adaptation in the EU and Regional Mobilization: The European Commission and the Structural Funds', paper prepared for presentation to the IXth International Conference of Europeanists, Council for European Studies, Chicago, 30 March–1 April 1994.

Hooghe, L. (1995) 'Subnational Mobilisation in the European Union', *West European Politics*, vol. 18, no. 3, July, pp. 175–98.

Hooghe, L. and Keating, M. (1994) 'The Politics of European Union Regional Policy', *Journal of European Public Policy*, vol. 1, no. 3, pp. 367–93.

Hooghe, L. and Marks, G. (1996) ' "Europe With the Regions:" Channels of Regional Representation in the European Union', *Publius*, vol. 26, no. 1, Winter, pp. 1–20.

Hull, R. (1993) 'Lobbying the European Community; a view from within', in S. Mazey and J. Richardson (eds), *Lobbying in the European Community* (Oxford: Oxford University Press) pp. 82–92.

Jacek, H. (1995) 'The American Organization of Firms', in J. Greenwood (ed.), *European Casebook on Business Alliances* (Hemel Hempstead: Prentice-Hall) pp. 197–207.

Jacobs, F., Corbett, R. and Shackleton, M. (1995) *The European Parliament* (London: Cartermill).

Jacquemin, A. and Wright, D. (1994) 'Corporate Strategies and European Challenges post 1992', in S. Bulmer and A. Scott (eds), *Economic and Political Integration in Europe: Internal Dynamics and Global Context* (Oxford: Blackwell) pp. 218–31.

Jeffery, C. and O'Sullivan, B. (1994) *The Role of Socio-Economic Interest Groups vis-a-vis Local and Regional Authorities*, University of the West of England Papers in Politics no. 4.

John, P. (1994) 'UK Sub-National Offices in Brussels: Diversification or Regionalization?' *Regional Studies*, vol. 28, no. 7, pp. 739–59.

John, P. (1995) *Centralisation, Decentralisation and the European Union: the Dynamics of Triadic Relationships* (Keele: Department of Politics, University of Keele).

John, P. (1996) 'The Presence and Influence of UK Local Authorities in Brussels', *Public Administration*, vol. 74, no. 2, pp. 293–313.

Jordan, A. G. and McLaughlin, A. M. (1991) 'The Rationality of Lobbying in Europe; Why are Euro Groups So Numerous and So Weak'?, paper prepared for presentation to the Conference on Euro Lobbying, Nuffield College, Oxford, 17 May.

Jordan, A. G., Maloney, W. A. and McLaughlin, A. M. (1992) *What is Studied when Pressure Groups are Studied?*, British Interest Group Project, Working Paper no. 1 (Aberdeen: University of Aberdeen).

Jordan, A. G. and Wadsworth, A. (1995) 'The Representation of Retailing in Europe', in J. Greenwood (ed.), *European Casebook on Business Alliances* (Hemel Hempstead: Prentice-Hall) pp. 114–27.

Kamarotos, A. S. (1992) 'The Challenge of Environmental Interdependence and Non-Governmental Networks', paper prepared for presentation to the 33rd Annual Convention of the International Studies Association, Atlanta, Georgia, 31 March–4 April.

Keating, M. (1993) 'The Continental Meso: Regions in the European Community', in L. J. Sharpe (ed.), *The Rise of Meso Government in Europe* (Oxford: Oxford University Press), pp. 296–311.

Keating, M. (1995) 'Europeanism and Regionalism', in B. Jones and M. Keating (eds), *The European Union and the Regions* (Oxford: Clarendon Press) pp. 1–22.

Keating, M. and Waters, N. (1985) 'Scotland in the European Community', in Keating, M (1985) *Regions in the European Community* (Oxford: Clarendon Press.

Keohane, R. O. and Hoffman, S. (1990) 'Institutional Change in Europe in the 1980's', in W. Wallace (ed.), *The Dynamics of European Integration* (London: Pinter).

Kitt, R. (1995) 'Local Authorities and Europe', paper prepared for presentation to the European Parliament Conference organised by the Institute of European Studies, Queens University Belfast, 1 June.

Kirchner, E. (1977) *Trade Unions as a Pressure Group in the European Community* (Westmead: Saxon House).

Kirchner, E. and Schwaiger, H. (1981) *The Role of Interest Groups in the European Community* (Aldershot: Gower).

Landmarks Publications (1995) *European Public Affairs Directory 1995*, 5th edn (Brussels: Landmarks).

Lange, P. (1992) 'The Politics of the Social Dimension', in A. M. Sbragia (ed.), *Euro Politics: Institutions and Policymaking in the "New" European Community* (Washington, DC: Brookings) pp. 225–56.

Lanzalaco, P. and Schmitter, P. C. (1992) 'Europe's Internal Market, Business Associability and the Labour Movement', in M. Regini (ed.), *The Future of Labour Movements* (London: Sage) pp. 188–216.

Laslett, J. (1991) 'The Mutual Recognition of Diplomas, Certificates, and Other Evidence of Formal Qualifications in the European Community', *Legal Issues of European Integration 1990/1*, Amsterdam.

Leisink, P., van Leemput, J. and Vilrokx, J. (1996) *The Challenges to Trade Unions in Europe* (Cheltenham: Edward Elgar).

Lenschow, A. (1996) 'The Nature and Transformation of Governance in European Environmental Policy', paper prepared for presentation to the Joint Sessions of the European Consortium for Political Research, Oslo, 29 March–3 April.

Leonardi, R. and Nanetti, R. Y. (1990) *The Regions and European Integration: The Case of Emilia Romagna* (London: Pinter).

Lewin, L. (1994) 'The Rise and Decline of Corporatism: The Case of Sweden', *European Journal of Political Research*, vol. 26, no. 1, pp. 59–80.

Liefferink, J. D., Lowe, P. and Mol, A. P. J. (1993) 'The Environment and the European Community: the analysis of political integration', in J. D.

Liefferink, P. D. Lowe and A. P. J. Mol (1993) (eds), *European Integration and Environmental Policy* (London: Belhaven Press), pp. 1–14.

Lijphart, A. (1971) 'Comparative Politics and the Comparative Method', *American Political Science Review*, vol. 65, pp. 682–93.

Lindblom, C. E. (1977) *Politics and Markets: The World's Political Economic Systems* (New York: Basic Books).

Long, T. (1995) 'Shaping Public Policy in the European Union: A Case Study of the Structural Funds', *Journal of European Public Policy*, vol. 2, no. 4, pp. 672–9.

Lovecy, J. (1993) 'Regulating Professional Services in the Single European Market: the Cases of Legal and Medical Services in France and the United Kingdom', paper prepared for presentation to the Third Biennial International Conference of the European Community Studies Association, Washington, DC: 27–29 May.

Lovecy, J. (1996) 'Interest Intermediation in France and the UK and the Europeanisation of Professional Regulation: A Comparative Study in the Transformation of National Governance Structures', paper prepared for presentation to the Joint Sessions of the European Consortium for Political Research, University of Oslo, 29 March–3 April.

Lowi, T. J. (1964) 'American Business, Public Policy, Case Studies and Political Theory', *World Politics*, vol. 16, pp. 677–715.

Lukes, S. (1974) *Power: A Radical View* (London: Macmillan).

Lund, H. (1995) 'Monitoring of Consumer Products by Producers in the Netherlands', paper prepared for presentation to the Third International Conference for Product Safety Research, Amsterdam, 6–7 March.

McAleavy, P. (1994) *The Political Logic of the European Community Structural Funds Budget: Lobbying Efforts by Declining Industrial Regions*, EUI Working Paper Robert Schuman Centre no. 94/2 (Florence: European University Institute).

McAleavy, P. and Mitchell, J. (1994) 'Industrial Regions and Lobbying in the Structural Funds Reform Process', *Journal of Common Market Studies*, vol. 32, no. 2, June, pp. 237–48.

McGowan, L. and Wilks, S. (1995) 'The First Supranational Policy in the European Union: competition policy', *European Journal of Political Research*, 28, 2, pp. 141–169.

McKinney, D. (1994) 'Animal Welfare Groups in the European Union', paper prepared for presentation to the Joint Sessions of the European Consortium for Political Research, Madrid, 17–24 April.

McLaughlin, A. M. (1992) 'Underfed Euro Feds', paper prepared for presentation to the Annual Conference of the Political Studies Association, Queens University Belfast, 21 April.

McLaughlin, A. M. (1995) 'Automobiles: Dynamic Organization in Turbulent Times?', in J. Greenwood (ed.), *European Casebook on Business Alliances* (Hemel Hempstead: Prentice-Hall) pp. 172–83.

McLaughlin, A. M. and Greenwood, J. (1995) 'The Management of Interest Representation in the European Union', *Journal of Common Market Studies*, vol. 33, no. 1, March, pp. 143–56.

McLaughlin, A. M., Maloney, W. A. and Jordan, A. G. (1993) 'Corporate Lobbying in the European Community', *Journal of Common Market Studies*, vol. 31, no. 2, June, pp. 191–212.

Machmer, A. (1995) Untitled paper, prepared for presentation to a conference on the European Parliament, Institute of European Studies, Queens University Belfast, 1 June.

Maier, L. (1993) 'Institutional Consumer Representation in the European Community', *Journal of Consumer Policy*, vol. 16, pp. 355–74.

Majone, G. (1993) 'The European Community Between Social Policy and Social Regulation', *Journal of Common Market Studies*, vol. 31, no. 2, June, pp. 153–70.

Maloney, W. A., Jordan, A. G. and McLaughlin, A. M. (1995) 'Interest Groups and Public Policy: The Insider/Outsider Model Revisited' *Journal of Public Policy*, vol. 14, no. 1, pp. 17–38.

Mann, M. (1996) 'Cutting Report Ploughs into Farm Lobby', *European Voice*, vol. 2, no. 41, 7–13 November 1996, p. 5.

Marginson, P. and Sisson, K. (1996) 'Multinational Companies and the Future of Collective Bargaining: A Review of the Research Issues, *European Journal of Industrial Relations*, vol. 2, no. 2, pp. 173–97.

Marks, G. (1992) 'Structural Policy in the European Community', in A. Sbragia (ed.), *Euro Politics: Institutions and Policy Making in the 'New' European Community* (Washington, DC: Brookings) pp. 191–224.

Marks, G. (1993) 'Structural Policy and Multilevel Governance in the EC', in A. Cafruny and G. Rosenthal (eds), *The State of the European Community*, vol. 2 (Boulder, Colorado: Lynne Reinner) pp. 391–410.

Marks, G., Nielsen, F., Ray, L. and Salk, J. (1995) 'Competencies, Cracks and Conflicts: Regional Mobilisation in the European Union', typescript, Department of Political Science, University of North Carolina-Chapel Hill.

Marks, G., Scharpf, F., Schmitter, P. and Streeck, W. (1996) *Governance in the European Union* (London: Sage).

Martin, S. (1993) 'The Europeanisation of Local Authorities: Challenges for Rural Areas', *Journal of Rural Studies*, vol. 9, no. 2, pp. 153–61.

Metcalfe, L. (1992) 'After 1992: Can the Commission Manage Europe', *Australian Journal of Public Administration*, vol. 51, no. 1, March, pp. 117–30.

Millman, T. (1994) 'The UK Engineering Profession: The Case for Unification', *Policy Studies*, vol. 15, no. 1, pp. 26–41.

Mitnick, B. M. (1980) *The Political Economy of Regulation* (New York: Columbia).

Mitrany, P. (1943) 'A Working Peace System' (London: Quadrangle Books).

Moe, T. (1980) *The Organization of Interests: Incentives and the Internal Dynamics of Political Interest Groups* (Chicago: University of Chicago Press).

Moran, M. (1985) *Politics and Society in Britain* (London: Macmillan).

Moravcsik, A. (1991) 'Negotiating the Single European Act: National Interests and Conventional Statecraft in the European Community', *International Organisation*, vol. 45, pp. 19–56.

Moravcsik, A. (1993) 'Preferences and Power in the European Community: A Liberal Intergovernmentalist Approach', *Journal of Common Market Studies*, vol. 31, no. 4, December, pp. 473–524.

Mundo, P. A. (1992) *Interest Groups: Cases and Characteristics* (Chicago: Nelson-Hall).

Murphy, R. (1988) *Social Closure* (Oxford: Clarendon Press).

National Consumer Council (1988) *Consumers and the Common Agricultural Policy* (London: HMSO).

Neale, P. (1994) 'Expert Interest Groups and the European Commission: Professional Influence on EC Legislation', *International Journal of Sociology and Social Policy*, vol. 14, nos. 6/7, pp. 1–24.

Nello, S. (1989) 'European Interest Groups and the CAP', *Food Policy*, May, pp. 101–06.

Nelsen, B. and Stubb, A. C. (1994) *Readings on the Theory and Practice of European Integration* (Boulder, Colorado: Lynne Rienner).

Nentwich, M. (1995) 'Citizens' Involvement in European Union Politics: Towards a More Participatory Democracy?', paper prepared for presentation to the Fourth Biennial Conference European Community Studies Association, 11–14 May, South Carolina.

Neville-Rolfe, E. (1984) *The Politics of Agriculture in the European Community* (London: Policy Studies Institute).

Nugent, N. (1994) *The Government and Politics of the European Union* (London: Macmillan).

Obradovic, D. (1994) 'Interest Representation and the Legitimacy of the EC Decision Making Process', paper prepared for presentation to the Joint Sessions of the European Consortium for Political Research, Madrid, 17–22 April.

Olson, M. (1965) *The Logic of Collective Action* (Cambridge, Massachusetts: Harvard University Press).

O'Neill, M. (1996) *The Politics of European Integration: A Reader* (London: Routledge).

Orzack, L. (1991) 'The General Systems Directive and the Liberal Professions', in L. Hurwitz and C. Lequesne (eds), *The State of the European Community* (Boulder, Colorado: Lynne Rienner) pp. 137–51.

Orzack, L. (1992) *International Authority and the Professions: The State Beyond the Nation State*, Jean Monnet Chair Papers, European Policy Unit at the European University Institute (Florence: EUI).

Paterson, W. (1991) 'Regulatory Change and Environmental Protection in the British and German Chemical Industries', *European Journal of Political Research*, vol. 19, pp. 307–26.

Pedler, R. (1994) 'ETUC and the Pregnant Woman', in R. H. Pedler and M. P. C. M. van Schendelen (eds), *Lobbying the European Union: Companies, Trade Associations And Issue Groups* (Aldershot: Dartmouth) pp. 241–58.

Pedler, R. and van Schendelen, M. P. C. M. (eds) (1994) *Lobbying the European Union: Companies, Trade Associations And Issue Groups* (Aldershot: Dartmouth).

Peterson, J. (1995a) 'Playing the Transparency Game', *Public Administration*, Autumn, vol. 7, no. 3, pp. 473–92.

Peterson, J. (1995b) 'Decision Making in the European Union: Towards a Framework for Analysis', *Journal of European Public Policy*, vol. 2, no. 1, pp. 69–93.

Petracca, M. P. (ed.) (1992) *The Politics of Interests: Interest Groups Transformed* (Boulder, Colorado: Westview Press).

Petre, L. (1991) 'Interest Intermediation at the European Level: A Study of European Consumer Policy', paper prepared for presentation to the Joint

Sessions of the European Consortium for Political Research, University of Essex, 22–28 March.

Pijnenburg, B. (1996) 'EU Lobbying By Ad Hoc Coalitions: An Exploratory Case Study', paper prepared for presentation to the Annual Meeting of the Western Political Science Association, San Francisco, 14–16 March.

Porter, M. (1994) 'The Packaging and Packaging Waste Directive: Scientific Uncertainty, The Role of Expertise and North–South Variations in the EU Environmental Policy Process', paper prepared for presentation to the Conference on Environmental Standards and the Politics of Expertise in Europe, University of Bristol, 9–11 December.

Preston, J. (1995) 'EU Issue Emergence – The Case of Policy for Small and Medium Sized Enterprises', paper presented to UACES Research Conference on Integration within a Wider Europe, University of Birmingham, 18–19 September.

Rath, F. (1994) 'The Co-ordinates of Trade Union Policy for Europe', in W. Lecher (ed.), *Trade Unions in the European Union: A Handbook* (London: Lawrence & Wishart) pp. 237–74.

Reuters (1994) 'Lobbyists Agree Code of Conduct', Reuters, Brussels, 28 September.

Reuters (1995b) 'Belgium: EU Parliament Cracks Down on Lobbyists', Reuters, Brussels, 24 February.

Rhodes, M. (1991) 'The Social Dimension of the Single European Market: National Versus Transnational Regulation', *European Journal of Political Research*, vol. 19, pp. 245–80.

Rhodes, M. (1994) 'Labour Markets and Industrial Relations', in N. Nugent and R. O'Donnell (1994) (eds), *The European Business Environment* (London: Macmillan) pp. 124–54.

Rhodes, M. (1995) 'A Regulatory Conundrum: Industrial Relations and the Social Dimension', paper prepared for presentation to the Fourth Biennial International Conference of the European Community Studies Association, Charleston, South Carolina, 11–14 May.

Rhodes, R. A. W. (1988) *Beyond Westminster and Whitehall* (London: Unwin Hyman).

Richardson, J. J. and Jordan, A. G. (1979) *Governing Under Pressure* (London: Martin Robertson).

Roethig, O. (1994) 'Transnational Cooperation Amongst Labour Groups', paper prepared for presentation to the Joint Sessions of the European Consortium for Political Research, Madrid, 17–22 April.

Roethig, O. (1995) 'ETUC and Trade Unions in Europe', in J. Greenwood (ed.), *European Casebook on Business Alliances* (Hemel Hempstead: Prentice-Hall) pp. 271–82.

Rose, R. (1993) *Lesson Drawing in Public Policy: A Guide to Learning Across Time and Space* (New Jersey: Chatham House).

Ross, G. (1994) 'Inside the Delors Cabinet', *Journal of Common Market Studies*, vol. 32, no. 4, pp. 499–523.

Rucht, D. (1993) 'Think Globally, Act Locally? Needs, Forms and Problems of Cross-National Cooperation Among Environmental Groups', in J. D., Lowe, P. D. Liefferink and A. P. J. Mol (1993) (eds), *European Integration and Environmental Policy* (London: Belhaven Press) pp. 75–96.

Sandholtz, W. (1993) 'Choosing Union: Monetary Politics and Maastricht', *World Politics*, vol. 47, no. 1, pp. 95–128.

Sargent, J. A. (1985) 'Corporatism and the EC', in W. Grant (ed.), *The Political Economy of Corporatism* (London: Macmillan).

Sargent, J. A. (1987) 'The Organisation of Business Interests for European Community Representation', in W. Grant with J. Sargent, *Business and Politics in Britain* (London: Macmillan) pp. 213–38.

Sasseen, J. (1992) 'Getting Through to Brussels', *International Management*, vol. 47, no. 2, March, p. 63.

Sbragia, A. (1996) 'Environmental Policy', in H. Wallace and W. Wallace (eds), *Policy Making in the European Union* (Oxford: Oxford University Press) pp. 235–56.

Scotland Europa (1995) 'Consumer Organisation Welcomes Commission Three Year Plan', *Monthly Report*, December (Brussels: Scotland Europa).

Scotland Europa (1996) *European Regional Offices* (Brussels: Scotland Europa).

SEPLIS (1996a) *The Liberal Professions and Europe* (Brussels: SEPLIS).

SEPLIS (1996b) 'Members List' (Brussels: SEPLIS).

Sidenius, N. (1994) 'The Logic of Business Political Organization in Western Europe', paper prepared for presentation to the Joint Sessions of the European Consortium for Politcal Research, Madrid, 17–22 April.

Sidjanski, D. (1967) 'Pressure Groups and the European Community', *Government and Opposition*, vol. 2, no. 3, pp. 397–416.

Stern, A. (1994) *Lobbying in Europe After Maastricht: How to Keep Abreast and Wield Influence in the European Union* (Brussels: Club de Bruxelles).

Story, J. (1996) 'Strategy, Ideology and Politics: The Relaunch of Social Europe, 1987–1989', in O. Cadot, L. Gabel, J. Story and D. Webber (eds), *European Casebook on Industrial and Trade Policy* (Hemel Hempstead: Prentice-Hall) pp. 312–54.

Stow, B. (1991) 'UK Coordination of EC Policy', paper prepared for presentation to the Conference on Europe 2000 at the Netherlands Management Studies Centre, Noordwijk, 28 November.

Streeck, W. and Schmitter, P. C. (1985) *Private Interest Government* (London: Sage).

Streeck, W. and Schmitter, P. C. (1991) 'From National Corporatism to Transnational Pluralism' *Politics and Society*, vol. 19, no. 2, pp. 133–65.

Streeck, W. and Vitols, S. (1993) *European Works Councils: Between Statutory Enactment and Voluntary Adoption*, Discussion Paper FS/I/93–312 (Berlin: Wissenschaftszentrum) September.

Sutherland, P. (1992) *The Internal Market After 1992: Meeting the Challenge*, Report to the European Commission by the High Level Group on the Operation of the Internal Market (Brussels: Commission of the European Communities).

Trades Union Congress (TUC) (1988) *Minutes of Congress 1988* (London: TUC).

Traxler, F. and Schmitter, P. C. (1994) 'Prospective Thoughts on Regional Integration, Interest Politics and Policy Formation in the European Community/Union', paper prepared for presentation to the XVth World Congress of the International Political Science Association, Berlin, 20–24 August.

Tsinsizelis, M. (1990) 'Neo Corporatism and the Common Agricultural Policy: The Case of Adjustment of the CAP', paper prepared for presentation to the Joint Sessions of the European Consortium for Political Research, Bochum, 1–6 April.

Turner, L. (1995) 'The Europeanization of Labor: Structure Before Action', paper prepared for presentation to the Fourth Biennial International Conference of the European Community Studies Association, Charleston, South Carolina, 11–14 May.

Underhill, G. (1997) 'From Ships Passing in the Dark to a Dialogue of the Deaf: The Contribution of International Relations Theory to Understanding Organised Business', in J. Greenwood and H. Jacek (eds), *Organised Business and the New Global Order* (London: Macmillan).

van Schendelen, M. P. C. M. (1993) 'Introduction: The Relevance of National Public and Private EC Lobbying' in M. P. C. M. van Schendelen (ed.), *National Public and Private EC Lobbying* (Aldershot: Dartmouth) pp. 1–20.

van Schendelen, M. P. C. M. (1994) 'Introduction: Studying EU Public Affairs Cases: Does it Matter?', in R. H Pedler and van Schendelen, M. P. C. M. (eds), *Lobbying the European Union: Companies, Trade Associations And Issue Groups*, (Aldershot: Dartmouth) pp. 3–22.

van der Klaauw, J. (1994) 'Amnesty Lobby for Refugees', in R.H. Pedler and M. P. C. M. van Schendelen (eds), *Lobbying the European Union: Companies, Trade Associations And Issue Groups* (Aldershot: Dartmouth) pp. 259–82.

Visser, J and Ebbinghaus, B. (1992) 'Making the Most of Diversity? European Integration and Transnational Organization of Labour', in J. Greenwood, J. Grote and K. Ronit (eds), *Organized Interests and the European Community* (London: Sage) pp. 206–37.

Wallace, W. (1996) 'Government Without Statehood: The Unstable Equilibrium', in H. Wallace and W. Wallace (eds) *Policy Making in the European Union* (Oxford: Oxford University Press) pp. 439–60.

Weale, A. and Williams, A. (1994) 'The Single Market and Environmental Policy', paper prepared for presentation to the ESRC Conference on the Evolution of Rules for a Single European Market, University of Exeter, 8–10 September.

Webster, R. (1997) 'Coalition Formation and Collective Action: The Case of the Environmental G7', in M. Aspinwall and J. Greenwood (eds), *Collective Action in the European Union: Interests and the New Politics of Associability* (London: Routledge) forthcoming.

Western Mail (1995) 'Euro MPs face Cash Scandal Allegation', *Western Mail*, 22 September, p. 1.

Wilding, P. (1982) *Professional Power and Social Welfare* (London: Routledge & Kegan Paul).

Yin, R. (1994) *Case Study Research* (Newbury Park, California: Sage).

Young, A. (1995) 'Participation and Policy Making in the European Community: Mediating Between Competing Interests', paper prepared for presentation to the Fourth Biennial International Conference of the European Community Studies Association, Charleston, South Carolina, 11–14 May.

Index

287